SOUL EXPLOSION

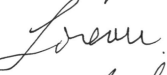

May God Bless You,
Watch Over You, and
Guide You onward
Forever.

Best wishes,

Dr. _____ _____

SOUL EXPLOSION

DR. RICK SCARNATI

Tate Publishing & Enterprises

Published by Tate Publishing & Enterprises, LLC
127 E. Trade Center Terrace | Mustang, Oklahoma 73064 USA
1.888.361.9473 | www.tatepublishing.com

Tate Publishing is committed to excellence in the publishing industry. The company reflects the philosophy established by the founders, based on Psalm 68:11,
"The Lord gave the word and great was the company of those who published it."

Book design copyright © 2011 by Tate Publishing, LLC. All rights reserved.
Cover design by Kellie Southerland
Interior design by Blake Brasor

Published in the United States of America

ISBN: 978-1-61777-588-8
1. Biography & Autobiography / General
2. Religion / General
11.07.12

Dedication

To Jesus Christ, my Good Shepherd

When a soul is reborn in the Holy Spirit, it is likened to a supernova.

The light from such a soul touches everything in its path forever.

Acknowledgments

This is a story of a Pittsburgh Steel City street kid's transformation through his Shepherd, Jesus Christ, and the Fire Power of the Holy Spirit, a Christ-centered journey from Delinquent to Physician

The writer wishes to express his deep appreciation to all his teachers, both past and present, who through their teaching and inspirational efforts, resulted in this finished physician. To my family and friends who have been encouraging, and my patients who have been my real "textbooks" in medicine and psychiatry, I am further indebted.

Specifically, as regards the book, a special expression of appreciation is addressed to my sister, Vivian, in transcribing and deciphering the extensive preliminary manuscript into a typed product.

I remain deeply indebted to my Publisher, Tate Publishing for all the care they provided in helping create a sparkling diamond!

Table of Contents

Childhood

This story begins on December 18, 1940, when I was born in Pittsburgh, Pennsylvania, during the Second World War.

I remember some of my infancy.

One thing that I can remember during childhood that stand out is that I had one of these little pull Snoopy dogs with a string, and you would pull it and it would make bark like noise.

One incident vivid in my mind happened was when I was dressed up with a brand new pair of white shoes. I had a tendency to play in the cabinets, and I got my hands on blue dye, drank it, and spilled it; my shoes had blue dye all over them. My mother was upset about the whole thing.

We lived in the Oakland area of Pittsburgh during my very early years. Then my dad bought our first home on Potomac Avenue near Dormont, south of Pittsburgh. It was a very large brick home with many rooms. At the time, we used the downstairs of the home, and he would rent the upstairs, thereby helping to pay on the mortgage. Our home was on a big hill, and in the back there were woods. It was quite enchanting for me spending most of my time in those early years playing in the woods.

My brother, Bob, and I would dig in the dirt. We had toy trucks. We would take our shoes off and play in the dirt and have dirt battles.

My father and mother were been born in this country. My dad was from a small town, Brockway, Pa.; he came from a very large family. My grandmother had ten children. My mother came from the Hazelwood area of Pittsburgh, by the steel mills. I don't know the circumstances under which my parents met, but I think they were going together for some time before they got married. At the time we moved to Potomac Avenue, my dad was working at the Neville Chemical Company.

Since we had an old house, we had a coal furnace. As a small child, I would go up to the coal pile and carry coal in a bucket and dump it into the basement window into a coal bin.

My parents always fought. They were always arguing back and forth, and at times unfortunately, my dad would beat my mother, which I found extremely distressful. I also was constantly being beat for some reason or another. My dad had an extremely violent temper.

Around 1944, my father was drafted into the Army; he had served in the Army and had been stationed in Panama some years earlier when he was around eighteen years of age. When he was drafted during the Second World War, he had a home and three children. My sister had just been born around that time. After my dad had been drafted, my mother had a very difficult time controlling me.

I had the tendency to get up early in the morning and go out on neighborhood excursions. I would go to the five and ten cent store that was twenty or thirty blocks from where we lived. I would go in there and get a wagon and candy and toys and bring them home. My mother had remarked some years later that she found it quite curious that no one had really stopped me. She told me that some of those candy counters were so high that there was no way that I could have reached that candy myself, and she believed the girls that worked in that five and ten cent store gave me the candy and toys. One wooden wagon had been so cheap that as soon as I brought it home, one of the wheels had rolled off it.

My mother and I enjoyed sitting out in the sun. We would talk. She would tell me about her childhood, about my dad being in the Army, and her hopes of when he would be coming home.

At that time, the government had issued ration books for meats and dairy products. There was a page of little wooden coins that you would break out when you went to the store to buy something. You had to give so many of these coins to the storekeeper. The coins were red and blue. Karklick's Corner Store was one block from our home. I would shop there for my mother. Mr. Karklick was so kind, he always gave me a free pop out of the pop cooler. I would stand there drinking my pop, and we would chat.

There were times when I would take my brother and sister on excursions. One day, we had gone some distance. A nice lady saw us and invited us in and made us some lunch. She asked us where we were from; we had no idea. She called the police, and we were returned to my mother. My mother was unable to keep me home. She decided that I should be sent to my grandfather's farm in Brockway, Pennsylvania.

Sometime later, my Aunt Mary and grandparents came down to collect me, and I was taken to Brockway on the train. It was great fun on the train, because I had never been on a train before. I would be running from car to car, creating commotion.

I didn't like the farm much, because my activity had been strongly curtailed. My grandfather was an extremely controlling person.

He worked as a laborer on the railroad and was a coalminer and farmer. They had pigs and chickens on the farm. I had various chores to do. Some of the chores were feeding the chickens and going along with my grandfather in the morning when he would milk the cow. I also helped him patch up the fences and so forth. Since my grandfather had a large family, I had cousins to play with. Cousins Billy and Sis lived close to us. I played with them whenever the opportunity would arise. Francis, an older cousin, also lived with us for some time. It was great fun when he'd wheel us around in a wheelbarrow. He also helped my grandfather with the chores.

There was a creek out back that was great fun. I would drag old potato sacks through the creek and bring up all kinds of crabs and small fish. I had a large collection of different colored stones that I kept on the back porch of my grandfather's house, along with various spears that I had made out of wooden weeds. My grandmother would get very upset about all my weapons on the back porch, and from time to time, I would have to take them back into the woods.

At the end of the day when my grandfather was all finished working and had milked the cow, we would go to the farmhouse basement. In the basement was a gigantic wine barrel. I don't know if he had built this himself or whatever. He made his own wine. I enjoyed going to the basement with him, because he had an old grinding stone there. I would sharpen his knife for him. It was fun, because the stone would give off sparks. He would help himself to a few drinks and get smashed, and during the process, he gave me a few. This wine was rather powerful, and I had a hard time drinking it, but then later on, I would get looped myself. My Aunt Mary got very upset about this.

After some time, the war was ending. One day, my grandparents were very excited, telling me that we dropped a real big bomb on Japan, and that my dad would be coming home. I think at that time, my dad was in the Guadalcanal region in the Pacific. I had no concept of what an atomic bomb was, but I remember people were excited about the war coming to an end. I remember a picture in the newspapers of General Macarthur and other soldiers accepting the surrender of Japan.

Shortly thereafter, a young, decorated soldier came to visit my grandparents, and they asked me who he was. I took a look at him and told them it was my Uncle Jim. My Uncle Jim had come to see us from time to time. Since I hadn't seen him for sometime, I confused this soldier with my Uncle Jim. It was my dad. He was very happy to see me. He picked me up and told me, "I'm your dad, and I am taking you back home." I was quite pleased about this, because I didn't like the strictness of my grandparents. After a great welcoming celebration at my grandparents' home for my dad and uncles' coming home from the war, I was taken back to Pittsburgh.

After the war had ended, there were parades in Pittsburgh. Everyone was very happy that the war had ended and there were big parades—tanks rolling through the city and just a lot of good cheer. My cousin Tootsie had an American flag dress, with a real tall hat. Everyone had purchased small American flags and stood around waving them. It was really great the war was over.

My punishments were extreme. At times when my dad would get angry with me, he would hold me by my feet and swing me over the stairs—the basement stairs—and then throw me down the stairs. When I think about it now, I consider it an extreme form of punishment for some minor infractions.

My dad had gone to work at the Neville Chemical Company, working nights. After he would leave for work, my brother Bob and I, and my sisters, Vivian and Linda, would jump around on the couches and have fun.

Many times after my parents fought, my mother would put us in juvenile court and she'd go and stay with my grandmother.

The effects of being in juvenile court were severe for my younger siblings.

My brother Bob would cry and cry and wouldn't stop. At that time, I had adapted to being separated from my parents, and it didn't seem to bother me as much as it did the younger ones. Later on, my parents would come and get us and bring us back home after arriving at some agreement about their current problems.

My dad had made a couple of grape arbors, and he built one of them in the form of a playhouse. He had built benches where we could sit outside and eat. He also built a seesaw for us. When it would rain, we would go in there and play and not get wet. The woods were really a fascinating place. We would go back there and pick violets for my mother, dig holes, and chop down trees.

The basement of our home was large. We would ride our tricycles through the rooms in the basement. There was a sun porch on the first floor where we could play, and it was rather pleasant.

About a year after the Second World War, I was of school age and ready to go to school. For some reason, my parents had never sent me to kindergarten. The school was too far away, and there was highway that I had to cross. They were probably concerned that I might get killed on the way to school. I started the first grade at Banksville Public School, which a good three miles from where we lived. Every morning, my father would take me to school so that I would learn the route. He had instructed me to only cross the highway where the school crossing guard was. There were actually two routes to school that I could take. One of the routes by which I had to go where the crossing guard was and that was the route I had been instructed to take.

I started school, and it was fun. My dad would take me in the morning with my lunch bucket, and my mother would come at the end of the day and bring me home. I started to make some friends with children who lived in the Banksville school district. These children lived along the route that I wasn't supposed to take.

When my parents were no longer taking me to school. I continued to take the route that I was forbidden to take. I believed I was capable of going that route, and I decided to take it. I had made some very close friends. One was Mary, along with three or four other children. We went to go to school together and came home at the end of the day together. It was fun. We made pinwheels at the school and were in art class. My parents had been very angry because school was getting on, and I was unable to write my name. They had grave concerns about the quality of teaching that I was receiving.

One day when I was going home from school, an unfortunate incident happened. Somehow my shoelaces got untied, and I tripped and fell in the path of a car. The lady driver had hit the break and the car skidded right into me and stopped right on me; it hadn't run over me, but I had a big bruise on the side of my chest where the car had stopped. The school crossing guard lady ran down, and everyone was very concerned. At first, they wanted to take me to the hospital but then decided to take me home and tell my parents what had happened. After this incident, and the fact that my dad didn't believe that I was getting a good education, he took me out of this school. Dad had me enrolled in St. Catherine's Grade School in Beechview, a suburb of Pittsburgh. When I started at St. Catherine's, it was necessary for me to take a streetcar, because the school was quite far from where we lived. St. Catherine's School was quite a change from the Banksville Public School.

I was in the second grade in Sister Saint James' Class. It was a very strict class, and we were required to stay in our seats at all times. I had a very difficult time adjusting to this, because I wasn't accustomed to authoritative teaching. I was constantly acting out in class and therefore was constantly being paddled in the cloakroom, because I wouldn't stay in my seat. I believe I hold the world's record for the most paddled second-grader on the planet.

My parents were pleased with this educational program, because I was learning the things that I was supposed to learn. The difference between this school and the public school was that I got Catechism. I liked the nuns very much, even though they were ritualistic. In those days, they wore long black robes with large rosary beads around their waist hanging down their side. The nuns would have parties for us around special holidays like Thanksgiving, Halloween, Christmas, and Easter. It was great fun.

My parents' bickering and fighting was going on as usual. I decided I would run away from home. I ran away from home and slept in cars. In those days, people did not lock their cars. The next day when I woke up, I went to school. When I arrived at school, I was quite dirty, and the sister took me to the principal. The principal had called the police, because unknown to myself, during the night, my parents had called the police and told them they thought I was kidnapped. My picture had been in the paper, and everyone had been frantically searching for me. When the police arrived, I was quite upset. I told them I had been out sleeping in a car.

From this one episode, any time there would be a lot of fighting at home or my dad's beatings of me became intolerable, I would run away and stay out for a night or two, and then return home. After a while, my parents came to accept this, because I ran away from home so much that there wasn't really anything they could do about it.

During those years, my mother had taken me over to my grandmother's frequently. Once I learned the streetcar route, when I would run away, I stayed with my grandmother. It took two streetcars to travel to my grandmother's house. Since I was such a young child, I would go on the streetcar with people, and the driver just expected that I was with somebody. Or when people would be paying, I would sneak on the streetcar. I became very good at doing this and got on streetcars without paying anything. Sometimes the conductors would catch me. I just made up some story that they seemed to accept, such as "I thought my mother got on this streetcar with me, but I guess she stayed in the store too long."

The old streetcars in those days were fun to ride. There were two operating places on the streetcar, in the front and in the back. Depending on what direction the streetcar was going, only one end would be in use at the time. I would usually go in the back and sit on the seat and play with the steering wheels, which were fun. These old streetcars really rattled.

I had been running away from home so much and going to my grandmother's; she finally accepted the fact that I would be constantly going there. She would get up at all hours of the night to let me in and make a place on the couch for me to sleep. I would stay there for a few days until I felt like going back home. I don't know what I would have done if I wouldn't have had my grandmother to watch over me.

My Uncle Richard was an auto mechanic and truck driver. He would haul coal. I would go with him in his dump truck, which was fun. We would go down to these large dump platforms, where the train's coal cars were turned over by a big machine. The coal would be emptied into a big bin under which a truck would pass to be filled with coal. It was a happy time when I could go with my uncle on these various trips.

I had been running away from home so much during the second grade that when school was over, the authorities from juvenile court decided that I should be taken out of my parents' home. It was recommended that I be sent back to my grandfather's farm. My Aunt Mary agreed they would take care of me. The summer before I entered the third grade, I went back to Brockway, Pa. I took my dog Champ with me. He was a spotty mongrel, mostly terrier and begal, that I had gotten for my birthday. I wasn't about to leave my dog.

My Dog Champ

When I lived with my grandparents this time, my grandfather had retired from the railroad. He still had a cow and some chickens. I would help him with the various chores around the farm. He also had a big garden. When school started, I entered Brockway Public School. I don't remember my teacher's name; it may have been Mrs. Johnson or Mrs. Thompson. There were two grades within one classroom. I was in the same class with my cousin, Sissy. My cousin, Billy, was in a class ahead of me on the other side of the room.

During school, we had group singing. I became quite a singer. I was so good that the teacher would have me come in front of the room, and I would sing in front of the class. I had a crush on a young blond girl, Ranitha. I would sing to her, "When it's Springtime in the Rockies." Everyone was always quite pleased with my performances. The school playground was great. They had an old fashioned merry-go-round. It had to be pumped by hand. The faster you would pump, the faster it would go. There were also swings, seesaws, and horseshoes.

One of my chores was to feed the chickens. When I would go into this one particular chicken coop, there was a blasted rooster there who would peck at me. I would bring in chicken feed and scatter it all over the place so the chickens and hens could have something to eat, and this blasted rooster would peck at me all the time. Since my grandparents were farm folks, from time to time, my Aunt Mary would make chicken for dinner. Whenever she did, she would go out and grab one of the chickens and chop off its head.

On one particular occasion, I asked her if I could pick the unlucky victim, and she agreed. I went through the coop and sure enough, there was that blasted rooster. She ran after him, grabbed him, and pulled him over to the tree stump. She laid his head on the stump, and held him by the feet. He was squawking. She came down with the axe, chopping off his head. I was really surprised to see he was able to run around without his head for a few seconds.

There was a sawmill in the area where we lived that was really great. The neighborhood kids and I would go over to this mill, which had pump cars. One could pump up and down so that we could travel a fair distance on these cars. We would sneak into this place and ride these cars. There was lot of sawdust from the mill that would be taken by small rail cars to a high platform and be dropped off. As a result, there was a mountain of sawdust several stories under this drop-off. We would run to the end of this drop-off and leap off onto the mountain of sawdust. None of us were ever hurt, because the sawdust was a tremendous buffer. It was fun to roll down this gigantic mountain of sawdust.

A watchdog was there to guard the premises. He knew us, and we gave him candy. He never chased us. He was always happy to see us whenever we would come around and would run with us. The elderly night watchman was always chasing us but could never catch us.

Another very enjoyable activity was going over to a mill where a train had stopped, and we would get on the flat cars after they had been unloaded. When the train would be moving, we would run from the far end of the flatcar and jump across each one. It was a miracle that none of us were killed doing this. One day when we were doing this, my grandfather, coming down from the barn, happened to spot me on a flatcar. He beat me that night. That curtailed any of our fooling around on trains.

In the spring, summer, and early fall, we would go on picnics. In one particular wooden area, there were tree vines. We would swing on these vines like Tarzan; it was great fun.

My Aunt Mary worked for the Brockway Glass Works. She had a black Ford sedan. She would pick me up after school on Main Street after work. She drove to the neighborhood news store to buy a newspaper and an ice cream bar for me. This was a fun activity I would await every day.

One of the town's performances of great interest to us was Saturday's local movie house ongoing serial, *Rocket Man*. If I had been good during the week, I could attend with my cousins. These episodes were great! They were similar to the serial, *Superman*. Rocket Man had a lot of gadgets to hook himself up to.

One day in the late fall, I had a very bad fight with my cousin when we were going to confession at the church. As a result, I hid in another church. Since I was there for a few hours, everyone believed I was lost. The whole town was out looking for me. They even had the fire department searching for me. At this time, it was quite cold and some of the searchers had gone off into the forest to look for me, while I was very warm in the church. Later that evening, when I had no idea what was going on, I decided to go home. On the way, my Aunt Mary happened to be driving down the road and spotted me. They were very happy to have found me, but they decided I was such a nuisance that I should be sent back to Pittsburgh. My uncle Jim and my dad came to Brockway for me. They took me back to Pittsburgh with my dog.

When I returned to Pittsburgh, I returned to St. Catherine's Grade School. I was in the fourth grade in Sr. Evangelista's class.

I found out that during the time that I had been gone, one of the neighborhood boys, Chucky, had been picking on my brother, Bob. When I found out about this, I started punching him every time I saw him. Finally his dad came down to complain to my dad about it. My dad told him that his son had been picking on my little brother, and he hadn't done anything about it at the time, so he really didn't get upset about this. After a while, when I believed he got what he deserved, I quit hitting him. Our neighborhood gang, Chucky M., Chucky W., Harvey A., Joe D., Billy H., and I were always into shenanigans.

I became a paperboy, and I had one of the largest paper routes in Pittsburgh. In the evening after school, I would deliver my papers. Many times, my friends would come with me. At times, we would all get cigarettes and smoke on the paper route. We felt pretty big doing this.

I saved my money on my paper route, and I bought a single-shot Daisy B-B Gun.

Back in those days, they had old-fashioned streetlamps; a flat piece of tin with a very large light bulb. It didn't have a globe on it. I'd become such a good shot that a block away, I would aim higher than the bulb and drop the bulb with one shot. Usually after the paper route, some of the streetlights in the neighborhood were out.

I really liked school; I never played hooky. If there were times when I had run away from home and Sister Evangelista knew that I hadn't eaten, she would send me over to the convent, and the cook would make me something to eat. I always got good care at school.

Sister Gerald was the principal at St. Catherine's School. She was a very old nun. Everybody was terrified of her. No one wanted to see her, especially if it had to do with disciplinary action.

On Stracken Avenue adjacent to our house, there were two tall, flexible pine trees. We would climb to the top of these trees and just hang on, and swing back and forth in the wind. It was great fun. There wasn't too much danger as long as one held on to the tree. Fortunately, none of us ever fell and got seriously hurt.

I saved up enough money from my paper route that year that when Christmas came, I bought my dad a Bulova watch. He was quite surprised, and I was quite pleased.

I was indoctrinated in Catholicism during my time in Catholic schools; especially around the time of Lent. On Ash Wednesday, everybody would get ashes for the beginning of Lent. Everyone would try to give up something they liked to do for Lent. Every Friday, all of the school children would go to church and make the Stations of the Cross. You would go around to various stations that were pictures of each of the steps to the crucifixion that Christ had to undergo.

A girl who sat behind me in class, Sandy S., would tease me all the time. She always showed me her petticoat, but she also wanted to fight, too. We had an incident during our First Communion. Actually, it wasn't really my First Communion, because before this when everyone went up to the altar to receive Communion, I went along. After old Father McCann gave me the Host he realized that I had not yet made my First Holy Communion. He stopped right in the middle of Communion Services and told me that I was not supposed to be there and to go back to my seat. I was really embarrassed, because the church was packed.

Regarding, my "First Communion." The boys were dressed in black, and the girls all had white dresses. All of us got a kit with a prayer book and rosaries. I had a black prayer book; Sandy had a white one. After the ceremony, we were outside; it had just stopped raining. She came over to me and said, "Let me see your prayer book; here look at mine."

I was looking at hers and I said, "It looks all right, but I like mine better."

Then, she said, "You can keep mine; I like yours better."

I said, "Listen, I want mine back."

I tried to get it back. She started pulling on my prayer book. I let go, and she fell right back into a large mud puddle behind her. She was covered with mud! Unfortunately, just then her mother pulled up in a car and got out and ran over to me and started to hit me. I told her Sandy took my book, and I finally got it back. Sandy and I still remained friends.

I was one of the few kids in class that had a paper route and was able to make money on my own. While I was in school I also had a paper route and made spending money.

Even though I never played hooky, I was quite a hell raiser in school. If I didn't like the class, I would take in a comic book and insert it in the book. While everybody was studying geography or something I didn't like, I would be reading a comic book. Another favorite pastime in class was to shoot gum bands. You would use a ruler as a base and put the gum band on the end and pull it back and release it. It was almost like an arrow. I and a few other kids in the class would have gum band battles each time the nun wasn't observing us. From time to time, the kids who got in trouble in class had to stay after school and write on the blackboard a hundred or several hundred times, "I will be a good student."

At times, we sold chance tickets for the school. I enjoyed doing this, because it was a good way to make some spending money. A book of tickets was $5. For each book that a student would sell, one would get fifty cents or $1.00. When I was on my paper route, I would sell chances to my customers.

The fifth and sixth grades were located in portable buildings. St. Catherine's was a small school, and they had built these additional buildings that had coal stoves. It was an old type one-room schoolhouse, and there were small rooms in the back where one would hang one's clothes.

Sister Gabriella was about two hundred years old but very kind. We spent an inordinate amount of time on the multiplication tables. She was a real bear on memorization. There is no way I could ever forget those tables.

Since I was the eldest of ten, I would take my brothers and sisters back and forth to school. I also took them to church on Sunday.

My brother helped me on my paper route. Our dream was to buy a '48 or '49 MG. It was a beautiful roadster with horns on the front, and a wheel in the back, on top of the trunk, and side runners. At the time, the car was $1,900.

All through grade school, I had a crush on an Irish girl, Denise K. Her family lived about seven or eight blocks from our home, and she came from a large family also. Her dad was a plumber.

I was also spending time at my grandmother's in Hazelwood when I would run away from home. I had my BB gun with me and would shoot out the neighborhood streetlights. The police were always after me. They finally caught up with me. Although they didn't take me to jail, they did take my BB gun. I was pretty upset about not having it anymore. When my mother came to take me back home, I wanted her to go to the police station with me and get my BB gun, but she wouldn't do it.

It was just matter of time before I saved up enough money on my paper route to buy a Daisy 1000 shot repeater BB gun. It was much better than the single-shot BB gun. I could load many BBs and shoot at my leisure. I was really pleased with it. Usually, after school, my dog and I, with my friends, would go to the woods down by a creek and fill bottles up with water and shoot at them. This would produce a hole in the bottle, and a stream of water would come running out. It was a lot of fun.

During the summer of that year, I spent a lot of time over my grandmother's. I may have been there the entire summer. I palled around with some the neighborhood boys. We would go down to the B&O Railroad train yards by the river and throw rocks in the river and ride river rafts. At night, we would socialize with our other friends.

In the summer, I would go to the swimming pool or to the movies. I enjoy scary movies.

When TV first came out, my grandmother was one of the first people in her neighborhood to get a TV. She was so kind; she would invite the neighbors over to watch TV. She would serve coffee or ice tea and cookies, and they all would chat and watch TV. I wasn't too keen on watching TV during those years, because I was always out doing things with my buddies.

In the fall, I was in the sixth grade. My sixth grade nun was Sister Avangala. Sister Avangala was really foxy. One afternoon, she sent me over to the principal with a message for her. She usually sent the class hell raisers on chores during the day. On the way back to the school portable, I stood on the porch by the front door and was making faces at my classmates. They all kept a straight face and did not give me away. The next thing I knew, the nun flew around the corner and had me by the neck, shaking me.

I had to stay after school and write on the blackboard several hundred times that I would be a good boy. I told her I couldn't figure out how she knew I was there. Her desk faced the class, and her back was to the front wall, where the door was. She showed me how the picture on the back wall hung. All she had to do was look up at it, and it gave off a reflection of the front porch and anyone who was there. Of course, she saw me when I was doing my stunts and I was "caught in the act."

My dog, Champ, started coming to school with me. He would lie on the porch until school was out and then go home with me. He did this even when I would go back and forth on my bike. One day, Sister Gerard, the principal, came by. She tried to chase him away. He started barking at her and even attempted to bite her. It caused quite a commotion and disrupted the class. After it was discovered that Champ was my dog, I was told to take him home and not bring him back to school anymore.

She told me if she ever saw him at school again, she would send a letter off to my dad. So I didn't bring Champ to school anymore.

During my paper route, I would pick up all the Popsicle Pete bags I found on the street. One could get nice gifts for hundreds of Popsicle bags. Well, I believed I saved up several thousand, and I sent them into the Popsicle Pete Company. I got a beautiful, large Bowie Knife. I took it to school to show my classmates. The nun took it away from me and gave it to Father McCann.

I complained about it, because I had worked very hard for a long time collecting bags to be able to get it. My mother finally went and got it back for me. My mother was very surprised to see that I even had it. Eventually, I ended up trading it to my friend, Chucky W, for a Japanese Rifle his dad had given him from the war. During these years, I had developed the largest paper route in Pittsburgh.

In fact, I had acquired so many new customers that I won a trip to Conneaut Lake, PA.

The Pittsburgh Post Gazette Newspaper sent me there on a train, and everything was free. Unfortunately, it rained that day, but I still had a very nice time there. Another time, I sold so many papers that I got to go to the Pittsburgh Pirates Club Room, and I met some of the ball players. I even got an autographed baseball bat. It was really great.

My pals would go on my paper route with me, and we would smoke. We thought this was a big deal, although we would get pretty sick on strong cigars. During the winter on my paper route, we would take our BB guns along. When we would find an outside tree with Christmas lights on it, we would lie under other trees in the snow and shoot out the lights. When you hit a light, it would explode with a very loud pop.

On my paper route, I met the son of one of my customers. He asked me if I wanted to buy some cherry bombs. I said sure. I liked to blow them up. They were really powerful! Later, I learned from him that his older brother worked for the city and used dynamite on his job. The kid informed me he knew how to take the explosive apart and use the powder to make cherry bombs. He talked me into helping him make cherry bombs. I would get old TV antennas. We would cut them up and put powder in them and pound the ends together. He used a hole-punch and put a fuse in it for lighting. As I think on this now, it was a miracle we were not blown up with all the pounding we did making the bombs. I am sure God was watching over us. Later, his older brother discovered what was going on, and had a "meltdown." After that, I was forbidden to ever see my bomb-making friend again.

I had to go shopping with my mother from time to time. Sometimes I would swipe a six-pack of candy bars and hide them in my shirt for my friends and I. On Sundays, I was expected to take my brothers and sisters to church, but we preferred to go for long walks. My dad had given each of us a church envelope with coins in it.

We always spent it on ice cream or candy. We were poor as church mice.

Carklick's Corner Store was a block up from our home. I would make deliveries for Mr. Carklick, and he would give me pop, ice cream, or candy.

In the fall of this year, the stores started selling bean shooters. It was a large, thick plastic straw. We would buy beans for shooting. I believe they were navy beans. It was a hard, white bean. One would fill one's mouth up and blow out beans. It was a good shooter and my pals and I would have bean battles. It was great fun.

You would see the neighborhood kids running down the street with baggy pockets filled with beans. One night, we went over to the Dormont football field. There were stands where spectators sat and on the outside, there was a very high fence. We would stand there and peer in. We were making jokes and laughing when a man on the stands walked down and peered through the fence and yelled as us. We stood there listening to him and then all of a sudden, we took out our bean shooters and really plastered him.

We fell on the ground, we were laughing so hard. He said, "I am going to kill you kids." This guy was really fast. We were some of the fastest runners in the neighborhood. Nobody could catch us. It was remarkable was that he took off from those bleachers and ran all the way up to the entrance on the other side of the field. He ended up catching my brother. He was super fast. He took my brother's bean shooter and broke it. He turned Bob upside down, held him by his ankles, shaking him, and all his beans fell out of his pockets onto the street.

I told him I was going to call the police. He said he was going to kill me if he ever caught me. My buddies were scared; they had all scattered like rabbits. Later on, I got another bean shooter for Bob, but we didn't go back there anymore.

In the summer of '53, when I was over my grandmother's, I started hanging around a gang. Two of my best friends were Joe and Hank. They were much older than me, about seventeen or eighteen. They had old cars that they worked on. They would go out drinking, riding around, and playing cards. They always stole parts from cars because they were poor. They didn't take me with them then; they were fearful I would get caught. Joe was the best fighter in the neighborhood. A lot of these guys had hot rods. I would spend a lot of time with them and help them work on their cars. I learned a lot about motors this way.

At this time, I met a girl who lived down from my grandmother's, Trudy D, and I liked her. Her mother was a religious fanatic. She always told us about the Bible. I really loved this woman. I went over there frequently. They were as poor as church mice. They had a big family. They later moved to California.

I had also joined the Boy Scouts this year, because my friends had joined. The scoutmaster, Mr. K, was a plumber. He also employed me part-time, working on the home he was building. It was an opportunity to make more money for myself. I liked scouting and had gone on several camping trips with my friends. Since we were a neighborhood gang, we always went off by ourselves and did not stay in formation. I advanced quickly and got several badges. I could identify sassafras. I was always found digging up sassafras roots to chew on or for making tea. It tasted like root beer; it's really good. Unfortunately, when we were at the Jamboree, we were supposed to be with the rest of the scouts, but we were in our tent reading comic books. I decided to make sassafras tea but had not kept my eye on it. When I went out to get the tea, the whole field was on fire. Fortunately, since there were many scouts at the Jamboree, we put out the fire in a short period of time.

When fall rolled around, I was in the seventh grade at St. Catherine's. We were now in the main school building. It was quite a difference. We had a homeroom and had different classes in other rooms. My homeroom nun was Sister Saint Francis, and she was fairly flexible. She liked boys and tended to favor them. Most nuns like girls and don't like to put up with hell-raising boys, but Sister Saint Francis could put up with things. She would give us different responsibilities. My job was to dust erasers at the end of the last class. I was happy to do this, because I got to skip history. I liked her very much and would help her scrub the Convent basement floor after school. I visited her all my life. She died at age ninety-three a few years ago.

As usual, we were back to our gum band battles. During class, someone shot off a gum band, and Sister Martin was at her desk, and it landed right in front of her. She was quite startled, and everyone laughed. Since no one would own up to the deed, we all had to stay in after school. She said if it happened again, she would report it to the principal.

We then brought squirt guns to school and would shoot all the girls in between classes.

I was doing very well in seventh grade English. Sister Judith was a very good English teacher. I was good in math, too.

This year I gave up my paper route, because I was chosen for a better job. I had a paper stand, and I also got to do all the bars in our paper district. The paper man drove me around to all the bars, and I would go in and sell papers. The only problem was that I didn't get home until after midnight, but my parents didn't mind.

I always bought my own clothes. I got a lot of tips, and sometimes someone would buy all my papers. My stand was in front of a drugstore. The counter girls always gave me free cokes. One day, the druggist saw the girl give me a free coke, and he yelled at her. I got very angry and told him that I worked very hard selling papers, especially to his customers, and deserved a free coke now and then. He told me to get out of the drugstore and that if he saw me in there anymore, he would call the police. I was really angry that he had yelled at that girl, so I got my squirt gun and shot up his store windows. He was so angry about this that he called up the paper company and had them move my paper stand to the other corner near the movie house. The paper company was not about to fire me; I was probably the best paperboy they had ever had.

I was very good friends with the Mt. Lebanon police. They had a foot policeman who would go around to all the stores and alleys to check the doors to see if anyone had broken in. I would go along with him, when I wasn't too busy on my paper stand. It was a lot of fun. They gave me police hats. Actually, the druggist had called the police and since they knew me, they wouldn't do anything about it. However, I did shoot the police with my squirt gun but later, they got me. One night they invited me to the station, which was adjacent to the fire station. They drenched me with the fire hose, because I wouldn't promise not to shoot anymore. I was soaked and wet. I knew I couldn't use my squirt gun anymore, because I liked to go on walks with them, and they always bought me a bottle of pop.

This year was especially bad one for me at home; I got into constant fights with my parents. I stayed away from home more and more. I had been in juvenile court probably three hundred times for running away from home over the years. I would sleep outside in the neighborhood with my dog. Many times, if I couldn't find a place to sleep, or it was too cold, I would go to court myself and sleep there until my mother came for me.

In June when I completed seventh grade, I decided to leave home altogether. I was building an underground hut in the woods to live in, and my pals were helping me dig it. I thought I could break into a plumbing line to get water. I had planned to live there, and my pals would bring me food. My mother believed I had to be put away, because I wouldn't obey her anymore. One day when I was working on the hut, my dog started to bark and I heard a lot of noise. I saw police running down the hill so I took off, but they caught me in the jagger bushes. They took my BB gun and took me to court.

I was in Juvenile Detention Home all that summer. In the fall, they had a trial for me. My mother told the judge I should be put away. I was sent to reform school; Thorn Hill in Warrendale, Pennsylvania. I was thirteen years old at that time. I was sent there in September of 1954, and I was very upset about it. I finally arrived there. There were very large cottages, and many boys were there. There were probably several hundred. I was placed in Cottage Ten after a week in an infirmary cottage. Mr. and Mrs. F were the house parents. It was a very large farm. We had beef and dairy cattle, large planting areas, and acres of apple orchards. We produced most of our food. We grew grains, corn, and just about anything you can think of. We went to school for half days. One group would work in the morning and one in the afternoon. It was very hard work. We would get up about 5:30 a.m., and all of us would do the morning chores, such as feeding the livestock. Our life was extremely regimented. We were marched in line most of the time. Their form of punishment was very brutal. When I got there in September, we were working in the orchards and that wasn't too bad. The apples were so good that I was sick constantly because I ate too many apples. You were able to eat all you wanted.

In a way it was fun, too. We would ride a wagon and then load it up. Mrs. F did a lot of canning, and a few boys were left at the cottage to help her during the day. We saw a movie once a week. The academic program was very poor. We did boxing a lot.

I was considered the best worker. Farm work is very hard and during the thirteen months I was there, I got to be quite strong.

On Sundays at Thorn Hill, a group of young Sisters of Mercy (nuns) would come and spend time with us. One nun, Sister Mary Paul, has been a lifelong friend of mine. She later got a Ph.D. in Educational Psychology at Fordham University and was the Chairman of Education at Mt. Mercy College in Pittsburgh. She then became a principal at the grade school there. Even though she is retired, she teaches reading to foreigners.

I didn't like the house parents. Mr. F was brutal. You really didn't have anyone you could sit down and talk with about problems. I developed strong relationships with my peers. We would talk about all the jobs we were going to pull when we got out, such as stealing cars and robbing banks. We were going to start gangs.

We went to bed about 8:30 p.m., because we had to get up early in the a.m. After awhile, I became a squad leader; like being a drill sergeant. I was a trustee and would take my peers back and forth to whatever places we had to go to such as school. I became a squad leader very fast. I worked very hard, and I was used as an example to the other kids. I could handle myself in a fight pretty good. Once a month you could get visitors, and once a month, my mother or dad would come. I couldn't see my brothers and sisters. I learned to weave there, too. I wove a very wide, very colorful belt. It was a series of knots, and it took nine months to make. I still have this belt today; it's beautiful. A couple of Indian boys had taught us how to do this, as I recall.

We had a big incident one day as we were going up to feed the pigs garbage. We always rode on the wagon that was pulled by a tractor. There was a pack of wild dogs that attacked the pigs. The farmers in the area got their guns and went out and shot the dogs, but by then, they had killed most of the pigs. I had never seen any-thing like this. I didn't know that dogs would run in packs like that. Later we found some pups, but they were taken away from us.

Our food at the cottage was very good. Every Friday, Mrs. F would bake devils' food cake with egg white icing. It was simply delicious. She used to irritate me with her bragging about the cake, but I have to admit it was the best devils' food cake I ever ate

One time when I was on rotation doing kitchen duty, I was clean-ing out the cupboard and the usual thing was to throw out anything there. Well, there were some cupcakes there, and we ate them. Mr. F beat us severely for having eaten those cakes. From then on, I felt he was a terrible person. I realized then that these people really didn't care about us. I was a trustee the last few months I was there.

In the fall, we harvested; in the winter, we took care of the livestock mostly, and in the spring, we would start the planting season. They had very good farm equipment.

In August of 1955, my dad wanted the court to release me so that I could begin high school at the start of the year. The court would not release me until my thirteen months were up, and I was placed on parole. Finally, I was released. I was taken back to juvenile court to be released. I didn't recognize my sister, Vivian.

I was fourteen then. My family had a big party for me at home. My dog didn't remember me. It was wonderful to have my freedom. How terrible it is to be without freedom. It can't be described. You really have to live through it. I prefer death than to be without my freedom.

I enrolled in South Hills Public High School and started ninth grade. Unfortunately, it was only little over a month before more problems arose in the family. The court again got involved and decided that it would be best for me to be out of my family situation.

I was sent to the Philadelphia Protectory for Boys in Phoenixville, Pa. A state trooper drove me there by way of the Pennsylvania Turnpike. The institution was in a large valley. There was a large clock tower there surrounded by walls. It was very foreboding. This place was run by the Christian Brothers. I was placed in the oldest group. I think there were about two hundred boys in my group. The work pattern was like Thorn Hill; you would work half a day and go to school half a day. I was placed in the tailor shop. I didn't want to do this type of work, but I was assigned there anyway. I was taught a trade. The tailor taught me skills. We made a lot of things there. I worked in the tailor shop the whole thirteen months that I was there. They had farming there, but I was not among the group who did the farming.

As far as academics, I was supposed to be in the ninth grade but I was given a test and was placed in the seventh grade. I was very angry about this, but there wasn't anything I could do about it. I had made the school honor roll every month of the thirteen months I was there. The brothers were too ignorant to realize that I belonged in a higher grade, where I would have intellectual challenge. The recreation period was at night and one could watch TV, work in the woodworking area, or read or whatever. There was a weightlifting area, and I began a bodybuilding program. It became an obsession with me. The problem was that they would only let you use the 110-pound barbell set. They had 4–25-pound plates, but we couldn't use these, because they were fearful that the boys would hurt themselves. I became one of the strongest kids in the place.

Their methods of punishment were really brutal. For some minor infraction they would shave one's head, and you would to stand on a line for a whole month or so. You even had to stand while eating. One's legs would swell because of the stasis that would result because of no movement. You didn't get the pumping action of the muscles milking the blood back to the heart. As a result, a lot of blood would be in the legs and one would get hypotensive and faint. We also received lectures at the end of the day. Sex was described as filth. Masturbation was considered abnormal and animalistic. Even though these were Christian brothers I really didn't see anything Christian in them; I believed they were monsters. I was angry at the Roman Catholic faith because of the ugly experience in this place. Natural feelings or normal desires of adolescence were never discussed. Empathy, love, and caring were unknowns here. We were servants only. There were many religious rituals but totally without meaning.

We had a recess in the evening.

I developed strong friendships, and we had big plans when we were going to get out. We planned to rob banks. At the time, we thought of many plans. I had girls on the mind all the time.

I was quite apathetic about the whole place. I was extremely bitter at society; I believed I was the victim of family circumstances and didn't belong in these institutions.

I was beaten quite severely for smuggling out letters from my buddies through the tailor shop. Mail was always read before it was permitted to be sent out.

The food was terrible; I took the bugs out of my food before I would eat it. In fact, later when I was home, my family would ask me why I always looked through my food before I ate it. The habit is still with me to this day. We got jungle stew and hash that we all hated. The hash looked like dog food. The brothers never ate this slop. That was real hypocrisy. Something that I really liked was scrapple. It's ironic that years later when I saw a can in a store and read the ingredients, I couldn't eat it anymore.

I went though a lot of soul searching in this place. Because of the hypocrisy and lack of love in this place, I dropped Catholicism. I started to believe that Christ and the Bible were a lot of hooey.

I decided to read the Bible from cover to cover to discover its falsehood. It took almost a year to read it. It was the most beautiful book I had ever read; a story of God with his people.

Christ was the most wonderful person I had ever discovered.

I accepted him as my King and my God forever. I could not find any fault with Jesus. The power of His courage and His love was overwhelming. I made a commitment in my mind, heart, and soul at that time, since everyone else in my life had failed me, that I would accept Christ as my Shepherd forever.

A certain sense of serenity resulted from this, and a courage to go on. From the depths of my soul, Christ had spoken to me, "I will lead you to all your dreams." I had no idea what that meant. Even though I had felt extremely vengeful and wanted to get back at all the people that had hurt me, all of these feelings were suddenly gone. I had been reborn. I knew I could go on and endure all that was expected of me, to do my best with the help of my Lord. I made up my mind to prove to people that I wasn't bad. I had the capacity to become something better than what I was.

On December 14, 1956, I was released, and I was sent back to Pittsburgh on a train. I had a meeting with the court. A PhD court psychologist tested me and informed me that I did not have the academic ability to complete high school and that I should learn a trade. I asked him what PhD meant. He answered Doctor of Philosophy. I didn't understand that because he was a psychologist. He told me that was what a Ph.D. meant but it did not make any sense to me at the time.

My family was happy to have me back home since they had not seen me in over a year.

Teenage Years

Two days after my release from court I turned sixteen.

When I went out with my friends, they suggested we go to a pizza place. I had no idea what pizza was, and I thought it was strange my friends wanted to get bread with tomato sauce on it. When I first ate it, I knew I would eat it all my life. It was that good. The pizza place was a teen hangout place, too.

I had no desire to go to school at that time, because of the poor academic experience I had had in reform school. Since I was quite strong, I wanted to get a job in a steel mill and make a lot of money. Unfortunately, even though employers wanted to hire me, they couldn't because I was under age and unable to get into a union. I finally got a job as a magazine salesman. I wasn't a very good salesman.

I didn't get many subscriptions; even though my employers were satisfied with my work and wanted me to stay on, I decided to quit.

I then got a job at the Supersonic Car Wash a few miles from my home. I worked full-time and was doing a good job. I believe I was paid $1 /hour. Well, after a few weeks, they hired an older man. I found out that he was paid 25¢ an hour more than they were paying me. I went to the manager and complained about it. He said that because he was a man and I was just a kid, he had to pay him more. I told him that I was doing the same work he was, and I wanted the same pay or I would quit. Since he wouldn't pay me more, I quit. I realized at that point that I had to go back to school and get an education. I couldn't get a good job that paid well enough to satisfy me.

Since I had always been in Catholic Schools, I decided to apply to St. Justin's for the tenth grade because at age of sixteen, that is the class I should have been in.

I informed the principal, a nun, that I wanted to start school and be placed in the tenth grade. When I told her that I had been through two reform schools, she informed me she couldn't accept me. She said I needed to see the Monsignor at the Arch Diocese of Pittsburgh. She told me I would have to start at the beginning of the ninth grade, but I didn't want to do that because I was sixteen. Actually, I could pass for mid-twenties. I met the monsignor, but he wasn't willing to take me in any of the schools. He believed I might be a problem. I was very, very angry about this. I had the motivation to go to school and learn, but no one would help me get back in school. Because of the monsignor's response, it solidified my split with the Catholic Church. These people didn't care about me and therefore, I didn't care about them or anything they stood for. When I told my dad about it, he couldn't believe that they wouldn't take me back in school.

He went down there with me to meet the monsignor to check this out himself. The monsignor told my dad the same thing he had told me. My dad said he would check into this further.

It was during this time that we had a neighbor, Dr. Jonstantin Jaroshezich. He gave sermons in Pittsburgh on WPIT. Dr. Jaroshezich was on the Council of Christian Churches. He visited with my parents several nights a week. He was Russian; he had escaped from Russia. He had been destined for Siberia, but the underground got him out in time with his family. The first time I saw him, I made fun of him, because he was begging me to go back to school. I was irritated about it, because I had tried to go to school and had been unable to get back in school. When I told him my story, he told me he would take me himself and try to get me in school.

I very reluctantly decided that I would go with him. He called the board of education and made an appointment for us. He believed he would be able to get me in one of the public schools. He had rheumatism and suffered a lot. He always had a bad cough. I think he was in his eighties. It was an extremely cold day in Pittsburgh when we left for the board of education. He was coughing severely that day as we were standing» waiting for the streetcar. He was very distinguished looking. I was a "street-kid" in Levi jeans, motorcycle boots, and a Levi jacket with studs all over it. I realized he cared about me. He cared about my future and had faith in me.

A lot of my relatives had condemned me. They believed I wouldn't amount to anything. From that moment on, I loved this minister. I realized he was genuine, and I was happy about it.

He reflected Christian qualities.

We got to the board of education, and he met with the director. He told me he would get me into any public high school in Pittsburgh.

He got me into South Hills High School. I became one of the best students in my class. A lot of kids would goof off, but I took my education extremely seriously. I wanted to learn all I could. I studied very hard. All of my friends in the neighborhood went to Dormont High School, which was within walking distance from my home. I had not applied there, because we did not live in the Dormont Borough.

I later developed more friends from Dormont High School. They informed me I could go there too. Because the city school was so far away, the City of Pittsburgh paid their tuition to Dormont High School. I decided to see if I could transfer, too, because most of my neighborhood friends went to Dormont High. I met Mr. Neff, the principal. He told me they would accept me in the sophomore year, but I would be required to take tests for the ninth grade courses. If I passed, I would get credit for those courses.

I told him I was willing to do that. The teachers were extremely helpful, and it was through their efforts that I was able to go on into higher education.

When I began school, I was so fearful of failing that I decided that I would read each book twenty-five times. That became a standard throughout my education. The exception was medical school. The medical books are so thick; I was fortunate when I could read them three times.

To keep from getting fatigued while studying, I would lift weights every fifteen minutes. If one does this, one is able to study indefinitely without fatigue.

In algebra, I started in the middle of the year in the course. Since Dormont High didn't have semesters, the course was already into the sixth month. It was hopeless. I was unable to learn it on my own. Miss Beatty, the teacher, informed me I could stay after school, and she would be happy to teach me. I ended up with a C plus; actually on my first test, I got a B.

After I became a physician, I searched for her. She was retired. When I visited her, I reminded her what she had done for me. She informed me that she didn't remember doing that. I informed her she was such an outstanding educator, always giving up her free time to help students, that her extraordinary had become ordinary, so she wouldn't remember it. I informed her I could have never have become a physician without her help, because math is necessary for advanced science. I was crying. I told her, her name was written on my soul.

I was lost in biology, but with Mr. Babyak's help, I got through the course. I did so well in geography that I got A's in all the tests. Dr. McLaughlin informed me I would not need to take the final exam, and I was to make up the final exam. However, Dr. McLaughlin had to grade it on the curve, because the students had complained bitterly about how hard the test was that I had created for them.

I had Mr. Brown for gym, and I got a B in gym.

In English, I had Mrs. Sawhill. I have a speech defect, and my stuttering was severe then. She always gave me encouragement to give talks in front of the room, which I did. My overall average at the end of my sophomore year was a B average, and I got credit for a whole year. Without god's help I would not have been able to complete my sophomore year.

In the summer of 1957, I got a job with the Cagni Construction Company as a hod-carrier. A hod is a tool with a very long handle that you rap your arm around and the top part has a V-shapped carrier, that lays on one's shoulder, that one puts in bricks or mortor to carry on one's shoulder to the brick layers and stone masons. It was non-union. He hired a group of college kids. Since I had walked up at the same time they did, he thought I was a part of their group. He had no idea that I was only sixteen. It was the hardest work I had ever done. I worked six days a week at $1.75/hour. I decided to save up for college. At the end of the summer, I had an unbelievable tan. I told him I had to quit to go back to school. When I told him I was sixteen, he got quite angry. He said that if I would have got hurt my parents could have sued him. I told him I was my own boss, and my parents would not have sued him. He told me he hadn't seen a sixteen-year-old work like me.

The bricklayers had taught me some bricklaying. The stonemasons from Italy had attempted to teach me how to cut stone. I just couldn't do it; they were real artists.

I went back to Dormont High in my junior year.

When I first started school, even though I was much more mature than most students, I didn't have the dating experience they had. I had never kissed a girl until I was sixteen.

In high school, I had a "gift" for "counseling" girls. When a girl was upset about something, she would come and talk to me about it. Afterwards, she said she felt so much better after talking with me. Word got around, and I found myself doing this when friends would ask me to talk to their friends. I had forgotten all about this until recently. An old high school classmate that I had not seen for years, remarked to me that I was a natural for psychiatry, because of the "counseling" I had done in high school. I was so surprised, because I had completely forgotten all about it.

In January, 1958, I was seventeen, and we had a family tragedy. Our home burned down.

My dad didn't have fire insurance and lost everything. He had to place most of the children in St. Paul's Orphanage. I decided that I would quit Dormont High, get a full-time job to try to help my dad, and go to night school.

Mr. Neff, the Dormont High principal, advised me against this, as did my dad. There was a big steel strike in Pittsburgh in 1958, and jobs were scarce. I was only seventeen.

We stayed with my grandmother for a few weeks until my dad got an apartment in Hazelwood. He sold the lot. I looked everywhere for work but couldn't find anything.

My buddy's dad worked for the Pennsylvania State Employment Office, and he got me a job as a dockworker loading trucks. Since it was non-union, they hired me. It was in Leetsdale, Pa., far from Pittsburgh. I started night school at Schenley Evening High in Pittsburgh. It was an accredited high school. My grades were good; I got A's and B's, because I studied hard. I still lifted weights off and on. About a year later, my dad had enough money to get a mortgage on a home in Beechview.

We moved there, and he got the rest of the children out of the orphanage. About a year later, I was laid off because work was down in Pittsburgh. I collected unemployment. I still attended night school.

I started having a very intense affair with a divorcee. It was the first time I had "made it" with a woman. I was nineteen at the time.

I didn't graduate until June 1960. I graduated seventh out of a class of 94. I had high academic standing. I decided to go into the Army, because employers didn't want to hire me, because they believed I would be drafted. The draft board informed me I probably would not be drafted because of my record. I then believed that I had to get into the military to prove to society that I could do a good job. I believed it was a way of proving myself. I got a recommendation from my congressman, and the Army said they would take me. If one volunteered for the draft, it was a two-year hitch.

I went down to the draft board to volunteer, and the lady there told me that since I was a high school graduate, I should enlist in the Army and obtain guaranteed training, but I would have to do a three-year hitch. I wasn't too keen on doing three years, but I decided to go down to the Army recruiter to see what options I had. I looked through the programs, and the X-ray technician course appealed to me. I told the recruiter I would think about it. I called up all the hospitals in Pittsburgh to find out if Army-trained X-ray technicians were acceptable. All the hospitals told me they were good training programs; in fact, one chief X-ray tech I talked with had been Navy-trained. He told me I could get good part-time jobs, too.

I had been thinking about becoming a doctor some day. I planed that after discharge from the Army, I would work my way through college, and save up for medical school.

I went down to the recruiting station for my entrance physical. The doctor who examined me told me that I did not pass the physical, and I could leave because I would not be drafted. I was shocked! He informed me that the arches of my feet were completely flat. I told him I was not being drafted, and I was enlisting because the

Army was going to send me to X-ray technician school, and that some day I planned to go to medical school. I asked him to give me a break, because I had spent years in reform school, and the Army was the only way I could prove myself. He told me if I wanted to go in that bad, he would let me do it.

Military Years

I enlisted in the Army on June 3, 1960. I didn't attend my high school graduation on June 10, because I had to go into the Army before the X-ray school started. Schenley Evening High School sent me my diploma. I was sent to Fort Knox, Kentucky for eight weeks of basic training. I went down on a train. I had had very long hair and used to comb it into something called a "DA." Well, they practically shaved my head. I felt pretty bad about it and started wondering if I did the right thing joining the Army. I was assigned to Company C, 6th Training Regiment, 3rd Battalion. Our drill sergeant was Staff Sgt. Negron. He was Puerto Rican and was "gung-ho" all the way, a highly decorated Korean War soldier, too.

My first encounter with him was a disaster. During my first night in basic training, I had not been told what time we got up in the morning. Well, it must have been around 3:00 a.m., and it was pitch black. I was sleeping on the top bunk when I heard this screaming, "Fallout, Fallout." I couldn't see a thing, and I yelled back, "Hey, man, get some sleep; it's still night." I had believed it must be someone who had had too much to drink. The next thing I knew, he had grabbed me and threw me to the floor. Suddenly, the lights went on, and I saw this sergeant standing before me, yelling at the top of his lungs. I thought, *Oh my God, this must be the Army!* We all got ready. I was the last one to get to the sink, and the water was cold by then. I was upset.

I had to shave with cold water, but it did bring me out of my stupor. When we fell out into formation, the sergeant was still barking. We got into formation, and then he called us "candy asses" and said in eight weeks, he would make soldiers out of us.

He said, "Before we get started, I want to clear one thing up. If any of you candy asses think you can kick my ass, step forward." There were two jackasses that stepped forward that day. I was one of them. He came up to me first. "You throw the first punch," he said. I told him I was a boxer in reform school. I could bench press 315 pounds on a standard barbell and could strick-curl 165 pounds. I was a Pittsburgh steel city street kid, and if I hit him with my sledgehammer (my right fist), I would send him into the twilight zone.

He responded, "Are you finished?"

I told him, "There is no way I am going to hit you; I will be sent to the stockade."

He turned to our company standing in formation, and said, "You have all these witnesses that I gave you an order to hit me." I am ashamed to admit this, but I was going to lay him out. I threw a right jab, but I never connected. I was still in the air after he flipped me, and he was already on the other soldier. He moved faster than lighting. He knew every form of martial arts on the planet. From that day on, he made my life hell on earth. Every day, we put in about eighteen hours of very rough training.

I had a problem with my M1 rifle. I would clean this weapon very good each night. In the a.m., the 2nd Lieutenant would come with a rod with cotton on the end and put it down the barrel of one's weapon and pull it out to see if it had been cleaned. He raised hell with me and said my weapon was dirty. I couldn't understand why, because I had cleaned it very good the night before. The following day, I spent hours on it and in the morning, the same thing happened again.

I believed it wasn't my weapon. I told him it wasn't my weapon.

He screamed at me, "What is your serial number?" I shouted back my weapon serial number. He looked at my weapon and threw it back at me. I looked and sure enough, it was my weapon. I couldn't believe it was dirty. Later, the sergeant asked me if I had cleaned my weapon in the a.m. and I told him I didn't, only the night before. He told me that the bore "sweats" at night, and that was why my weapon was dirty in the a.m. So, I started to clean my weapon in the a.m.

I lost a lot of weight with all the training I got.

I was one of the best shots in the company. If one made a high score on the shooting range, one got to ride back to camp in a truck. I was happy about this, because I could get a hot shower then. One day, we were setting up pop-up targets, and I was down range with a buddy of mine. It was getting dark, and several companies were there getting ready to fire down range; it was hilly, and the 2nd Lieutenant had forgotten about us. Believe it or not, they opened fire on us. We hit the dirt and started yelling, "Cease fire!" I was angry as hell. It was a miracle we weren't killed. The 2nd Lieutenant was pretty shook up.

Another problem was I never got enough chow. I was always hungry. I happened to notice a couple of times that there were other companies of troops on the other hills. Some companies would serve lunch later than us. After I ate my lunch, I would pretend that I was going over the hill to take a crap. Then I would hightail it over to another company and get in their chow line. I thought they wouldn't know the difference. One time I was stopped, a sergeant asked who I was and what I was doing in their chow line. I told him I was in a skirmish, and I got hungry and thought I might get some chow. He let me go through their chow line. The next morning when I was in formation in my own company, our 1st Sergeant, an "old soldier" more decorated than most generals, stood up and said he got wind of a infiltrator who has been going into other companies and getting their chow. He said the next time they catch him, he would be shot. My buddies were laughing, because they knew I went over to other companies to get an extra chow.

When I got on to the qualifying firing range to qualify for my medal, I had thought I would get a trophy, because I had always been a very good shot. I had done a lot of work on the elevation of my sight and had it at a perfect adjustment for myself. Drill Sergeant Negron was in the next foxhole with one of my buddies. He was watching me. My elevation on that day was all fowled up.

I was missing targets right and left. I was really angry. I threw my weapon down, and the line officer ran up and asked me what was wrong. I told him my elevation was off.

He told me if I didn't continue firing, they would fail me on the firing range, and I would have to go through basic training again. I was such a good shot, I ended up getting a Marksman Medal, but I really should have got a trophy.

One of the soldiers in our company who received the top trophy attempted to give it to me, because I had always been the best shot in the company. I told him I deeply appreciated the offer, but he had won it on the qualifying day, and it was his as far as I was concerned.

Since Sergeant Negron had always been "steamed" when I got to ride back in the truck each day for my good shooting, I believe that it was he who changed my elevation when my weapon was in the rack during the night. He did "teach me a lesson." My M1 was my responsibility, and I should have also memorized my sight elevation.

When we went down to the grenade range, I was first in line. The 2nd Lieutenant was shaky. He gave us instructions after we all threw mock grenades. We were up to throw real ones. I was first in line. I pulled the pin and threw it down the hill. We were in a bunker. I got up to watch it explode down the hill. The next thing I knew, the 2nd Lieutenant tackled me and as we hit the ground, it went off like a bomb.

I hadn't known how powerful it was. It would have blown my head off.

One big pain for me was there was never enough hot water to take a shower. We had coal stoves that had to be fed coal to heat the water pipes. Each day, someone would be left behind on coal duty. Finally, my day of duty arrived. I decided that there would be enough hot water in the barracks for everyone. I worked very hard all day shoveling coal; the furnace got white hot. I was one of the first ones into the latrine to take a shower. At that moment, this very tall, lanky boy from Mississippi, who was also our Squad Leader, flushed the toilet. I heard a loud explosion, and he was blown completely over the divider. The skin had been burnt off his rump. I yelled out, "Don't touch the water spigots! Hey everyone get out of the barracks!" Someone went to call an ambulance. I stood to the side of the water fountain and turned it on; steam shot out.

By then, I was quite upset; I couldn't understand what had happened. The 1st Sergeant called me up, and I told him I had been working hard all day; unfortunately, too hard. What had happened was that the hot water got so hot, it turned to steam, and the cold water pipes were so close to the hot water pipes that they too turned to steam. Unfortunately, the squad leader had to go to the hospital; he was out of basic training. The plumber was sent for to correct the problem.

In the last week of basic training, we spent the whole week out in the field.

We marched with full packs. In Fort Knox, there are two mountains you must climb with full packs, *misery* and *heartbreak*. It was nighttime by the time we reached the top of one of the mountains. We were then on a gravel road. I was in real trouble because of my flat feet. My feet had also been bleeding probably because of blisters. I was in extreme pain, and I fell down. Drill Sergeant Negron came back to see what was wrong with me. I told him about my feet, and I couldn't walk. He told me if he brought up the jeep, he would need to report what happened and I might be medically discharged. I told him I would crawl the rest of the way. He told me we only had a little way to go, and that I had to get up and march the rest of the way. He helped me up. I made it to camp. It started to rain. I fell down into the mud to sleep. My tent buddy didn't want to sleep in the rain.

Since I had part of a tent, I helped make a pup tent in the rain as best as I could.

Later that night, I went down the ridge to take a crap. I couldn't see anything, except I felt a sharp incline. I went back to the tent and went to sleep. The next morning when I got up and I looked out, I was in shock. The sharp incline led to a cliff that went several hundred feet below. I was very angry that no one had told us about this. If I had fallen off this cliff, I would have not only been killed but would have been caught with my pants down, so to speak.

Later that morning after I had shaved, I was sitting down cleaning my bayonet, when lo and behold right in front of me was a sassafras tree. I recognized the leaf from when I had been in the boy scouts. I immediately whipped out my entrenching tool, a small shovel, and I began to dig up the roots. I cleaned the root with my bayonet. My buddy had been observing me with much trepidation. He thought I had lost my mind. He told me he hadn't realized how hungry I was, and he offered me some candy. I laughed and gave him a piece of root. I told him it was sassafras and to chew on it. He said it was great and it tasted like root beer. Soon, the whole company was comparing leaves and digging up sassafras roots. Just then, the 2nd Lieutenant happened to come by. I don't think he had been a boy scout. He was extremely unhappy about the rooting activities, and we were back to war games.

The "neatest" toy was an automatic weapon with an infrared scope. I could see everything in total darkness. It was fun shooting at targets in the dark with this. I had a great time firing tracer bullets. They would give off a stream of light.

I must have gone through that range a hundred times. I was sorry the next day, because it left a lot of residue in my Ml, and I had to work several hours cleaning it.

I could take an Ml apart and put it together blindfolded.

One of the big obstacles one had to crawl through was an infiltration course. It had barbed wire and mounds that would explode while mounted machine guns were being fired overhead to simulate war. I was about halfway through when I got a severe "charley horse" in my leg. I flipped over and my weapon went to the side and I started rubbing my leg frantically.

Then the 2nd Lieutenant yelled "Cease Fire!" He ran out to the course and asked, "What in the hell is going on?" I told him I got a cramp in my leg and was rubbing it out. He was really upset. He had everyone stand on the side. He put a stake in the ground at the height I had been, and he ordered the machine gunner to commence firing. It hit the top of the stake. I couldn't believe how low the shells had dropped; it was a wonder I hadn't been killed. Unfortunately, he ordered me to crawl back through the course several times until everyone was through it.

We were taught bayonet training and Judo.

They were never happy with the way I marched. My feet were the problem. I was not permitted to march in graduation. I got the day off. On that day, I had an interesting experience. Drill Sergeant Negron met with me. He informed me that he was going to be transferred to armor (tank division). He told me he wanted me to be his buck sergeant. I was very surprised! I was only a private at the time, and he was telling me he would see to it that I received a triple promotion. I told him I was highly honored by his request, but I wanted to go to Army X-ray Tech. School.

Soon basic training was over; I think it was the worst eight weeks of my life.

Me in the Army

I had a few days leave, and I went home in my uniform. I thought it was a big deal being a soldier. I was gung-ho about the Army; I think it was because my dad had been in twice. I had uncles and aunts who had served in World War II and were decorated. Two of my cousins had been in the Korean War. It was a family tradition to serve in the military.

I was then on orders for the Brooke Army Medical Center in Fort Sam Houston, Texas. Before I could go to the Army Medical Service School to become an X-ray technician, I had to become a medical corpsman. That training was eight to ten weeks. We were a good group of soldiers. My best buddy was a lab technician who had been drafted into the Army. He went on into the paramedics as a paratrooper. I wanted to go with him, but I didn't like the idea of jumping out of an airplane. I went up to the training range, but I didn't like the looks of the jump tower. You did get extra pay.

I learned a lot of basic emergency medical care as a corpsman. In the last week, we went out on bivouac. They set up station hospitals and had simulated injuries. We were to treat the "injuries," put the "patient" on a stretcher, and bring him back to the station hospital. We even had to go across a river on a raft. We had to go back to the forward area and start all over again. It was set up just like it would be in combat. I had been working all day long, very hard. A lot of guys had been sitting around goofing off. I was sitting down with the stretcher on a hill when I heard a lot of racket behind me. I jumped up, but all it was an armadillo.

Soon it was dark, and I decided to lay down on the stretcher for a while, because I was very tired. I fell asleep. They had decided to call off the bivouac, because everyone had done so well. Everyone got into formation. Roll call was taken, and it was noted that I wasn't there. They sent everyone out to look for me. I had been in the far forward area fast asleep.

I heard all this commotion, and I heard my name being called. I jumped up and put the stretcher on my shoulder and walked down out of the forward area. A searchlight was placed on me and some-one yelled out, "What is your name, soldier?" and I told him my name. This major came running up cursing and said, "Where in the hell have you been?" I told him I had been up in the forward area looking for some injured. He told me they had been looking all over for me. He told me he wanted to see me in his office in the a.m.

I was worried. The next morning, I went over to see the major. He told me, "Get out of here!" while he was laughing, and so I assumed he wasn't going to do anything to me.

The Army training fields in San Antonio were interesting. They have real big colorful spiders.

I don't know if they are desert spiders but they weave webs in trees. Also, there are a lot of rattlesnakes in the area.

When I completed my corpsman training, I was sent to the Army Medical Service School. There were twenty-nine soldiers in my X-ray school class, some of which were draftees. Most of the draftees were college graduates. I "automatically" became a squad leader. I went into the barracks and all the beds were full, so the only two beds left were in the squad room, so I helped myself to one of those. The other soldier there was Mike L, who turned out to be one of my best Army buddies.

For some reason beyond me, I was elected to be the barracks "Commander." I was still a "private" at the time. We soon got our assignments and started class. We had assumed that there would not be any inspections. I thought we would just be responsible for school. Our barracks wasn't very clean. We swept all the dirt to one huge pile in one of the corners at the end of the barracks. One day when we were at class, class was called off. We were told to return to the barracks.

They had had a major inspection. When we got back to the barracks, the inspecting officer was awaiting our arrival. He was red with rage and barked out, "Who is in charge here?" Everyone pointed at me. He was like Mount Vesuvius erupting. He said he was in the Army for over thirty years, and ours was the filthiest barracks he had ever seen. He informed us that we would learn "clean." We were placed on extra K-P duty after spending the entire day cleaning up the barracks.

I was not relieved of my "command" by my peers, though.

The X-ray school was excellent training. We even learned how to set up field equipment. In March 1961, we graduated. My rank was sixth in a class of twenty-nine. I had done well academically. I was assigned for on-the-job training in X-ray at Letterman General

Hospital in the presidium of San Francisco right near the Golden Gate Bridge. I had my first plane ride from Texas to San Francisco. I loved San Francisco. It was one of the best assignments I had in the Army. Unfortunately, I was ill when I got there. I had had a bad abscess in my gum, and I also got sinusitis, which I had never had before. It's very damp in San Francisco.

I visited Chinatown and Fisherman's Wharf.

It was like being on vacation. After my on-the-job training was over, I had wanted to stay at Letterman General Hospital, but their positions were all filled. I then wanted to go overseas, but the Army wouldn't send me overseas.

I was assigned to Munsion Army Hospital in Fort Leavenworth, Kansas, as an X-ray technician. It was about thirty miles from Kansas City. I didn't like it there. The Command General Staff College was there, and we were constantly subjected to inspections.

I spent time in the college library. They had complete records on the Nazis. I was horrified by the picture books on the Nazi experiments on the Jews. For me, the worst was seeing a picture of a so-called doctor sitting on a stool by a bathtub with a Jew in it filled with ice. This devil was freezing the man to death. They wanted to find out how long one could survive in frigid conditions. Another picture showed a little Jewish man hanging by his neck on a hook as a monster doctor was suffocating him. The cruelest pictures were the ones of children marked for experiments.

When these devil dictators stand up and harm others, the good must stand up against them at all costs!

I had to be on emergency call so that I couldn't go to college at night. I did start taking college correspondence courses through the United States Armed Forces Institute. The courses were very hard. I "worked out" in the gym a lot.

I became a chief X-ray technician there. I was promoted to SP4, which is equal to corporal. I had been promoted to Private 1st Class at Letterman General Hospital.

After awhile, I was fortunate to be transferred to Fitzsimmons General Hospital in Denver, Colorado. It was one of the most beautiful places I had ever been.

During one of the times I had been working out in the gym, I was instructing a few patients in exercise. The occupational therapist there told me I should think about becoming a physical therapist. At that time, my goal was becoming a doctor.

There was a big police scandal when I was in Denver. The police had been robbing homes.

I still wanted to go overseas. Since my tour of duty was now under two years, I could not be sent to Europe, where I wanted to go, because the tour of duty there was two years. I volunteered for Korea. Soon I was on orders for Korea. I flew to Oakland, California, to be shipped overseas. I was put on the USS MANN, a naval troop transport ship.

The first woman administrative naval officer ever to be put to sea was on that ship. She was constantly photographed. One of the nurses complained that she had been on ships for years, and no one was taking her picture.

The navy divided us up into two groups; half were assigned to guard duty, and the other half were assigned to K-P. I was assigned as a cook's helper. I was extremely seasick; actually, it's a misnomer, I wasn't sick of the sea; it's the motion, the rocking back and forth of the ship that made me sick. When I was down in the galley of the ship early in the a.m. cooking eggs, I would be vomiting all over the floor. The sailors were quite amused. They told me to suck on lemons and eat crackers, which I did, but nothing seemed to help. I was sea sick the whole three weeks I was on the ship.

I had five real good buddies. Bob S was with the Army Security Agency outside of Seoul, Korea, going back to Korea for a second tour of duty. Another soldier was an M-P and three others. I was lucky, because they had all been overseas before and knew the "ropes." They knew the best places we should travel to each time the ship docked.

I had a really funny experience one day while being a cook. There were these very large, metal caldrons. When we put food in there, it was usually by the case.

We were making chili con carne. After I had filled the very large metal caldron with ground beef, the chief cook said to throw in a couple of boxes of chili powder. Unfortunately, I thought he meant cases. I was on the second case when I had been coughing, and he came over to see what was wrong. I told him the aroma was pretty strong.

He gasped and said, "My God, how much chili powder did you put in here?" I told him I was only starting on the second case. He said he only meant two boxes. There were twelve boxes to a case. I asked him if we should throw everything out. He said we would serve it. Ironically, we received a lot of favorable comments concerning the chili.

Our first stop was Honolulu, Hawaii. The harbor was loaded with subs and battleships. The food was very good, and we saw several floorshows. I still felt like I was rocking when I got off the ship. After a few days, we were off to Japan.

I never had a twenty-first birthday. When we crossed the International Date Line, we went from December 17 to the 19, skipping my birthday.

In the Yellow Sea, we had a typhoon. From the ship's galley, I went up the back steps to the deck and hung on; it was great! The waves were like mountains. This was the only time I wasn't seasick.

As we came into Japan, all I could see was Mt. Fuji. It appeared like Japan was nothing but one gigantic volcano. It was one of the most beautiful sights I have ever seen. We docked at Yokohoma on Christmas Eve. It was like a place out of a storybook, very enchanting. The Japanese were extremely friendly.

We went to a very good restaurant; even though they had booths, we decided to take a platform loft. I can't sit in Lotus position, so I put my legs under the low table. I decided to eat with chopsticks. The waitress was giggling. They served sake. I didn't know that it was a Japanese alcoholic beverage of fermented rice. I thought it was tea. I told my buddies I didn't care to drink, as they wanted to, so I decided to drink the "tea." They ordered OB beer, which is great Japanese beer. They pushed the "tea" pots of sake to me. It was great. We had Sukiyaki, and I must have some oriental blood in me, because I was an expert with chopsticks. My buddies had really pulled one over one me. I had downed several jugs of warm "tea" without realizing what I had gotten myself into. We even had some whale blubber. Then everything started to spin; I couldn't stand up. My buddies were laughing. I staggered out of the place.

We had a lot of exotic food there. Japan was the most fascinating place I have ever been. In a few days, we left Japan for Taipei Formosa. It was the most beautiful island I had ever seen. Living conditions were very primitive. Young women had racks on their backs and carried water jugs. Young children came to the ship dock and begged for coins.

Coolies were pulling rickshaws.

It, too, was like being in a place in a storybook. The hillside was dotted with small huts.

After some time, we were on our way to Inchon, Korea. The water was very rough by the Korean peninsula. It was extremely cold. On New Year's Day, we docked and were loaded into large army trucks. I was sitting in the back of the Army truck feeling down and cold, when suddenly I was hit with a large bag filled with donuts. A Red Cross girl had passed out donuts and wished us a Happy New Year.

Korea appeared very primitive. The farmers worked very hard.

When we reached Ascom, we were put in temporary barracks until we received our assignments. We were issued very heavy warm clothing, and "Mickey mouse" boots. They are very heavy, well insulated, and go over regular army boots.

When I spoke to a Korean War Veteran years later, I was upset to learn they did not have "Mickey mouse" boots back then, and many troops lost toes and feet because of frost-bite.

In Ascom, I went to personnel and requested an inter-theater transfer back to Japan. The personnel office was not pleased. They told me I just arrived in Korea, and I would be stationed there. They did accept my transfer request, though.

I was assigned as an X-ray technician to the Seoul Military Hospital in Seoul, Korea.

Even though it was a military hospital, we treated military personnel, military dependants, and embassy personnel. My night call wasn't too difficult; therefore, I was able to take courses at night at the University of Maryland/Far East Extension Program on Post.

I did a lot of sightseeing in Seoul. People were extremely poor here; it was like being back in the Stone Age. I dated quite a few Korean women. I never got involved in the black market, although I had many opportunities to do so. I had too much to lose. My best army buddy was Larry B, the chief X-ray technician. Dr. J, a radiologist, would come up from the 121 Evac Hospital to take X-rays for us. Bok was also an X-ray technician who worked with us and was also the hospital mail clerk.

I went to visit another army buddy of mine, Bob S. He had been on the troop ship with me. He was in the Army Security Agency. When I arrived at the site, the Army Guards would not let me in. Finally they called Bob, and he came down for me. After I informed him about all the problems I had crossing checkpoint areas, he decided to make up area IDs for me. That enabled me unrestricted travel, even though Korea was under martial law.

When I told my Air force buddy, who was in college with me, about the IDs, he requested some too. Bob made him some, too. He worked in air transport. When there were extra seats, he would see to it that my buddies would fly out. I never did fly out. I was too busy with work and college study. When my friends did fly out, I had a lot of extra work to do, but I was still able to get it done. I would take a day off from time to time to be with my girlfriends.

One day there was a catastrophe. I had taken the previous day off and was in town. Dr. J was in Hong Kong, and Larry B was in the Azores. Bok was supposed to be in the X-ray department that morning but went on mail call instead. No one was in the X-ray department! At noon, I returned to the post. I saw the Hospital Commander Major S. walking up the road. He called me over. He was speaking in a matter-of-fact way. He told me how he had come up the ranks as an infantry soldier and had especially enjoyed administering at the Army Medical Service School in Fort Sam Houston, Texas. He had been my commander when I was there and was impressed with my performance. He informed me that he was pleased with his last "elite" assignment, the Seoul Military Hospital. He said that after nineteen challenging years, he was looking forward to his twenty-year retirement. He informed me he was quite distraught to learn that morning that even though he was commander of this elite hospital, he was absent an X-ray department. He informed me that he had picked a nice burial spot in the rice patty for us on the way to the post. He informed me he then decided not to shoot us, because he did not want to go to the stockade. He ordered me to gather up my X-ray comrades, and he would have a nice lunch discussion with us. When I told him where everyone was, he requested that I not say another word. He ordered me to the X-ray department immediately. He informed me that I was to stay there until all the work was done, and all the patients had happy smiles. As for him, he was going to have a very pleasant afternoon working on our transfers out of the hospital. He informed me that he would try to find a spot for me in "outer Mongolia."

I was transferred to the 44th Mobile Army Surgical Hospital (MASH unit) in the 1st Cavalry Division. When I arrived at Camp

House, I was issued a weapon and a lot of field gear. I informed the quartermaster sergeant that they were making a mistake issuing me all this equipment, because I was an X-ray tech. The quartermaster officer came out and asked me what the problem was, and I repeated myself.

"Where are you from soldier?" he asked.

I responded, "Seoul."

He responded, "Your party is over, we soldier here! Get your gear soldier," he barked back at me. I realized I was back to "soldiering" again.

There was a Heliport in the MASH unit to transport the injured by helicopter. Injured were to be flown to the 121 Evac Hospital in Ascom.

We lived in Quonset Huts, a prefabricated metal shelter.

I started night school at University of Maryland Extension in Yongjko.

Osani was the village next to the MASH unit.

We had a ROK soldier assigned to us. Corporal Pak was assigned to our X-ray department. My salary as a corporal was $180/month; his was $1.24 /month. These were extremely poor people. I taught Pak X-ray. He was a very good worker. He didn't joke much, and did not like my constant" kidding around." He had had a couple of years of college.

I could have gone to Rest and Recuperation in Hong Kong, but I never did. The First Calvary Division had a lot of field operations, and our medical support group went along. I set up X-ray equipment and darkroom tents.

Around October of 1962, our MASH unit had come back from a field operation. Early that morning, I decided to go on pass to Seoul. I had probably been on the army bus for about an hour. We arrived at a checkpoint. Our Korean bus driver was talking to one of the ROK army checkpoint soldiers. The bus driver then started turning the bus around. I went up and pointed back and told him, "Seoul that way,"

He responded, "GI go back to post."

I told him, "GI not go back to post, GI go to Seoul." Since he refused to turn the bus around, I thought I had a crazy bus driver. I told him to let me off the bus, which he did. I was out in the wilderness, and I assumed someone would come and give me a lift to Seoul.

As I was standing at the checkpoint, I noted a jeep was coming down the road from the side mountain. I crossed over the road. The jeep stopped. A sergeant from artillery was driving. He asked me where my post was. I informed him I was at the MASH Unit, but I was trying to get to Seoul. I was surprised to see tears running down his face, and I asked him what was wrong. He told me the U.S. had been attacked that morning. I was stunned! I told him I needed to get back to my unit ASAP. He informed me he would be driving past Osonee and would drop me off at the MASH Unit. It was noteworthy that we had been in the jeep for sometime and didn't speak. I only thought about my family and assumed they were probably all dead. The silence was broken by a number of Air Force fighter jets flying overhead. When we got back to the MASH unit, I was surprised to see we were completely mobilized. Major Mosbar ordered me to get into full field gear and get in formation ASAP.

President John Kennedy had stopped the Russian ships from going to Cuba. All the military around the world was on high alert. I did not appreciate the fact that we had been lied to, but the military believed at the time it was the quickest way for us to get mobilized. It was successful.

The Koreans were very concerned. They thought we would be at war again.

Fortunately for everyone, the Russians went back home.

I only had a few more months left in Korea by then.

In November, I was called down to headquarters. A First Lieutenant informed me they had approved of my inter-theater transfer. I had forgotten all about it. I told him I would be happy to spend the rest of my tour in Japan. He informed me that it was not Japan, but Vietnam. I told him I did not know anything about Vietnam. He handed me an Army information accordion type packet on Vietnam. On each section was an artwork, and standing next to the art work were some of the most beautiful women I had ever seen. Since I had never seen anything produced by the Army like this, I had a bad feeling about it. I informed him I had only put in for Japan, and I didn't want to go to Vietnam. At that time, we were sending advisors to Vietnam. A year later, we had a full-scale war there.

Living conditions were harsh in Korea. It stunk all the time, because human poop is used for manure for fertilizer. During the spring monsoons, it would pour buckets of water, and the ground would be like quicksand.

I was "deeply" involved with a girl there, Bonnie, and thought about bringing her home with me. She did not want to leave Korea. I liked the Koreans very much. They are good, hardworking people. The Army had good gyms in Korea. The Koreans learn Karate at a very young age and would put on demonstrations for the American troops.

I had an extremely strong religious experience one day. I had always questioned things, especially the fact that people here had to live in such poverty and suffering. One day, a laborer came to the clinic. There were quite a few times that we gave medical care to the Koreans. The laborer had a very large family. His wife had committed suicide because of the terrible conditions they lived under. I will never forget him as long as I live.

It was reported by staff that he had been seen to be having "chest pain." We x-rayed him. The doctor diagnosed an anomaly of his heart that would cause pain. The doctors had wanted to do surgery on him, but he was fearful that he would lose his job. He was pounding on his chest to show that he was hardy.

Later after work, I was standing on the road waiting for the bus. It was dusk; the sun was beginning to set. That same man was walking up the dirt road with his small son. He must have been about three. His son was dressed adequately. They stopped for a moment. So many times in life had I questioned the tragedy of life. Suddenly, the voice of God came to me in my heart and said to look upon the moment and dare curse it.

The divine Michelangelo had painted the moment. With the setting sun the background, I looked upon the moment. As the man was looking down at his son, the Book of Job came to mind. This man was like Job. I couldn't understand how he could suffer more than he had. It was plain to see that his child was well cared for, for he was looking up into his dad's face with happiness. One could see the pain of uncertainty in the father's face, and the harsh reality of life had left its mark allover him. And, yet there was such force of strength and courage in him, that as long as there was one ounce of breath left in him, he would meet the challenge of life.

I could not curse the moment. The power and beauty of it moved me such that I was overwhelmed with tears, for this personage held more splendor than adorned kings.

Whenever, I have been puffed up with my so-called spirituality, I remember an encounter I had in Korea long ago. I was in downtown Seoul and had walked into a shop. The proprietor was at the counter. A Korean popason (elderly man) was standing in the aisle. He was dressed in the traditional all-white outfit. He had a handsome face with sharp features. He had long black, coarse, irregularly cut hair. One of his eyes was diseased oozing green pus. His eyelids stitched together with a coarse thread. He was in rags. A makeshift A-frame was tied to his back. His pants were torn. He had wooden sandals on his feet tied with a rope. He put out his hand to me.

He must have been in agony, for it was extremely uncommon for a popason to beg.

I gave him not. I must have been in a stupefied stupor. At that moment, I had achieved the station of a great grand pig!

In December, I was back on ship transported back to the U.S.A.

I had prepared myself and had got some motion sickness prevention pills from the MASH unit. However, before we boarded the ship, our belongings were searched, and my pills had been taken away from me.

As soon as we got on ship, we were divided up into two groups; one for guard duty and the other for K-P. I was assigned to K-P. That night, someone fell and broke an ankle. It was discovered that I was the only X-ray tech on the ship. They had asked over the loud speaker if there was an army medic who could take X-rays. When I reported I was an X-ray tech, I was assigned to the ship dispensary and taken off K-P. I was really happy about that. We stopped in Japan, Okinawa, the Philippines, Hawaii, and we docked in Oakland, California. It was great to be back in the U.S.A.

I was assigned to the United States Army Hospital at Fort McArthur in San Pedro, California, next to Long Beach.

I spent my last six months there. I was on night call again. I took USAFI College Correspondence Courses again. I was the chief X-ray technician. Captain G, who had been the radiologist at the 121 Evac Hospital in Korea, was my radiologist here. I did a lot of sightseeing in California.

I had a very significant encounter with the hospital commander there. A Wac who worked under me was known to be gay. Becky was an outstanding X-ray technician. Since I wanted her to be promoted in rank because of her outstanding work, I was required to complete a full evaluation on her. She received an "Outstanding" performance evaluation from me. Sometime later, the hospital commander met with me. He was extremely angry.

He asked me, "Do you know anything about this woman?" I knew he was referring to the fact that she was gay. I informed him that her personal life was none of my business, but I was responsible for evaluating her work performance. He threw the evaluation at me and ordered me to change it at once. I informed him that I stood by the evaluation that I had completed and was not going to change it. He was extremely angered. I expected him to demote me to private right on the spot or worse, have me thrown in the stockade for disobeying an order. He then informed me that he would see to it that I did not receive a good conduct medal on discharge.

I did not tell Becky what had happened. She spoke to me some time later. She informed me that she had learned what I had done for her. She informed me that her barracks footlocker had been broken into and her personal letters had been taken, and she was going to receive a dishonorable discharge. I was extremely shocked about what had happened to her. I remain angry about it to this day when I think about it.

Right before I was discharged, Captain G, my radiologist, informed me that I was going to get a good conduct medal, and he was the one to make the decision, not the hospital commander. He informed me he had not forgotten the night I agreed to be flown from the MASH Unit to the 121 Evac Hospital to take X-rays for him.

On May 31, 1963, I received an honorable discharge. I had achieved a lot in the Army. I had been able to travel, I received training, and I had completed one-and-a-half years of college.

College Years

I returned to Pittsburgh, lived at home, and attended the University of Pittsburgh, majoring in pre-med. I planned to work part-time in one of the hospitals as an X-ray technician.

After I had applied to all the hospitals and didn't get any replies, I wrote to all the medical directors about my plans.

I received several very good replies. Shadyside Hospital offered to train me further to be in nuclear medicine as an X-ray technician, and the salary was good.

I also received a call from Dr. Michael James Kehoe, a research psychiatrist at the Western Psychiatric Institute and Clinic, a part of the University of Pittsburgh's School of Medicine.

I met with Dr. Kehoe.

Dr. Kehoe informed me that my hours would be flexible, so that I could take the pre-med courses I needed. I could work day or night for him. I began working with him full time and going to school full-time at the same time.

I had saved all that I could in the Army for school.

When I was a student in the University of Pittsburgh, it was a private school then, and tuition was very high.

He sent me to St. John's Hospital to be trained as an EEG Tech under Nancy F.

The first study involved dream studies in identical twins. We had a soundproof room with a one-way mirror where we could observe the subjects. I would apply the electrodes to each subject. We used a sixteen-channel EEG Machine, eight channels for each subject. Electrodes were also placed around the eyes to pick up rapid eye movement during a subject's dreaming. An earplug was placed in each subject's ear and connected to a tape recorder that had a prerecorded set of instructions. Each subject was then placed in bed with a partition between them. A microphone was placed above each subject's head. They would go to sleep. The EEG would be running, and the subject would enter various stages of sleep. Deep sleep is stage 4. As the subject would come up to the lighter stages of sleep, they would start dreaming, and we would pick this up by the rapid eye movement artifact on the electroencephalogram. After about fifteen minutes, the dream would end, and they usually displayed some body movement. We then played the prerecorded tape. The sleeping subject would be awakened by the ringing and would follow the instructions on the tape that instructed them to record their dream into the microphone above their head. This was done all night long, all year long, on many sets of identical twins. It was interesting to find that even though one identical twin had mental illness, and one did not, their dreams were similar.

I also helped Dr. Kehoe with his reprint file and would research the literature on various topics that he wanted to explore for research.

We had a psychiatric resident, a Dr. Earl B, and a medical student, Rich C, who worked with us. They became life long friends.

I liked my job. Dr. Kehoe had strongly encouraged me to go into medicine. I was having a lot of problems with general chemistry, and I didn't like the course. I did well in my biology courses. I enjoyed the art courses.

I had been going to school full-time and working full-time. I was "burned out." I did not desire to take organic chemistry.

I decided to switch my major to physical therapy. Dr. Kehoe was distraught that I wanted to drop pre-med. He informed me that he would meet with the dean of the medical school for me, but I had made up my mind about physical therapy. He informed me that I would never be satisfied in the end if I did not go into medicine.

I changed my major. I wanted to have money and buy a car. I changed my major to physical therapy with a minor in biology.

I had taken a drama course and liked it so much that I asked Dr. Whitman, the professor, if there were any other courses as good as his. He suggested that I take Tragic Literature from the English department chairman, Dr. Lee.

He too had been a Harvard professor. I had noted that all the Harvard professors I had were very outstanding. I decided to take Dr. Lee's course. Some students told me not to take his course, because he gave bad grades.

I signed up for the course based on Dr. Whitman's recommendation. The course was really great.

We read some of the world's great novels. Dr. Lee was one of the greatest professors I had ever had. He loved teaching so much that he created a living subject before me. I could feel myself in Troy among the battles. I could experience it all. He made the course come alive.

He ran a tight ship. He would throw students out of class who disrupted class. He wouldn't stand for any nonsense. On my first test I got a D, even though I had answered all the questions correctly. I was very upset. I had never gone to see a professor about a grade before, but I decided to see Dr. Lee. He informed me that my spelling was terrible, my English horrible, and that since this was an upper-level English course, I had little chance of passing.

When I told him my major was physical therapy, he told me that I was in the wrong class and needed to be in a lower division humanities course, where I would have a better chance at a better grade. He informed me that the trimester had just begun, and I could transfer to another class without any problems. He handed me a transfer slip and told me to take it over to the registrar.

I told him there was a problem. He asked, "What's that?" I told him I loved his course, and he was the greatest teacher I had ever had, and it was impossible for me to drop his course. This was no small matter. If I failed this course, I would not be able to complete my junior year on time to enter the school of physical therapy in the fall.

He gave me a very stern warning, "I have told you to transfer from my course. You have no business being in an upper division English course with your major. If you earn an F in my class, that is what you will receive. It's on your head."

I replied, "I am sorry Dr. Lee, I cannot drop this course."

One night while reading Leo Tolstoy's book, *Anna Karina*, I got to the part where she was at the railroad station. I hoped that at the last moment her lover, Vronski, would show up, but unfortunately he did not, and the train roared her into eternity as she jumped on the tracks. I was torn apart.

I find it frightful to imagine going through this life without having read some of the world's greatest literature. Fortunately, I did pass Dr. Lee's course. I received a "D." He wrote me a note. He stated that not all of his best students were "A" students, and that he imagined that I would travel a very long distance in my chosen career. He was correct. I have studied all my life.

Dr. Kehoe began a second long-term experiment, in which I assisted him. He trained me to do analysis of gastric juice. The study also involved identical twins. He would slide a tube in the subject's nose and pass it down the throat into the stomach. On the other end was a syringe to draw out gastric juice. We taped the entire experiment and had tubes marked at five-minute intervals for the gastric juice. It was an analysis of gastric secretion under different stages of emotion under hypnosis.

In September 1965, I resigned my position at Pitt and entered the School of Physical Therapy under the University of Pittsburgh, the D. T. Watson School of Physiatrics in Leetsdale, Pa. It was also a home for crippled children. It was a year-long course and counted as my senior year at the University of Pittsburgh. It was a very challenging program. As usual, I had to study all the time. I liked physical therapy. They had an extensive anatomy course: the study of muscles, was given great emphasis. We learned gait training. We did muscle testing on crippled children. We would do group pool therapy with the kids, and that was a lot of fun. We evaluated joint range. We used whirlpools, ultrasound, microwave, massage, bandaging. We taught patients how to use braces and crutches. We taught therapeutic exercises.

I would commute back and forth from home. It was a one to one-and-a-half hour trip each way. I studied on the bus.

In the summer of 1966, I did my clinical training in the various hospitals in Pittsburgh: St. Francis General Hospital, Children's Hospital, South Side Hospital, and Presbyterian Hospital.

I received my diploma in physical therapy from the D. T. Watson School of Physiatrics in September 1966. I received my Bachelor of Science degree in physical therapy from the University of Pittsburgh in December 1966. Even though I graduated in September 1966, the university issued degrees only in June and December.

I was in Los Angeles when my degree was sent to me.

In October 1966, I went to San Francisco to take my State Board Exam in Physical Therapy. I took the California test because it was the most difficult state board exam, and most states would issue me a license based on my California license. Fortunately, I passed the test.

I had gone to California to study for a Master's degree in physical therapy at the University of Southern California. I stayed in a hotel in Los Angeles and applied at most of the hospitals in the city to decide where I would like to work. Fortunately, every hospital needed a physical therapist.

After a few days, I had a horrible reaction to the smog. I was in Hollywood, and I was unable to talk. My throat was burning. I was extremely worried, because I believed I would need to leave California. I noticed a doctor's sign on an old building that looked as if it should be torn down. I went inside and walked up the steps. It appeared like an old movie set. The doctor looked to be a thousand years old. I pointed to my throat.

He looked inside my mouth and said, "You have just arrived here in Los Angeles?" I nodded my head in agreement. He told me to come in the lab. He had a very long flask and put a number of medicines in it. Then he heated it with a Bunsen burner until it formed a cloud. He told me to put my nose over the flask and to start breathing in the cloud. It was a miracle, but he cured me. I was happy, because I wanted to stay in California.

I met one of the physical therapy professors at the University of Southern California. She suggested that I do a Master's Degree in Public Health. She informed me such degree would be more valuable for me, since I wanted to end up with a doctorate degree.

I took the Graduate Record Exam and made an acceptable score for graduate school.

I took a position as a physical therapist with the Los Angeles County Crippled Children's Service. I wanted to work at the school in Inglewood California a west suburb of Los Angeles. I liked the Chief Therapist there. I got an apartment across the street from the school.

I had to be trained in special physical therapy techniques at the Selery School in Gardena California. Unfortunately, they had a big turnover and the Chief Therapist left the Inglewood School. After two months I was informed I would have to stay at the Gardena School. I didn't want to do that so I quit.

I accepted a full-time position as a registered physical therapist at the Daniel Freeman General Hospital in Inglewood California. It was run by the Sisters of St. Joseph. I loved my job.

I started taking driving lessons. I was twenty-five years old at the time. One needs a car in Los Angeles, because bus service is terrible. After a few short lessons, I passed my driving test and got my license. The driving instructor had been pretty surprised that I had not had a license. Even though I had only worked at the hospital for a few weeks the credit union loaned me $2,000 to put down on a new car. I liked my job very much.

In February 1967, I started graduate school at night at California State at Los Angeles in the Health Science Department. Even though I was carrying a heavy course load in grad school and working full-time, I still found time to do a lot of sightseeing. I went to Disneyland and Knots Berry Farm several times. I went to the ocean a lot. There is a lot to do in Los Angeles. I dated a lot and was a member of a few social clubs. Most of the girls I met were members of the clubs such as the Los Angeles Catholic Alumni Club and the Scott Club in Long Beach California. I went to Hollywood frequently, especially to see the places on Hollywood Boulevard.

I had passed the Church of Scientology near Hollywood several times. Since I had always seen cute girls around there I thought I would look into it. It appeared to be a "healing cult" that attempts to help people get rid of their problems through something called "clearing." It was an extensive program of classes with "advanced" stages. The ultimate stage in the process is becoming a "clear." I had signed up for the basic course, the HAS course. I don't remember what those initials stand for. The first course was $15. I had attended the course several times. Each time, I was there for about two hours. My instructor was called an auditor. The basic course had to do with communication. I was supposed to sit there and stare at the auditor without moving. After a couple of periods, I was getting severe headaches and since I hadn't met any cute girls, I felt it was a waste of my time. They used something called an E-meter, and it is a simple skin galvanometer.

I had seen in an article in the newspaper that the Federal Drug Administration had reported that the E-meter was a quack medical device, and it was unlawful to use this. The auditors that I had talked with had dropped out of school to become involved with Scientology. I believed it was rather tragic that they had quit school for this. I believed they should be doing something more constructive with their life.

Scientology had been founded by L. Ron Hubbard, an engineer and a science fiction writer. He wrote a book, *Dianetics*, supposedly the Modern Science of Mental Health. I believed the book was loaded with a lot of "outlandish" claims such as that Dianetics deletes all the pain of a lifetime. That is impossible.

In the winter quarter of 1968, I was taking three graduate courses at night at California State. One was a graduate course in recreation. It was Recreation for Special Groups.

I wrote a paper for the course on Cystic Fibrosis.

Cystic Fibrosis is a disease of youth, involving the exocrine glands of the body. It causes pancreatic and pulmonary disease, mostly. The cause of the disease is unknown. When I had been a student physical therapist at Children's Hospital in Pittsburgh, I did lung postural drainage on children with Cystic Fibrosis. I used fantasy games doing physical therapy with them for postural drainage, to get mucous out of their lungs so they could breathe better. I had them pretend they were the big, bad wolf, and they would huff and puff to blow down the little pig's house. In essence, they were using a lot of the respiratory muscles to do this. I had them blow pinwheels and do other games. From this, I had ideas for the paper for my Graduate School Recreation class. When I turned my paper in, my instructor was very impressed. She told me I should submit it for publication. I had never had a publication before, and I followed up with her suggestion. My paper was published.

During the next quarter at California State, I took was a graduate course in Accident Safety. For my class paper, I did an evaluation of Daniel Freeman's Hospital Safety Program. I not only revamped the hospital safety program, but also taught a safety course to the hospital staff. As a result, the hospital administrator elected me to be the safety chairman of the hospital. I was quite flattered about this. I was able to do this, along with being a staff physical therapist.

From time to time, I would go down to Mexico. I didn't like Tijuana, Mexico.

Living conditions were as poor, as in Korea. It was one of the poorest areas of the world I had seen.

One Easter Sunday, I went up to the Danish village, Solvang, with one of the girls I had been dating at that time. It's about thirty miles north of Santa Barbara, California. I had wanted to see Hurtz Castle, but I never got around to getting there.

There was a very heavy drug culture in California when I was there.

Most of my friends smoked pot and took "acid" LSD. I never had a desire for drugs. I didn't believe drugs were where it was. However, I had had an experience with "acid" once. One Saturday afternoon, I was in a "coffee house" on the Sunset Strip with a buddy of mine. We had a couple of drinks and someone had spiked my drink with LSD. The air became filled with purple globs. At the time, I thought it was amusing, but then I got quite angry, because I realized someone had put something in my drink. I called the police, and they were upset because I had called them. They informed me that if I didn't want drugs, I shouldn't be in the Sunset-strip area. I went home and slept it off.

In the spring of 1968, I was at a Catholic Singles Party in Manhattan Beach, California and met a nursing student, Barbara R. I started dating her. Later, I started going steady with her. We went to a lot of places together in California.

I was doing quite well in graduate school.

One day in the fall of 1968, after finishing work at the hospital, I was on my way to California State, on the east side of the city. I had to take several freeways to get to school. I was driving down Imperial Highway toward the Harbor Freeway. I was in the left lane, traveling east. On the other side of the road was a guy from Kentucky, who had his family with him. He was in the L-turn lane. You are not supposed to make an L-turn until the traffic is clear. He made an L-turn right in front of me. I hit the brake, and all I could say was, "I don't believe it!"

The oddest thing happened. At that time, I truly believed I would be killed. In an instant, it was as if I was in a slow motion movie floating in and with my car and into the other car. I could see all of the steel on my car bending up. I had a Corvair, which has the engine in the back of the car. I saw their car flip around. I was unconscious for a few minutes.

When I came to, there was a massive traffic jam because it was during rush hour. My car was demolished. Believe it or not, I was able to get out of my car. At the time, I didn't think I had been hurt. The California Highway Patrol was already on the scene. The officer taking the information from me informed me he had been on the force for over twenty years, and this was one of the worse accidents he had seen. He told me he couldn't believe I was standing there talking to him. The others had been taken to a hospital in an ambulance. I was so concerned about missing class that I called California State and told them about the accident. I was still in "shock." I started to have chest pain and went to the hospital to be examined. It was a miracle that I hadn't been killed. I had fractured ribs and was in pain for several months.

I was still seeing Barbara, but the relationship started to fade. Even though I liked her and her family very much, I wasn't in love with her. I believed the relationship was at a dead end. At the time, I was working on my master's degree thesis and didn't have time to spend with her. As a result, she started to see other guys. I did go to her wedding.

For my master's degree thesis, I developed a syllabus for student teaching, in physical therapy.

I joined a bowling coed group, the Scott's Club. It was a Catholic Singles Club in Long Beach, California. Even though it was twenty-five miles from where I lived, I enjoyed the group and didn't mind the drive.

At the end of the season, I had won a little bowling pin. My high game was 191. I also won a belt buckle for the most improved average. It's really funny, but when I started bowling, I was an extremely poor bowler. I had had a lot of reservations about joining the league, but the captain of the league talked me into it. I went out and got measured for a bowling ball and bought one and a bowling bag and shoes. What was remarkable was that the team I was on was good except for me. However, at the end of the bowling season, we were the highest team on the league and I won a big trophy. I got a lot of ribbing about it, because I had reservations about joining. I like bowling.

In the spring of 1969, I was at a social at the Numan Club at UCLA, and I met a teacher, Lorrain T. She was a widow with two daughters. Her husband had died of liver cancer. I started dating her. She lived in the San Fernando Valley. I enjoyed being with her and her children very much. We all went out together. We would go bowling and to the trampoline park a lot. We enjoyed bobbing up and down on the trampolines.

Usually on Sundays, I would go to the Pancake House in downtown Los Angeles. It's a flophouse but a very popular eating place. They had the best coleslaw I had ever eaten, and usually I don't even like coleslaw. They had excellent roast chicken. One Sunday, I had come out of the Pancake House and was walking toward my car.

On the other side was a large auditorium, and in front were a lot of interesting people, and a large sign with a very strange word on it. It looked foreign. There was this extremely gorgeous girl walking up to the auditorium. I smiled at her and she said hello. We started talking. I wanted to take her out, but she informed me she was with the conference. I didn't ask what the symbol was on the sign. Since I have a very curious nature, I went back and wrote the symbol name down, "Baha'i." Since I had seen a lot of cute girls around there, I decided to find out what this was all about. I looked the word up in the White Pages of the phone book. It was listed as the Baha'i faith. I called, and they informed me they had firesides at people's homes, and I was invited to attend.

I became very interested in this faith. This faith had come into being around 1844. A "great world teacher" was to be the prophet of our age. The Baha'is believe that every few centuries, a great teacher comes, such as Krishna, Zoroaster, Moses, Jesus, Buddha, and Muhammad, appears in the East to illuminate the darkened minds of men and awaken their souls. The Baha'is believe that these are all manifestations of God, and even though their teaching appears different for each age, they all represent the same "light" of God. A young man, Mirza Husayn Ali, took the title, "Bahaullah," which means the Glory of God. He was supposed to be the manifestation of God for our age. For some reason, I was extremely drawn to this faith. I was very impressed with the principles of the Baha'i faith. I read all their books and writings. I attended weekly firesides of the Baha'i faith.

From time to time, the desire to become a physician would keep coming back. I had thought about going into medicine. I made an appointment to see the medical school deans at both UCLA and University of Southern California. I had thought that by having a Master's degree, I could get into medical school on that basis. I didn't have the undergraduate prerequisite courses, though. Both deans informed me I would need to go back and take undergraduate pre-med courses, which I was unwilling to do at that time. I then decided that after I received my Master's degree, I would go on to a Doctor of Public Health Degree Program at UCLA or the University of California at Berkeley, California. I was interested in being a consultant with the Agency for International Development (AID), under the Department of State.

I planned on doing a major in international health and a minor in hospital administration.

I applied and was interviewed by Dr. Albert N in the Department of International Health in the School of Public Health at UCLA. I told him I wanted to get the degree in order to get a position with the Agency for International Development. Since he had been one of their advisors, he knew a lot about AID. He informed me he was impressed with my enthusiasm. He believed that even with a doctoral degree, my chances were poor of getting an immediate position with AID. The advisors chosen were professionals who had very outstanding experience in their field.

He informed me UCLA would be happy to consider me for their doctoral program in international health, but not for a minor in hospital administration. Hospital administrators were in great demand. Dr. N informed me they were only willing to accept students in that area who wanted to be administrators, not someone like me who just wanted the academic background. I then decided not to pursue a doctorate in public health.

I decided that after I received my master's degree, I would go to Europe, work as a physical therapist and in my free time, travel all over Europe.

I had been working very hard on my thesis. I had twelve chapters in my thesis. My advisor, Professor Bob F informed me that I had overwhelmed him with the amount of data that I had accumulated. I was certain I would have more than twelve chapters. He tossed my thirteenth chapter in the waste can and informed me that my twelve chapters completed my thesis. He informed me that my thesis was one of the largest in their department library. Since there was a possibility of California State developing a program in physical therapy, my advisor, also a physical therapist, informed me that my thesis might be used as a syllabus in their department.

In June 1969, I sold my car, because I was certain I would be going to Europe. I obtained a passport in Los Angeles. I felt bad about breaking up with Lorraine, but I wanted to go to Europe.

Since I hadn't seen my family in two and a half years, I decided I would spend a few months with my family in Pittsburgh, Pa. before going to Europe.

I received a Master of Arts Degree in Health and Safety on June 14, 1969.

I graduated with a GPA of 3.51 out of a possible 4.0. I had worked extremely hard in my graduate program.

It was a three-hour flight from Los Angeles to Pittsburgh. My family had been very happy to see me again. I was happy to see my family again. I spent a few weeks visiting all my friends. I applied for a license as a physiotherapist in London and on July 14, I was issued a license. I wrote to a few hospitals in England about a position. While I was waiting for a reply, I happened to hear that one of my physical therapy classmates had gone to London, worked at Guy's Hospital, and was back in Pennsylvania. I decided to visit her to find out about positions.

I visited her and to my dismay, I learned that the yearly salary of a physiotherapist in London was about $2,000. I had a master's degree and could obtain chief physical therapist positions in the USA for about $14,000 a year. I realized that it would not be reasonable for me to go to Europe to work. Shortly thereafter, I received replies from London, and the highest salary that I had been offered was $1,800 a year. Actually, a physical therapist in England does not have the "advanced" degree training that we have in the U.S.A. After I was home for a couple of months, I decided to apply for physical therapist positions in special education and work with handicapped children.

During the time I was in Pittsburgh, I had been very active with the Baha'is and had attended quite a few firesides. I had even taken some of my brothers and sisters along. However, they were not really interested in becoming Baha'is. Most of my friends felt that this new religion was very "strange."

In August 1969, after reading a year of Baha'i writings, I was convinced that Bahaullah was the prophet for our age and was the return of the manifestation of Jesus Christ. I joined the Baha'i faith in August 1969. At the time, I felt pretty good about joining.

The Bahai's had encouraged me to take a position in a rural area, so that I could "spread the faith."

I was interviewed for a position as a physical therapist in the Highlands Elementary School, a part of the Appleton Public Schools in Appleton Wisconsin. The school was new, and they had a large physical therapy department with a large pool. I decided to take the position. I signed a school year contract. I also applied for a teaching certificate that I received shortly thereafter.

The Appleton Public Schools kept a list of rooms that people rented out to single teachers. I was quite fortunate because I got a room in a beautiful, colonial home. It was in a home of a widow who worked for the University of Wisconsin. She spent most of her time in Europe. She had two grown children who lived away from home. I had the whole place to myself. I did check her mail for her.

I loved my job very much and looked forward to going to work. I liked all the children, and they liked me.

After spending a few weekends in Appleton, I realized I had made a very grave mistake in going there. I was twenty-eight and single, and there wasn't anything for me to do there. They didn't have all the social things going on that a large city had. I got involved in activities at Lawrence University. I was also driving to Milwaukee, a hundred miles south of Appleton, or going on to Chicago on the weekends.

Even though I was a Baha'i, I joined a Catholic social group.

I had talked with my landlady, Mrs. K, about the Baha'i faith. She informed me there was a girl in Appleton that had a religion somewhat similar to that, and that I should meet her because she was interesting. Her name was Lynne, and I called her. She informed me she was a member of the Unification Church, founded by a Rev. Sun Myung. Moon, and she was a "Moonie." I went over to see her. She was very charming, and I became attracted to her. She was a student at Lawrence University. I met a lot of her friends. I told them all about the Baha'i faith in the hopes that they would leave the Unification Church and become Baha'is.

Lynne had friends in Chicago. We would drive there and spend the weekend there at their homes fairly often. It was a two hundred-mile drive from Appleton. I liked Chicago very much.

On one trip, we decided to stop at the Baha'i temple in Wilmette, Illinois, a north suburb of Chicago. When I first saw the Baha'i temple, I was "beside myself." I had never seen a building more interesting than this temple. I had seen beautiful temples and palaces in the orient. It was beyond words. It's near Lake Michigan, and the garden around the temple is extremely beautiful. The Baha'is have no clergy. I purchased many books on Baha'i, because I wanted to read everything the Baha'i prophets had written. I was extremely enthusiastic about Baha'i. I wanted everyone to be Baha'i.

I met another Baha'i in Appleton, Don D. He was also from Los Angeles. He informed me he had been a drummer. He was married to an RN, and they had a son. I spent a lot of time with them. Since he had been a member of a rock group in Los Angeles, various "show people" would come to visit him and as a result, I met them too. A most interesting couple was a jazz musician who was married to a Syrian belly dancer. They were from Alaska.

I spent a lot of time with Lynne and her friends. I wanted her to be Baha'i, but she believed I would leave Baha'i and become a "Moonie."

After a few months, I was extremely unhappy with Appleton and wanted to break my contract, but the special education director talked me into staying there.

At Lynne's suggestion, I decided to read about the Unification Church. She gave me a book entitled *The Divine Principle* by Young Oon Kim. I read the book but found many grave discrepancies comparing it to biblical Scripture.

After I had talked to Lynne about all the discrepancies, I believed she would drop the "Moonie movement." She had no interest in leaving the "Moonies." She still had great hopes that I, too, would become a "Moonie." At this point, considering she was a young, dynamic, intelligent girl, and would not change, she was probably brainwashed. I don't see any other way she could have accepted principles that are in direct contradiction to biblical Scripture.

In more recent years, the Rev. Dr. Sun Myung Moon's organization had come out with paid advertisements in newspapers. On Monday, November 1, 2004, they had a full-page ad on page B7 of *The Columbus Dispatch*.

It appeared to me that according to Rev. Sun Myung Moon, Jesus Christ failed his mission because he was crucified. This concept comes from Satan and the proof for this is found in Matthew, Chapter 16, verses 21–23. In this key section Jesus informs the disciples that he is to suffer and be put to death and will rise up on the third day. Peter responds:"This must not happen to you." Jesus responds: Get behind me Satan! You are an obstacle in my path because the way you think is not God's way but man's." Now Jesus did not mean that Peter was Satan, only that the concept that Jesus was not to suffer the Passion was Satan's stance.

SATAN HATES THE CROSS!

Biblical Scripture has pointed to Jesus' passion and death over and over. There is no question about that Jesus came here as a savior.

In Matthew, chapter 1, verses 20–21, "…the angel of the Lord appeared unto him in a dream and said, Joseph son of David, do not be afraid to take Mary home as your wife, because she has conceived what is in her by the Holy Spirit. She will give birth to a son and you must name him Jesus, because he is the one who is to save his people from their sins."

In Matthew, chapter 12, verse 39–41: " It is an evil and unfaithful generation that asks for a sign! The only sign it will be given is the sign of the prophet Jonah. For as Jonah was in the belly of the sea-monster for three days and three nights, so will the Son of Man be in the heart of the earth for three days and three nights."

Matthew, chapter 16, verse 21: "From that time Jesus began to make it clear to his disciples that he was destined to go to Jerusalem and suffer grievously at the hands of the elders and chief priests and scribes, to be put to death, and to be raised up on the third day."

Mark, chapter 10, verse 45: " For the Son of Man himself did not come to be served but to serve, and to give his life as a ransom for many."

Luke, chapter 13, verse 32: "Learn that today and tomorrow I cast out devils and on the third day attain my end."

Luke, chapter 18, verse 31–33: "Then taking the twelve aside he said to them, now we are going up to Jerusalem, and everything that is written by the prophets, about the Son of Man is to come true. For he will be handed over to the pagans and will be mocked, maltreated and spat on, and when they have scourged him, they will put him to death: and on the third day he will rise again."

In John, chapter 10, an extremely beautiful part describing the Good Shepherd, verse 11: "I am the good shepherd: the Good Shepherd is the one who lays down his life for His sheep."

John, chapter 10, verses 17–18: "The Father loves me, because I lay down my life in order to take it up again. No one takes it from me; I lay it down of my own free will ... so it is in my power to take it up again ... "

In John, chapter 12, verse 27–28: " What shall I say: Father, save me from this hour? But it was for this very reason that I have come to this hour. Father, glorify your name!"

In Romans, chapter 3, verses 23–25: " Both Jew and pagan sinned and forfeited God's glory, and both are justified through the free gift of his grace by being redeemed in Christ Jesus who was appointed by God to sacrifice his life so as to win reconciliation through faith."

In I Timothy, chapter 2, verse 5–6: "For there is only one God, and there is only one mediator between God and mankind, himself a man, Christ Jesus, who sacrificed himself as a ransom for them all."

In Revelation, chapter 5, verse 9: " They sang a new hymn:

You are worthy to take the scroll, and break the seals of it, because you were sacrificed, and with your blood you bought men for God of every race, language, people and nation ... "

Well, brothers and sisters, from the biblical Scripture quoted above, we can see how important it is to read Scripture to find the truth for ourselves. Without biblical Scripture, it would be difficult for us to know what the Word of God is for us

Satan hates the cross!

There isn't anything that Satan hates more than the cross. Jesus' whole purpose was to go through the most horrible ordeal of the crucifixion and be the gate for sinners to enter into eternal life.

Rest assured that Satan and his devils will use every scheme imaginable to belittle the crucifixion and God's great sacrifice and the almost incomprehensible act of love ever to be accomplished by God for His creatures.

The Moonie movement is pretty sad. It is my belief that Moon has brainwashed slaves serving him. My Master Jesus Christ came as a servant to serve us and die on a cross so that we may have eternal life. There is no one in creation that did what my Master did for us. The only God I will serve is Jesus Christ!

I had been attracted to the Baha'i faith because of its extremely high principles of life.

Baha'is teach that God sends divine manifestations that are His representatives. Divine teachers who, even though they many bring a different message for each age, represent one and the same light. These "manifestations" in other words are equal and the same as the Light of God; they are: Abraham, Moses, Krishna, Buddha, Zoroaster, Christ, Mohammed, and the manifestation for our age, Baha'u'llah. I decided to learn about these other "manifestations" as well as I knew Christ and Bahaullah. However, things did not turn out as I had expected.

I read the *Encyclopedia of Religion and Ethics*; the editor was James Hastings. The publisher is New York: Charles Scribner's, Sons. When I read about the Bab, the forerunner of the Baha'i faith, I learned that there had been many who had claimed to be divine manifestations of God.

In *The History of Religions* by E. Washburn Hopkins, Ph.D., Ll.D., a professor of Sanskrit and comparative philosophy at Yale University, which was published in New York: by The Macmillan Co., 1928. I came to learn that Buddha did not believe in a creator or the soul.

I then read many other books about Buddha; all he believed in was self-enlightenment, and he did not acknowledge a divine Creator.

The real blow came when I read about Moses in Scripture. In Exodus, chapter 2, verses 11–13: "…he saw an Egyptian strike a Hebrew, one of his countrymen. Looking round he could see no one in sight, so he killed the Egyptian, and hid him in the sand." From this, I believed it was quite odd that a "manifestation" of God would be capable of killing anyone.

In Exodus, chapter 4, verse 24: "On the journey, when Moses had halted for the night, Yahweh came to meet him and tried to kill him." It seemed strange to me that if Moses was a manifestation of God, that God would want to kill His own manifestation.

In Numbers, chapter 20, verse 2: "There was no water for the community, and they were all united against Moses and against Aaron. The people challenged Moses..." In verses 7–12, "Yahweh spoke to Moses and said, "Take the branch and call the community together, you and your brother Aaron. Then in full view of them, order this rock to give water. You will make water flow for them out of the rock, and provide drink for the community and their cattle. Moses took up the branch from before Yahweh, as he had directed him. Then Moses and Aaron called the assembly together in front of the rock and addressed them, "Listen now, you rebels. Shall we make water gust from this rock for you?" And Moses raised his hand and struck the rock twice with the branch; water gushed in abundance, and the community drank and their cattle too." " Then Yahweh said to Moses and Aaron, 'Because you did not believe that I could proclaim my holiness in the eyes of the sons of Israel, you shall not lead this assembly into the land I am giving them.'"

In Deuteronomy, chapter 32, verse 48: " Yahweh spoke to Moses ... Climb Mount Nebo ..." Verses 51–52 state, "Because you broke faith with me among the sons of Israel that time at Meribath-kadesh in the wilderness of Zin, because you did not display my holiness among the sons of Israel, you may see this land only from afar; you cannot enter it, this land that I am giving to the sons of Israel."

This was the clincher; by his mistake, there was no possible way that Moses could be a "manifestation" of God. I could accept him as one of the greatest prophets that ever lived, but not on a par equal to Jesus Christ. These prophets are not equal to Jesus Christ. He is the Son of God, and He is God for He had said, "The Father and I are One." I now believed that even though the principles of Baha'i appeared desirable, the underlying foundation of Baha'i was false according to biblical Scripture, because Bahai had lowered the station of "The Son Of God" to a prophet. I could not accept that belief.

I resigned from the Baha'i faith, because I did not believe their teachings were from God. On December 11, 1969, I wrote a letter to the National Spiritual Assembly of the Baha'is of the USA. In the letter, I stated that I wanted to withdraw from the membership of the Baha'i faith. For me, my master, Jesus Christ, was the only path to God. I received a reply on December 17, 1969, acknowledging my withdrawal from Baha'i membership. I had only been a member for four months, even though I had done extensive study on the writings of the Baha'i faith for over a year.

In Proverbs, chapter 3, verse 5, it says to, "Trust wholeheartedly in Yahweh, put no faith in your own perception" Buddha had preached self-enlightenment, but we see biblical Scripture warns us against our own perception.

The essence of Hebrews, chapter 3, verses 1–3, is that Christ is held higher than Moses.

The Baha'is do not acknowledge Satan. To deny the existence of Satan is to deny the validity of Scripture, for he is mentioned throughout the Bible.

I saw the devil when I was sixteen. One night while I was sleeping in my and my brother's bedroom, I woke up and sat up in bed. My brother was asleep in the bed next to mine. I looked over to the left at the entrance door. A "spirit-like" thing came into the room. At first, it was almost formless, as I might imagine a ghost to be. It was as if it was going to go into the wall that was directly opposite to me. At that moment, it turned and looked at me; it was like a white, chalky mist, a face with very prominent, sharp features. The eyes were black and even though the face was completely expressionless, I looked into its eyes for a split second. It is impossible to describe what I saw. The eyes projected the most horrible hate I have ever experienced. I saw its soul. At that moment, I screamed, but no sound came from my mouth; I was frozen with fright. It was a feeling of extreme evil. We had a closet over on the right corner of the room; it had an open door. The door was always open; we never closed it. This thing flew across the room and while it was moving, I heard a very loud noise, like a team of horses galloping over cobblestones dragging heavy chains. It was loud enough to have awakened the whole neighborhood. It flew into the closet, and the door slammed shut. I sat there in shock, trying to gather my senses together. I couldn't believe my brother and family were still sleeping. I felt the floor in front of my bed. I expected it to have been broken up by the horses dragging the chains. To my surprise the floor was not broken.

I reached up on the wall and took hold of the crucifix; I held it up and went to the closet. I can't believe I had the courage to do that, but I believed as long as I held the cross, no harm could come to me. I opened the door, and there was nothing there. I went and woke my mother and told her what had happened. I told my dad the next day. My parents called the priest, and I told him about it. He believed I had a bad dream. But, the problem is, what shut the door? As far as I know, dreams don't close doors.

There is a phenomenon called a hypnopompic hallucination, in which one may awaken out of a dream and still be dreaming, believing that one is seeing things. However, I can't believe this is the case, because it doesn't answer the question how the door came to be shut. Furthermore I have had nightmares but I cannot believe there is any way I could conjure up the being that I had seen.

I believe that the thing I saw was completely separate from my imagination conscious or unconscious. I know it was the devil. That terrible hate and extreme evil was separate from me. It all came from the eyes. It is said, the eyes are the windows to the soul.

The only explanation that I can give as to why the whole household did not hear this was that I believe it may have some special significance for me whatever that may be.

The Baha'is disclaim his existence, but I know the devil exists as an entity in itself. Something extraordinary happened regarding what I had seen. I had been reading *Faust* years later in college. I don't remember if it was *Faust* by Marlowe or Goethe, but in the book was a picture of the devil. He was dressed in men's clothes and was looking back as he was running. It was the only picture in the paperback. The face in the picture was the same one I had seen. One of these authors may have been writing a true experience.

Even though Baha'i on the surface appears to have high principles, it could be inspired by the devil. In Matthew, chapter 12, verse 26, it states, "…if Satan casts out Satan, he is divided against himself." Since Baha'is don't acknowledge him, if he did inspire Baha'is, he is not acknowledged, thereby not attacked, and left free to go about his business. Baha'is claim to be the followers of the light. Lucifer means light bearing. In 2 Corinthians, chapter 11, verses 13–15, we see the essence of which is, if Satan himself goes disguised as an angel of light, there is no need to be surprised when his servants, too, disguise themselves as servants of righteousness. They will come to the end that they deserve.

Another thing that was interesting that may even be considered as a sign.

My physical therapy aide at the Highlands School was a Native American Karen W.

At one Baha'i Fireside, she and her girlfriend had gone with me. Neither had ever seen the Baha'i symbol. Karen asked me what the word "evil" was doing on the wall, and her girlfriend told me that she had thought it was the picture of a Viking ship. I had the association of the devil as a Viking king on a Viking ship. Since the Vikings loved war, he also could be thought of as a warlord for the battle for souls.

The night I dropped Baha'i, I was lying in bed, and the cross of the window pane threw a shadow on the wall, and scripture came to mind: "You will tell them by their fruits." It is the key! Evil cannot produce good fruit.

That same night, I had an extraordinary experience. I was sleeping in my bedroom but awoke and looked to the door window and saw a being of "contained fire." I believe it was an alien life form. I was not fearful but extremely fascinated by it. I got out of bed and went towards it, but it ran off the porch and over the snow towards the forest. It did turn around to "see" if I was coming after it. It appeared as pure flexible crystal, totally filled with flames. It had crystal arms and legs and a large square trunk. Even though it did not have a head, it acted as a complete living alien life form. I thought about it and went back to bed. As I think on it now, I cannot believe I did that. Today, I would have got dressed as fast as possible and would have gone after it. I am too fascinated with reports of aliens and UFOs to pass up such an encounter like that now. It is possible that it could have been an advanced mobile recorder.

I spent the holidays with my family. I had a lot of negative feelings about going back to Appleton. I was still trying to terminate my contract, because I wanted to go to Chicago to live.

I was starting to get the urge to go back to graduate school and obtain a doctorate degree. Since I enjoyed working in special education, I thought about getting a doctorate in special education. Mr. N, the Special Ed Administrator at the Appleton Public Schools, encouraged me to do this. He informed me that Dr. M at Northwestern University in Chicago had a good program. The superintendent released me from my contract.

On Easter, I left Appleton, Wisconsin, and decided to obtain a chief physical therapist position in Chicago. I was very fortunate to have several very good offers. On April 6, 1970, I took a position with Skokie Valley Community Hospital, in a north suburb of Chicago.

I called Northwestern to speak with Dr. M and was informed he had gone to Northern Illinois University in DeKalb, Illinois, to develop a doctorate program in special education. It was eighty-six miles west of Chicago. I went out to see him. We had a good meeting. He informed me that I had the requirements to do a doctorate in his program.

Since his program was not yet official, it was necessary for his doctorate students to apply to educational psychology or educational administration. When his program was accredited, we would then transfer to his program. I had to take the Graduate Record Exam again, because the university required a score of 1,000, and I had scored about 780 when I took it in California. This time, I scored close to 1,000. They accepted students who had had at least a 3.2 in their master's degree program. Since I had a GPA of 3.51 in my master's degree program, I was acceptable. I had been interviewed by a committee of thirteen professors, and I was accepted into the Department of Education Administration. I planned on obtaining a special education administration credential, besides working for a doctorate degree.

I planned to continue work at Skokie Valley Community Hospital until the fall of 1970, and then enter the doctoral program at Northern Illinois University.

I had a very active summer in 1970. I planned that in the fall, I would obtain a position as a physical therapist in special education and attend NIU at night. I wanted to get more experience in special ed, while working toward a doctorate degree. I contacted a large number of special ed cooperatives that oversee a large number of public school districts. Since most programs did not have a physical therapist, I informed them I would develop a physical therapy program for them. I did obtain a chief physical therapist position for the '70-'71 school year at the Southwest Cook County Cooperative Association for Special Education. They served over twenty-six school districts.

Fortunately, for Skokie Valley Community Hospital, the previous chief physical therapist, a graduate student at Kent State, was not satisfied with her program. She was willing to take her position back when I resigned there in August.

I developed a physical therapy program for the special education cooperative. I had to move from the north side to southwest suburb of Chicago. I went to NIU four nights a week. It took about one hour and forty minutes each way. I didn't mind the travel, because I got off from school about 3:00 p.m. I loved my job, and I looked forward to working with all the kids.

I developed a paper entitled, "The Role of the Physical Therapist in Special Education" which was published as the article of the month in the Journal *Rehabilitation Literature*.

I was also elected as the Program Planning Chairman of the Division of Physical Therapy in the Illinois Council for Exceptional Children, under the National Education Association.

I made all A's in my doctoral program.

In the fall, the Special Ed Director asked me if I would try to get some of our kids in the Special Olympics in Chicago, which are for the mentally retarded. I obtained the information on Special Olympics. Even though I was impressed with the program, I believed that since we had so many other types of disabilities, it would be better to develop our own Special Olympics, which would include all of our handicapped children.

I drew up plans. I got most of the ideas for the program from a Guide for Local Programs published by the Joseph P. Kennedy Foundation for Special Olympics. I developed a number of committees with their respective chairman who would develop their program. The response was great; all of the teachers volunteered. At first, I had some problems with high school bands; but in the end, they came through for me.

An Olympic motto was "Win or Lose. Let me do my Best."

I directed the entire Special Olympics Program.

A special education coach consultant developed a physical education Olympic training program for all the contestants. I assisted in a lot of the therapeutic exercises for the children.

A training guide was developed for each classroom teacher. Many teachers coordinated the Olympic Training Program with their respective school training programs.

A games event committee was responsible for developing and setting up each particular event.

An official for each event was to record names and scores.

A Promotion and publicity chairman developed all the media coverage, press conferences, and TV and promotional activities.

A printed materials chairman was responsible for all printed materials for the program, including the printed program for the day of the Olympics.

A medical and emergency service chairman was selected to obtain insurance, doctors and nurses, and a Red Cross Station and Ambulance standby service. An Olympics ceremony and parade chairman was responsible for the opening and closing ceremony and parade.

A Special Olympics announcer was chosen for the day of the Olympics.

An Olympic Village chairman was responsible for developing a luncheon for the contestants; this was developed by the Special Ed PTA.

A safety chairman developed an overall safety program for the Olympics.

A budget and fund chairman was selected to obtain pledges from organizations, businesses, and individuals to cover the cash needs of the program.

An awards chairman was selected to secure medals and awards for the contestants.

A special events chairman was selected to contact well-known personalities to take part in the Olympics.

A transportation chairman was selected to address transportation needs.

A parent communications chairman was selected corresponded with parents about the Olympics.

As the year went on, all the staff was very involved in training. Each classroom teacher encouraged their children to make a classroom Olympic flag or banner for the day of the Olympic parade. This was a big art project.

In the fall of 1970, I started "steady dating" a nurse, I had met at Skokie Valley Community Hospital. She had been a nun and a Peace Corps teacher before she became a nurse. Her name was Pat. She was now working at McNeil Hospital in Berwyn, Illinois, a suburb of Chicago. We had seen a lot of each other. Her family liked me very much.

I was thirty in December 1970. We went out on New Year's Eve. That evening I proposed to her, sad to say, in a very "matter of fact way," and she accepted. As I was driving home, about fifteen miles from where she lived, I started shaking all over, and I became extremely upset. I was very upset about the engagement and realized I was not in love with her. I called her immediately.

I felt bad because I didn't want to hurt her feelings. I talked to her about it. I informed her I would never have proposed if I believed something like this would have happened.

Afterward, we still dated but around February, she "stood me up" one night and didn't want to see me anymore. I started dating other girls again.

On Saturday, May 15, 1971, we held the Special Olympics at Tinley Park High School.

The weather couldn't have been better. It turned out to be a much greater event than

I had imagined. The events were a fifty-yard dash, three hundred-yard run, the softball throw, standing broad jump, and swimming meet with subdivisions.

For the physically handicapped, the events were Indianapolis 500, this was a Krazy Kar Race for the preschoolers; a shot put (ball), a discus that was a plastic ring; and a wheelchair race. Children were divided into ability teams. I will not list the businesses that gave us support; the list is too long. Red Cross, a funeral home, had donated their ambulance for the day.

Doctors had volunteered their time. The Jolly Jesters sent us a clown. McDonalds gave all of the contestants free tee-shirts and lunches, and all contestants were made automatic members of the Ronald McDonald Fun Club. Prizes were donated by various merchants. A raffle was also held. Painted gold, silver, and bronze medals were made and donated so that each child received a medal. Every child was a winner. Jaycees, Lions Club, Boy Scouts, American Legion, Tinley Park Police served without pay, and many others gave outstanding help.

Dave Hale, a Chicago Bears football player, was on hand to sign autographs.

I am crying as I am writing about this experience; it was one of the most beautiful experiences I had ever had.

There were over seventy classrooms in the meet, and each classroom had a flag in the big parade before the meet. We had two high school bands.

Eunice Kennedy Shriver of the Kennedy Olympics had said: "Special Olympics seems to do something for everyone; it touches not just the children, but also the parents, teachers, coaches, the officials, the volunteers, all of us. I know it will give you a lifetime of memories."

Go-cart Race

Wheel-chair Race

Special Olympic Race

Discuss Throw

Blind Girl Feels Her Olympic Medal

The last paragraph of the paper I had published entitled, "Special Olympics," sums up my feelings: "Before Saturday, May 15, 1971, I had never really seen a Special Olympics or any other type of Olympics, let alone develop one. But on that day it happened, a happening, and the beautiful things that took place on that day will remain with me always. I am very happy to have had the privilege of developing that program and will always be indebted to the people who made that day, a day of winning for our children."

During the summer of 1971, I was on vacation, and took two graduate special ed courses from Chicago State College. I went back east and spent time with my family. I visited my brother at Georgetown University in Washington, D.C. He was majoring in languages and linguistics.

For the fall of 1972, I was to start my dissertation project at NIU. I was going to develop a master's degree program in the area of the physically handicapped. I was going to receive a grant to do this. Even though all these good things were happening, the desire to pursue medicine became so strong that I realized I had to go back, take undergraduate pre-med courses, and get into medical school.

I informed my brother Gil what I planned to do. He couldn't believe it.

My advisors at NIU tried to discourage me from leaving the program, but I had made up my mind. I would become a physician, no matter what. The Special Ed Cooperative was upset that I would not be going back to them in the fall, but fortunately, a physical therapist was obtained for the program.

I obtained an acting chief physical therapist position on a part-time basis for the Oak Forest Hospital, a two thousand-bed county hospital.

I believed with my background that I would be able to get into any medical school. However, I was in for a big surprise.

I had been an X-ray technician, an EEG technician, and a physical therapist for six years; I believed I was an excellent candidate for medical school. I had no idea at the time of how difficult it was to get into medicine. I wanted to go to the School of Medicine at the University of Chicago. I went to see the Dean for a preliminary interview and to find out what courses I would need to take to get into medical school in the fall of 1972. He advised me not to drop my doctoral program in special education. He told me I would need too many preliminary courses, and because I was thirty, my chances of getting into medical school were nil. He said I needed to take the MCAT test and would need to have very high scores. He told me there were four thousand applicants for ninety positions. He told me not to apply there, because I would not be accepted there. I was very upset.

I decided to try Loyola University, School of Medicine. I met with the Dean Wells and I got almost the exact story I had gotten at the University of Chicago. I realized that I was in a real bind. I still made up my mind to take the courses I needed. If I could not get into medical school in the USA, I would go anywhere in the world that would accept me as a student of medicine, such as Guadalajara, Mexico, or the University of St. Thomas in the Philippines.

I went to see the director of physical therapy at Northwestern University. I believed that since it was part of the medical school there that she might be able to help me get into Northwestern. She told me that they had had a physical therapist in their department who had been in the same bind I was in. He had even taught residents rehabilitation but could not get into Northwestern Medical School. She informed me that he had been accepted into the Chicago College of Osteopathic Medicine. She suggested that I apply there.

I met with the dean, Dr. Robert Kistner. It was a good interview. He looked at my graduate transcripts and master's degree thesis. He told me he was impressed with what I had done with my life, and that I was medical school material. He told me I would need to take the MCAT, pre-med courses, make good grades, and forget about applying to foreign medical schools. I was so extremely happy, for in essence, he was telling me if I made an acceptable score on MCAT, and passed pre-med courses, I would be accepted. He was impressed with my publications, too.

In 1971, I was extremely happy to receive my letter of acceptance from the Chicago College of Osteopathic Medicine, with a stipulation that I had to pass the pre-med courses.

I had developed a comprehensive physical therapy teaching program for the Restorative Nursing Department of Oak Forest Hospital, besides supervising and teaching staff. Teams of RNs would be rotated with me, and I taught them aspects of physical therapy.

I took pre-med courses at St. Xavier College in the southwest suburb of Chicago. It was a beautiful small college with a very nice campus. I took Physics and Organic Chemistry.

During the fall, I was contacted by an RN named "Rose" who planned to become a physical therapist. She requested that I be so kind to meet with her a few times and tell her about physical therapy. I informed her I would be happy to do so. We set up a time in the afternoon at a small park rotunda.

I had parked my car and was walking down the long path to the rotunda.

It was on a clear, cool day. It is said that on a clear day, you can see forever.

I love the fall, always have. The maple leaves had painted the ground. The sun was streaming through the pillars at the rotunda as I walked up the incline. She was seated at a small table writing something on a pad.

She sat up, smiled, offered me her hand, and said hello. I don't know what happened, but from that moment on, she was on my mind all the time. I couldn't imagine going through life without her.

One day after I had met with her a couple of times, she asked me, "Why do you like me so much?" I told her how I felt about her. She was very angry. She replied, "Do you mean to tell me you felt this way, and you were not going to tell me?" She was separated and had children.

I informed her I was in pre-med, and medicine would become my life. Soon I would be completely broke and in extreme debt, once I entered medical school. It would not be possible for me to carry on a deep relationship during my medical school studies. I believed I had to give medicine everything I had, to study harder than I had ever studied in my life. I wanted to be a sponge soaking up knowledge.

She informed me I would not be seeing her again. After a short time, I called her. I informed her I was in absolute agony being away from her, and I wanted to continue seeing her. She gave in. We saw each other about a year. It was wonderful being with her. I lived in stardust with her; it was complete joy! She remains in my heart.

I studied very hard. In the spring term, I decided to go to Olive Harvey Junior College because it was a city college, and tuition was much more reasonable. I liked it there and made a lot of friends. It was just as challenging as St. Xavier College.

I always got to Organic Chemistry class early and would study before class. A student, Diannella W, was always at the blackboard working on her calculus problems, complaining about calculus, and the instructor, who was also early for class, would be joking with her. She was in pre-med. One day, she was no longer at the blackboard working on Calculus.

The instructor remarked, "Dianella girl, you done up and dropped that Calculus course." She acknowledged she had. I felt bad. I knew she would not get into medical school without completing Calculus. At the end of each term, the class had a big party. I took two watermelons, and my friends were quite amused. I must say the "soul spaghetti" that Dianella's mother made was some of the best spaghetti I had ever had.

My lab partner in microbiology, Dedra H, was a single mother, and had to take her child to day care before class. I was one of three who got an A in the class. The top student was a divorcee with four children. I can't remember her name. I had attempted to talk her into applying to med school, but she wouldn't do it. She wanted to be a nurse.

I had made a B in Organic Chemistry and an A in Microbiology.

Years later, I learned that Dedra H. had become the chief surgical nurse at South Chicago Hospital.

I worked full time at Oak Forest Hospital during the summer. I had purchased most of my medical school textbooks and decided to start studying before school began. My microscope was over $500, and the books were quite expensive.

I fell deeper and deeper in love with "Rose." I couldn't go a day without seeing her.

Medical School Years

The medical school had two fraternities. ITS had a home with rooms. I believed it would be cheaper for me to live there and be across the street from the school. I had never lived in a fraternity before. I signed a contract, paid my money, and moved in one of the rooms in July 1972. After the first night there, I realized there was too much noise, and the place was loaded with roaches. I terminated my contract. I lost my money but believed I would need a clean, quiet place to live.

I moved to Marquette Park, a southwest suburb of Chicago. Even though there was a Nazi organization there, it's a very clean neighborhood. I got a furnished apartment, fifteen miles from the school.

The Chicago College of Osteopathic Medicine is in Hyde Park, where the University of Chicago Campus is located. Hyde Park is about ten miles south of the Chicago Loop.

In September of 1972, I started my first year of med school. I quit my job, because it was not possible to work. Since I had had an "A" average in my doctoral program in education, I expected to be at the top of my medical school class. I had a lot of confidence that I would do well.

My first courses were anatomy with cadaver, biochemistry with lab; clinical orientation to the hospital clinics; medicine; and osteopathic principles and practice. We dissected our cadavers four hours each morning, five days a week. Since we had a female, we would switch tables and also work on a male cadaver, too. Anatomy was very fascinating. It's a great privilege to be able to take a body apart and see all of the internal organs such as the heart. It gives one a much deeper appreciation of the beautiful machine that God made.

Fortunately, I had had some anatomy before I came to medical school. I had learned osteology (the study of bones) as an X-ray technician, and myology (study of muscles) as a physical therapist, but still, the medical school anatomy course was so much deeper. In the first week, we received very intense lectures.

I believed that they were just trying to scare everybody. I believed it was not possible to memorize that amount of material in so short a time. Unfortunately, I was in for a rude awakening. We were given weekly examinations.

Around the third week when we were doing dissecting anatomy, our grand professor, Dr. Strachan was questioning one of the students about what he was dissecting. The student started yelling at Dr. Strachan. Everyone was stunned. He informed Dr. Strachan that he was an inhalation therapist making good money, and he was not going to take the crap of med school. He left the class. I told my dissection classmates that I would not want to be anywhere else in the world but in our program. One of my classmates remarked, "It is better that he left now, he would have never made it here."

Shortly thereafter, we got a new student to replace the one that quit. He was from New Jersey. Was he happy!

He informed us that he had just begun a master's degree program in microbiology, signed an apartment lease, and was settled in study. He said when our school called him, he immediately left all behind to study medicine. We told him, "You belong with us."

We were expected to memorize all the cycles of metabolism in biochemistry. Biochemistry was the "super-bear" for me. I was just barely passing the course. If it wasn't for the anatomy I had before medical school, I may have failed. I could spend more time on biochemistry, because I knew a lot of anatomy. It was a very humbling experience for me. After the first month I realized that medicine was my destiny. I wanted to be a doctor more than anything else.

I still saw "Rose," but not very often now, because I was very busy. On a Saturday, I met her children. After I met her children I realized that I was in no position at that time to be taking on the responsibility of a family.

I decided to meet with the biochemistry professor, because I was not satisfied with my performance. She was surprised to see me. She informed me that she had not called me up about grades. I informed her I was only used to making A's and was not happy about my grades. She informed me she believed my grades were fine. She informed me I was now with all the other "A" students, and we were competing against each other. "The best against the best," she remarked.

Fortunately, I passed the first quarter of medicine. Second quarter was November to February 1973. I now started Physiology with lab, along with the other courses I had had. Another added course was microbiology. I was still having a great challenge with biochemistry. Even though I had made an A in microbiology in junior college I was having problems just getting by in Microbiology, even though I was studying all the time.

I was thirty-one and had to "hit the sack" at midnight. Medical school was extremely demanding. I don't believe anyone can pass without giving it everything they got. It was like working for a PhD in each of the basic medical sciences. The courses were extremely interesting.

In physiology, we did experiments on animals. We had very sophisticated equipment.

In the second quarter, I was still having a very hard time with biochemistry. I believed my relationship with Rose was taking too much of my "energy" that I needed for med school.

In the winter of 1972, even though I was in love with Rose and didn't know how I could possibly go on without her, I realized I needed to break off the relationship. It wasn't going anywhere. I was unable to take on the responsibility of a family. I noted when I would be studying, I was preoccupied with the problems of the relationship. I was falling back in my courses, and didn't believe I could sacrifice medicine; it meant so much to me. The last thing I desired was to hurt her.

I prayed about all these things quite often. One night, I called her and told her I believed the relationship should end. It hurt me so bad, that I hurt her. I felt as if I had died. I had prayed for the strength to separate from her. It's beyond me as to how I was capable of separating from her. God helped me through this stage.

She told me years later that she did not want me to enter medical school, because she believed she would lose me. She believed we would have had a good life together, her being a nurse and I a physical therapist.

I would not have been satisfied, without being a physician.

I passed the second quarter. I began the third quarter in March 1973 to June; the only new course I picked up was psychiatry. Soon the year was over. I was in shock, because I could hardly believe I had made it through the year. It was the most difficult academic year of my life. My class average was 79.3.

For the summer of 1973, I worked full-time as a physical therapist at Oak Forest Hospital. Soon summer was over, and I began my second year.

In the first quarter of 1973 from September to November, I had Medicine, Osteopathic Medicine, Pathology, Physiology, and Psychiatry.

I had passed Biochemistry. I had a great interest in Psychiatry. I had also considered the possibility of specializing in physical medicine because of all the years of experience that I had had as a physical therapist. Since I had a master's degree in public health, I also thought about preventive medicine. I believed I would go into one of these areas.

In the next term, we started Pharmacology.

In December of 1973, during Christmas break, I returned to Oak Forest Hospital with the idea of developing an elective medical clerkship (medical student rotation) for our medical school. Since Oak Forest Hospital was a two thousand-bed hospital. There were a considerable number of patients that had rare conditions that one does not usually see in a regular practice. The patients could benefit from our help.

I approached the chairman of the hospital and told him of my ideas. He told me he would be happy to meet with our dean. I called our dean, Dr. Kistner, and they got together. I met with all the specialty areas at Oak Forest Hospital to help formulate a clerkship program. Each department drew up a program for a five-week clerkship. The medical director and a very good friend of mine, Dr. Sherman K, was in favor of the clerkship, too. He gave me a lot of assistance for developing the program. The clerkship became an approved program for a five-week senior elective clerkship for our medical school.

At the end of my first two years, we were required to take national board exams and pass them in order to go on to the clinical years of medicine. Fortunately, I passed Part 1 of national boards. My average now was 79.9.

In the spring of 1974, I had become very interested in biofeedback, and I did research in EEG biofeedback in the summer of 1974 with Norm D , a clinical psychologist at the University of Chicago. With biofeedback, one can learn to control one's physiological processes. Some have learned to control seizures, heart rate, blood pressure, blood flow, and headaches.

In EEG biofeedback, the most popular machine is an Alpha Trainer. Alpha brain wave state is usually a relaxed state. However, I was interested in Theta training, because the Theta brain wave state is supposedly the state of "creative-consciousness." It takes about eight months minimally to condition oneself to this state. I wanted to do this and remain in the Theta brain wave state for long periods of time to see what would happen. I wanted to explore creative consciousness.

Since I had been an EEG technician, I understood EEG biofeedback machines. I had worked with the Alpha Trainer for some weeks and began to get frustrated about the machine. I didn't believe it was sophisticated enough to give me feedback on the theta brain wave state. I needed a multichannel EEG biofeedback machine. Since the machine was over $10,000, I decided I would wait until I could get such a machine.

One day, I saw a movie on the psychic healers of the Philippines while I was in a singles bar with my friend, Nancy J. Barehanded "surgeons" were sticking their hands "into" people's bodies to remove damaged tissues. It appeared that they were massaging the area. It would be interesting to see such a person doing this in person.

It may be possible, but all I can say at this point is that "seeing is believing." Their claims are rather fantastic. I thought they would be worth investigating.

I had read about the psychic surgeon Arigo from Brazil; *Arigo, Surgeon of the Rusty Knife* by John G. Fuller. He had been born in a village. He had dreams about a surgeon called Fritz, who told him he should help people. This surgeon had died in the 1900s and took possession of Arigo. Arigo would speak in German and write prescriptions. He is reported to have seen over three hundred patients a day for twenty years. He operated with rusty knives, and no patient felt pain. Arigo said he did the surgery through Dr. Fritz and Jesus Christ.

It's extraordinary that Arigo had not gone beyond the third grade. Some of the scripts were for modern drugs. It's interesting that Dr. Fritz would have had knowledge of these new drugs.

The Catholic Church took a strong stance against Arigo; they believed he may have been in league with the devil. The legal system had put him in jail for witchcraft. Other spirits had possessed Arigo, too. The scripts were very bizarre at times. Arigo believed that the spirit of Dr. Fritz was the spirit of Christ.

It would be interesting to do a follow-up study on the people Arigo had treated and if their "cure" is still good, and what the long-term effects on these "patients" has been. In 1971, Arigo was killed in a car accident.

Looking at scripture as a means of interpretation this phenomena, in Leviticus, chapter 19, verse 31, it states: "Do not have recourse to the spirits of the dead or to magicians; they will defile you. I am Yahweh your God."

In Deuteronomy, chapter 18, verses 10–12, state, "There must never be anyone among you who makes his son or daughter pass through fire, who practices divination, who is a soothsayer, augur or sorcerer, who uses charms, consults ghosts or spirits, or calls up the dead. For the man who does these things is detestable to Yahweh your God..."

In 1 Samuel, chapter 28, verses 7–19, the essence is that King Saul had consulted with a necromancer to call up Samuel, and he was going to take advice from him. Samuel was called up and was angry. He told Saul he would be delivered in the hands of the Philistines. In 1 Chronicles, chapter 10, verse 13, we see that Saul died because he showed himself unfaithful to God, because he had consulted a necromancer instead of God.

We can see from the above that according to Scripture, we are not to conjure up spirits, and those that do so are not on the side of God.

It's interesting at this point to see what it says in 2 Thessalonians, chapter 2, verse 9, " ... when the Rebel comes, Satan will set to work: there will be all kinds of miracles and a deceptive show of signs ... "

I do not believe that Arigo's power was from God. But another interesting point is that it has been said that the largest sightings of UFO's were seen above Arigo's home. Did he get his power from UFOs? Could Arigo himself have been an extraterrestrial?

In America, Edgar Cayce had prescribed treatments while in a trance state. He was known as the sleeping prophet. In a trance state, he gave "readings," just about anything anyone could ask about such as reincarnation. I read several books on him and by him.

In *There Is a River*, he claimed the gospels did not condemn astrology or reincarnation. Actually this contradicts Scripture, for in Hebrews, chapter 9, verse 27, ... men only die once ... "

In Isaiah, chapter 47, verses 13–14: "those who analyse the heavens, who study the stars and announce month by month what will happen to you next. Oh, they will be like wisps of straw and the fire will burn them. This appears to be a very strong scriptural statement against the practice of astrology.

Jesus had spoken about being born again, but Jesus was talking about spiritual rebirth, not reincarnation. We are reborn in the Holy Spirit.

Phillip J. Swihard's book entitled *Reincarnation, Edgar Cayce and the Bible*, published by Intervarsity Press in Downers Grove, Illinois 60515, compares Cayce's writings with Scripture, and he

points out the major discrepancies of Cayce. It is interesting that
he has come up with arguments that I have been aware of for a
long time. It goes to show one, that we can all find the truth by
reading the Word ourselves.

I believe the Bible is the greatest book ever written. 2 Timothy,
chapter 3, verse 16, gives key guidance: "All scripture is inspired by
God, and can profitably be used for teaching, for refuting error, for
guiding people's lives and teaching them to be holy."

Another personality in the psychic world was Jeane Dixon. I read
two of her books and had corresponded with her.

Her books are *My Life and Prophecies* and *The Call to Glory*.
She claims that the Spirit of God is responsible for her prophecies.
However, it is known that her predictions do not always come true.
In Deuteronomy, chapter 18, verse 22, it states, "When a prophet
speaks in the name of Yahweh and the thing does not happen and
the word is not fulfilled, then it has not been spoken by Yahweh."

She also has a horoscope, and since Scripture condemns astrology, I believed she probably got her power from the devil. She
should have read Isaiah, chapter 47, verse 13–14: " ... these who analyse the heavens, and announce month by month what will happen to
you next. Oh, they will be like wisps of straw and the fire will burn
them." Again this appears to be a very strong Scriptural statement
against the practice of astrology.

One of the best critical articles I have read on astrology was *Reflec-
tions*, published by Merck-Sharp and Dohme, Vol. II, No.5, 1976. "A
Critical Look at Astrology" by Bart J. Bok, a professor emeritus of
astronomy at the University of Arizona, looks upon astrology as a
pseudoscience. He believes there is no scientific basis for astrological beliefs. He believes it is deplorable that newspapers publish the
astrological forecast nonsense. He believes it may affect one's personal judgment. For some, it's a religion.

Professor Bok had requested that his friend, and psychologist,
at Harvard University, Dr. Gordon W. Allport draft a statement

entitled, "Psychologists state their views on Astrology." It reported that psychologists find astrology of no value whatsoever as an indicator of past, present, or future trends in one's destiny. Nor is there ground for believing that social events can be foretold by divinations of the stars.

The reason people turn to astrology is that they lack resources in their personal lives to solve serious personal problems confronting them. Faith in astrology or the occult is harmful insofar that it encourages flight from the problems of real life. People who are interested in astrology should obtain Professor Bok's article. Our fates lie in ourselves and our relationship to God, not in the stars.

In the summer of 1974, I did a surgical clerkship from June to August 1974 at the Illinois Central Community Hospital in Chicago. I learned a lot about surgery.

In one of the rotations, I had a major confrontation with one of the gynecological surgeons. He was always "barking" at the surgical nurses. I was angry about it, because they seemed to be doing the best they could and did not deserve that kind of crap. He got on my case one day. I informed him that I could have been working all summer as a physical therapist making good money, but I took the surgical clerkship because I wanted to learn all I could about surgery. I informed him I did not appreciate how he treated his staff, and all he taught me was that I wanted to be the exact opposite of him when I became a physician.

The surgical intern was in shock after I said all this. After the operation, I was summoned to meet with the hospital medical director. He was Italian. He told me, "We Italians have bad tempers that get the best of us!" I informed him that was not the case with me. He had me transferred to Dr. Rama Row's surgical team. I was so fortunate in working with him. He was a wonderful teacher. Even though I had read the Schwartz Textbook of Surgery, he had me read the Indian textbook of surgery, too. It was a great book. He also taught me to do some minor procedures.

I also rotated with a cool eye surgeon. He reminded me of James Bond. He carried a stainless steel case with his instruments. He was a great ophthalmologist! After I assisted him with about thirty cases, I requested to do the next one, since I believed I had his surgical technique memorized. He had a fit. He was shaking his finger at me saying, "You are a medical student. You are here to assist me; you will not be doing any operations on my patients!" I was not happy about it. After I became a doctor, I remembered the encounter and said to myself, based on liability. If I was that Dr. I would have said, "Send this medical student to Siberia!"

At the end of August, I began my third year of medical school and was now in the hospital.

In the mornings we received lectures, and in the afternoons we rotated through the various specialty clinics.

My courses for the third year were Anesthesiology, Medicine, Medical Jurisprudence, Obstetrics and Gynecology, Oncology, Ophthalmology and Otorhinolaryngology, Osteopathic Medicine, Orthopedics, Pathology, Pediatrics, Psychiatry, Surgery, and Urology.

I saw patients in the family practice clinics and in specialty clinics.

In September, I met with Dr. Kelso, the professor of physiology. I requested that he purchase a multichannel EEG biofeedback machine for me. I planned to condition myself to the Theta Brain Wave State and do research on Creative Consciousness. He was interested, but informed me I would need to do a fellowship in physiology.

That meant an extra year in medical school that I did not want to do. He informed me that the department couldn't buy medical students $35,000 multichannel EEG biofeedback machines, unless they were willing to do a year of fellowship in the physiology department. I was unwilling to do that, because I wanted to graduate in 1976.

In November, I was fortunate to have another paper published:

"A Critical Evaluation of the Techniques of Manual Muscle Testing."

I was taking an elective seminar in psychiatry at night at my school. I was pretty certain that I would go into psychiatry. I had a tendency to spend too much time on psychiatry, rather than my other course work. Since most of our patients were black, I started reading books "of color" to learn more about their culture.

It is interesting to note the character change in Eldridge Cleaver through accepting the Word of God. His *Soul On Ice* and *Post Prison Writings and Speeches* contained racism and statements against America. George *Otis's Eldridge Cleaver; Ice and Fire* showed Eldridge had come back to America and taken responsibility for his actions. Eldridge's early heroes had been Fidel Castro, Mao Tse-Tung, Karl Marx. His final hero was Jesus Christ, and through Christ, he was born again.

For me, the biggest name in the civil rights movement was Dr. Martin L. King, Jr.

"The King Plan for Freedom," by Lerone Bennett, Jr. in *Ebony*, Nov. 1975, reported King had studied Gandhi known for passive resistance. King was urging blacks to emulate Gandhi.

I was extremely impressed with his eight points in his plan.

Headings:

Refuse to cooperate with injustice.

Use love in everyday relations.

Violence must be avoided at all cost.

Mobilize for citizenship.

Get out to vote.

Continue legal and legislative fight.

Awaken the Church to its social responsibility.

Close the gap between the classes and the masses.

Be ready.

Everyone should read his article. It was an extreme tragedy for America and the entire world when Dr. King was shot.

Like Dr. King, I had read many books on Mahatma Gandhi. I love Gandhi very much. He has had a great effect on my life. His faith was a living one. The book that I enjoyed the most by him was *All Men Are Brothers*, published by Navajivan Publishing House. It is one of the most beautiful books I have ever read. His life is of a great inspiration to me. I read his books frequently. They are loaded with wisdom. He was extremely well disciplined. He had read the *Vedas*, the earliest Hindu scriptures. He had read the Upanishads, which are ancient accounts of mystical revelations. I have read parts of the Vedas and the Upanishads. For me, Biblical Scripture is still my reference point.

The Upanishads put the law as its highest reference point. Looking at biblical scripture, law is held quite differently. Colossians, chapter 2, verse 14, in reference to Jesus Christ, says, "He has overridden the Law, and cancelled every record of the debt that we had to pay; he has done away with it by nailing it to the Cross."

First Corinthians, chapter 13, verses 1–13, contain the essence of Love which is, "If I have all the eloquence of men or of angels but speak without love, I am simply a gong booming, or a cymbal clashing.

- Love is always patient,
- Love is kind,
- Love is never jealous,
- Love is never boastful,
- Love is never conceited,
- Love is never rude,
- Love is never selfish,
- Love doesn't take offense,
- Love is not resentful,
- Love takes no pleasure in other people's sins,

- Love delights in the truth,
- Love is ready to excuse,
- Love always trusts,
- Love always hopes,
- Love endures whatever comes,
- Love will never end.

In short, there are three things that last: Faith, Hope, and Love: and the greatest of these is Love."

Love is the supreme principle in Christianity.

To enter life, God expects us to live a life of love. Years ago, I made myself a 3x5 card on 1 Corinthians, chapter 13, verses 1–13. Everywhere you see the word "love," substitute your name. For example, my card is the following and where my name is plug in yours:

Rick is patient

Rick is kind

Rick envies no one

Rick is never boastful

Rick is never conceited

Rick is never rude

Rick is never selfish

Rick is not quick to take offense

Rick keeps no score of wrongs

Rick does not gloat over other men's sins

Rick delights in the truth

Rick can face anything

Rick's faith, hope, and endurance has no limit

Rick will never come to an end

I read my above 3x5 card verses every morning at the start of my day. It is the key to life.

Those statements are so simple, and yet so powerful!

See if you can accomplish them in a lifetime!

That card is the greatest challenge you will ever face. I guarantee it!

I also have a holy card of the prayer of St. Francis Of Assisi that I like to read in the morning, too:

> *Lord, make me an instrument of Thy peace;*
> *where there is hatred, let me sow love;*
> *where there is injury, pardon;*
> *where there is doubt, faith;*
> *where there is despair, hope;*
> *where there is darkness, light;*
> *and where there is sadness, joy.*
> *O Divine Master,*
> *grant that I may not so much seek to be consoled as to console;*
> *to be understood, as to understand;*
> *to be loved, as to love;*
> *for it in giving that we receive,*
> *it is in pardoning that we are pardoned,*
> *and it is in dying that we are born to eternal life.*

In essence, by the law we stand condemned, but by the cross, Jesus has won us salvation.

Gandhi had stated that there was a time in his life when he had been wavering between Hinduism and Christianity, but he felt that salvation was only possible through the Hindu religion. This has been very puzzling to me, because I haven't been able to find anything about salvation in the Hindu writings. He did believe in reincarnation, and Scripture refutes reincarnation. In Hebrews, chapter 9, verse 27, its essence stated that men only die once.

He had also read John Ruskin's book, *Unto This Last*, and believed it had transformed his life. I have read this also and was very impressed by it. It's about political economy. If we followed the principles in this book, we would have a much better world to live in. This book is published by the University of Nebraska Press in Lincoln, Nebraska. It's loaded with wisdom.

Leo Tolstoy and Shaw had shown much interest also in Ruskin's book.

Nonviolence was a very great part of Gandhi's life. His life was service to others. His life is Christ-like. It's beautiful and amusing to note how Gandhi felt about material wealth. The essence of his position was seen when he registered with the customs official at Marseille on September 11, 1931. He stated, "I am a poor Mendicant, my earthly possessions consist of six spinning wheels, prison dishes, a can of goat's milk, six homespun loin cloth and towels, and my reputation which cannot be worth much."

I am overwhelmed by the power of this man. He had said that Leo Tolstoy had been the main influence on him for his stand of nonviolence.

I learned about Leo Tolstoy in Professor Lee's Tragic Literature Course at the University of Pittsburgh. Tolstoy's *Anna Karenina* was so beautiful and powerful. He also wrote *War and Peace*. I also liked his book *What is Art*.

Gandhi was influenced by Leo Tolstoy's book, *The Kingdom of God is Within You*. It turned his belief against violence. *The Kingdom of God is Within You* is Leo Tolstoy's interpretation of the Sermon on the Mount. Gandhi looked upon Tolstoy as his great teacher and spiritual guide. I believe since Tolstoy loved Christ, was Christ-like in his life, and since Gandhi looked to Tolstoy, Gandhi was really more Christian than Hindu, even though he believed he was Hindu.

The Kingdom of God is Within You stimulates one's soul. *The Kingdom of God is Within You* other title was *Or, Christianity Not As A Mystical Teaching But As A New Concept Of Life*, translated from the Russian by Leo Winner, published by Noonday Press. This is one of the greatest books I have ever read, a book of profound wisdom.

Gandhi believed his mission was to teach by example. What a profound model of human behavior he provided for us. Even up to the moment he was shot, he was an example of everything he believed in. Gandhi had stated the "Gita" was his spiritual reference point. He had been referring to the *Bhagavad-Gita*, "The Song of God" which is the Hindu gospel. This book described a battle in which Lord Krishna spoke to one of his warriors. It also speaks of rebirth. As a Christian, I cannot accept Krishna as incarnate god, but only Jesus Christ. For my Hindu friends, the "Gita" is their reference point.

I had also read Gandhi's *My Religion*, compiled and edited by Bharatan Kumarappa, published by Navajivan Publishing House. Gandhi believed that the biblical New Testament gave him comfort and boundless joy. He believed "The Sermon on the Mount" gave him the same joy as the "Gita." He did recognize Jesus as the Son of God. He believed that Jesus belongs to the entire world. Gandhi was living in my lifetime. I wish I could have met him. I love him very much. We need more professionals like him who are willing to take up the cause of the "underdog."

In Scripture, in Acts, chapter 10, verses 34–35, "…God does not have favorites, but that anybody of any nationality who fears God and does what is right is acceptable to him." I have a number of Jewish, Hindu, Muslim, and people of other "persuasions" who are my best friends.

In James, chapter 2, verse 9, "…keep the supreme law of scripture: you must love your neighbor as yourself; but as soon as you make distinctions between classes of people, you are committing sin."

Jesus knew the plight of the "have-nots" of the world well, having been born in a stable, an obscure village, a child of a peasant woman, having to flee for their lives. He never owned anything. He was uneducated. He himself didn't have a family. The only credential He possessed was Himself. When it came time to face His "ordeal," He was left standing alone. His disciples had scattered like rabbits.

His trial was a farce; He was mocked, spat upon, whipped, and lastly, lynched. He took man's pain upon Himself. A Lamb led to the slaughter. God's love for us is beyond my comprehension. It's beyond words; it can only be felt and experienced.

During the fall semester at school, I developed intractable tinnitus, which in lay terms is ringing in the ears, which was probably secondary to the sinus condition I had. The ringing was very bad, and I couldn't sleep at night. The medicines had not helped.

At Dr. Lee's suggestion, I did autogenic-training and self-hypnosis; both proved to be quite helpful.

A German doctor had developed auto-genic training, Johannes H. Schultz. There are standard exercises in this technique for general relaxation. Since the clinical years of medicine were so demanding and stressful, I used these techniques from time to time. I also used a therapeutic "saying" that may have been developed by Dr. Luthe: "Every day, in every way, I am getting better and better." I also taught these techniques to my clinic patients.

In November of 1974, "Rev." Sun Myung Moon gave a talk in Chicago. I received the literature after I had called the information number. His topic was "The New Future of Christianity," given at the Arie Crown Theater at the McCormick Place on the Lake on November 12, 1974. I wanted to see this "so-called" "God's Prophet" who I believe to be giving a presentation not based on biblical Scripture.

Three girls I knew went into the Unification Church, and I never heard from them again. They are Lynne, Sandra, and Patricia. I had written to them, but I never received a reply. I had talked my medical school buddy, Ralph, in attending this presentation with me. He had a PhD in history. I estimated about 4,000 people attended the program. I was extremely irritated by the program.

They put very high intensity spotlights on the audience. That was odd.

The "Rev." Moon doesn't speak English, which is quite strange for a so-called "God's prophet." He had an interpreter who had been a Lt. Col. in the Korean Army, Mr. Bo Hi Pak. He said "Rev." Moon would speak about a "new revelation." He said Jesus was not to die on the cross, but was to have had a family on the earth. It was stated that Jesus failed his mission.

Biblical Scripture does not support this.

During the presentation, they had the Korean Folk Ballet. They were extremely beautiful and very talented. I enjoyed them very much. They also had the New Hope Singers, and they were very talented also.

I found "Rev." Moon's presentation very irritating and after five minutes, I wanted to leave, but I felt a responsibility to stay to the end. Dr. Ralph (Ashod) slept through most of the presentation. He found it quite boring.

Checking Scripture regarding Jesus' sacrifice:

In Leviticus, chapter 17, verse 11, " ... it is blood that atones for a life."

In Isaiah, chapter 53, verses 6–7: " ... Yahweh burdened him with the sins of us all. Harshly dealt with , he bore it humbly, he never opened his mouth, like a lamb that is let to the slaughter-house ... "

The essence in Matthew, chapter 16, verse 21, Jesus is to be put to death and to be raised on the 3rd day. That same essence is in Matthew, chapter 17, verse 23, also in Matthew, chapter 20, verse 19; in Mark, chapter 8, verse 31; in Mark, chapter 9, verse 31; in Mark, chapter 10, verse 34; in Luke, chapter 9, Verse 22; and in Luke, chapter 18, verse 33.

In Mark, chapter 10, verse 44, " ... the Son of Man himself did not come to be served but to serve, and to give his life, a ransom for many." In Matthew, chapter 26, verse 2, "It will be Passover, as you know, in two days' time, and the Son of Man will be handed over to be crucified." In Luke, chapter 12, verse 50, "There is a baptism I must still receive, and how great is my distress, till it is over!"

In 1 Timothy, chapter 1, verse 15, "…Christ Jesus came into the world to save sinners…" In Revelation, chapter 5, verse 9, in reference to Jesus: "They sung a new hymn:

You are worthy to take the scroll

and break the seals of it,

because you were sacrificed, and with your blood

you bought men for god

of every race, language, "

This last quote is especially for "Rev." Moon: Deuteronomy, chapter 18, verse 20: "…the prophet, who presumes to say in my name, a thing I have not commanded him to say, or speaks in the name of other gods, that prophet shall die."

In reference to "Rev." Moon's "new revelations," Galatians, chapter 1, verse 9, "…if anyone preaches a version of the Good News different from the one you have already heard, he is to be condemned."

And, in Revelation, chapter 22, verse 18–19, "This is my solemn warning to all who hear the prophecies in this book: if any one adds anything to them, God will add to him every plague mentioned in the book; if anyone cuts anything out of the prophecies in this book, God will cut off his share of the tree of life and of the holy city, which are described in the book."

In Colossians, chapter 2, verse 8, " Make sure that no one traps you and deprives you of your freedom by some secondhand, empty, rational philosophy based on the principles of this world instead of on Christ."

In I Timothy, chapter 2, verse 5–6, "…there is only one God, and there is only one mediator between God and mankind, himself a man, Christ Jesus, who sacrificed himself as a ransom for them all."

John, Chapter 10, verse 30, "The Father and I are one."

Rest assured that when the antichrist, the Beast, and the false prophet arrive, they will do everything in their power to belittle the cross. They hate the cross, for by the cross they were defeated, and we are saved.

Satan hates the cross, for in Hebrews, chapter 2, verse 14, "...by his death he could take away all the power of the devil, who had power over death..."

Excellent books against the Moon Cult are: *The Moon Doctrine* by J. Ismu Yamamoto, published by InterVarsity Press in Downers Grove, Illinois 60515; and *The Puppet Master: Sun Myung Moon and the Unification Church* by same author and publisher. *The Spirit of Sun Myung Moon* by Zola Levitt is also good. At the end of the book, there is a reprinted article from *Seventeen Magazine* entitled, "Why I quit the Moon Cult," a story of a seventeen-month experience of a teenage girl who was at first drawn to, and then repelled by the Unification Church.

Another excellent article published in the *American Family Practice Journal*, Vol. 15, number 2, pp. 80–83, by Dr. Eli Shapiro, entitled: "Destructive Cultism." Dr. Shapiro lists the characteristics of a destructive cult.

Rev. Sun Myung Moon has had no small effect on American politics as is noted in the following Political Cartoon by Nick Anderson.

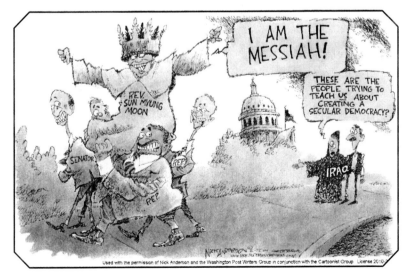

Used with the permission of Nick Anderson and the Washington Post Writer's Group in conjunction with the Cartoonist Group. License 2010-250

Biblical scripture does not support "Rev." Sun Myung Moon as the true messiah, only Jesus Christ.

One Sunday while I was in the Chicago Loop, I came across the I AM Temple. I stopped inside to see what this was all about. When I had been the chief physical therapist at Skokie Valley Community Hospital, I met a private duty nurse who had sold her home and everything, and went to Arizona to be with the I AM movement. All the men were dressed in white. I understand that this I AM is also Summit International, which used to be The Summit Lighthouse. Their most recent name is Church Universal and Triumphant. I read one of their books: *The Purpose of the Ascended Masters: I AM Activity*, published by the Saint Germaine Press, Inc. They have a concept of reembodiment, which I suppose is reincarnation, which Scripture refutes. They have multiple God-beings. In Christianity, we only have one God.

During Christmas vacation of my junior year, I was assigned to the internal medicine department and followed patients over the holidays. It was a very busy service; I was putting in over twelve hours a day treating patients. We were supervised by interns on the service.

In February 1975, I dated a psychiatry resident, Sharon. Since I was interested in going into psychiatry, she gave me a lot of helpful hints about applying to programs.

I had submitted a couple of papers to the 1974 Student Medical Writing Contest sponsored by the American Osteopathic Association and Marion Laboratories. I was fortunate to I receive first prize, in the essay category: "Psychological Considerations of the Physically Handicapped," and honorable mention in essay category for a paper: "Hospital Safety is Everybody's Business."

On May 23, 1975, I had completed my third year of medical school. It had been an extremely demanding year. I had treated hundreds of patients. I only had a week off before senior year. I went back to Pittsburgh to visit my family.

On the way back from Pittsburgh on the Ohio turnpike, I saw a young couple hitchhiking. I felt sorry for them and picked them up. Jay and Susie said they were from New York City and were going to Venice, California. I told them I was going to Chicago and would take them that far. Jay went in the back seat and "passed out." He must have really been tired. Susie wasn't sleeping; she was reading a book; her path. I told her to get some sleep and not worry about me, that I was harmless. But, she said she wasn't tired. She wanted to read her book. When I dropped them off at the end of the trip, she insisted that I write down the name of her book and get it. I did write the name down.

The next day, I took my car into the Firestone Company in the Evergreen Plaza to have my brakes checked. They told me I would have a long wait. I went into the shopping center, and since there was a bookstore there, I decided to see if they had the book Susie had told me about.

The title of the book was *The Greatest Salesman in the World* by Og Mandino, a paperback published by Bantam Books. It was non-fiction. I read it when I got back to the apartment. It was one of the most beautiful books I had ever read. Its spiritual wisdom was almost overwhelming. It was a very beautiful story of a camel boy who desired to become the greatest salesman in the world and how it came to be. In this, he received ten ancient scrolls, which gave him the secret to success. The spiritual wisdom in the scrolls is extremely beautiful. The secrets in these scrolls are beyond the price of gold or diamonds.

One can become completely transformed by adopting these scrolls as a part of one's life. I have recommended this book to my friends and patients many times.

Og Mandino also wrote other books that I have read such as *The Greatest Secret in the World* and *The Greatest Miracle in the World,* published by Frederick Fell in New York. These books are also in paperback in Bantam Books. *The Greatest Miracle in the World* was also extremely beautiful. It referred to a fiction paperback by Lloyd Douglas, *The Magnificent Obsession*, also a very good book. He had also written *The Robe*. *The Magnificent Obsession* is about a secret of success found in Scripture.

On June 2, 1975, I began my senior year in medical school. I was assigned rotations in the various specialty departments. My first five weeks was in Internal Medicine. I was assigned patients and was given full responsibility for working up and treating the patient. I was supervised by interns and residents and overall by the internists. I worked many hours; you might say I lived in the hospital. I attended seminars and grand rounds.

I had an agonizing experience on my first day on internal medicine. I was with my classmate, Roy S. When he went to lunch, I covered his patients for him. One of my patients was a very elderly lady in an end bed, in a room at the end of the hall. The RN requested that I put a nasograstic tube in her, so that she could be tube-fed. I complied. I iced the tube first, because it is easier to move it through the nasal cavity and down the esophagus into the stomach. I did the procedure and then tube-fed the patient. I then went up to the nursing station to write a note. In the next instant, a cardiac arrest code was called. The next thing I knew, the RNs were doing cardiac resuscitation to attempt to save the patient. I was in shock; I assumed at that point I had put the tube down the patient's trachea instead of the esophagus and had "killed" my patient. I assumed I would be thrown out of medical school. A few minutes later, Roy showed up and said, "What happened to my patient?" He said, "That's my patient." I ran down to the other end of the hall, and "my" patient was comfortably asleep. When I told Roy that both out patients looked alike and were at end beds at the end of the halls, I had confusedly thought his patient was my patient. I certainly sympathized with him about his patient, but I was so grateful that my patient was all right.

I rotated with all the subspecialties in Internal Medicine, Cardiology, Pulmonary Medicine, Nephrology, Gastroenterology, Endocrinology, Rheumatology, Hematology, Urology, Infectious Disease, and Nuclear Medicine.

I had to present the case (patient) to each of these doctors when they made rounds; therefore, I learned a great depth in internal medicine.

Our department chairman, Dr. Ward Perrin, was one of the best doctors I had ever worked with. He was a "super specialist."

Our rheumatologist, Dr. M was great to be with, he had trained at the University of Chicago in rheumatology.

Our infections disease specialist, Dr. S also on staff at Rush-Presbyterian Medical Center, had a great sense of humor. The interns that taught us were really outstanding. I liked them very much.

My resident in internal medicine, Dr. John G , was awarded the "Resident of the Year" plaque, at the end of the year. He was an outstanding teacher.

My worst experience was toward the end of the rotation. Dr. George C, an internal medicine board examiner was looked upon as "god" in our department. One evening, I was working up one of his private patients. I was so obsessive-compulsive about doing everything perfect that my intern and resident, both of whom were outstanding, started to sign off on what I had done. I had received additional study reports on the patient that showed a fluoroscopy study was needed. I called up radiology and scheduled the test for the morning. The intern and resident were pleased with my medical evaluation and test schedule, and signed off on the test. I placed the patient on a fasting diet for overnight. The next morning when I was at the nursing station, Dr. C came by. He read his patients' chart. I was sitting there waiting for a shower of accolades on how well I had worked up his patient.

He remarked, "I didn't know my patient had all those problems," set the chart on the desk and walked away. I thought for a moment, *If 'god' didn't know something, something had to be very wrong.* I checked the chart. The names on the studies were common names. The patient hospital numbers were not the same. I had only checked the name, not the hospital numbers. I did not take the elevator to the basement radiology department; I believe I may have jumped down flights of stairs getting there. Just as I got to the patient, the technician was getting ready to wheel him in for the study. I told him we were canceling the study because we decided he didn't need it. The patient was happy about it, because he was hungry and wanted something to eat.

My resident and intern, and I were devastated when I informed them of what had happened. I informed them, that from that day on, I would check the name and spelling and numbers on every patient I would ever see again. I have done that all my career. When I note mistakes in charts, I always bring it to the attention of my medical students, and also inform them of the mistake I had made on internal medicine, so that, hopefully, they will not make the same mistake.

For some reason beyond me, I was one of the best in the hospital for doing an IV. I could get into vessels when no one else could. As a result, I was called on from time to time to do an IV. I did fail on one asthma patient; it was impossible to get into her veins. They had to do a cut down on her.

One evening, I was called to one of the medicine floors to give packed cells. I asked the nurse if she had checked everything, and she told me she had. At this point, I checked everything. I got the patient's chart and compared the doctor's order with what was on the packed cell pack. They were not the same. I was very upset. I called hematology and spoke with the doctor in charge. I read off the order to him and what was on the pack cell pack. He told me I would kill the patient if I gave the patient that pack.

For the health professionals reading my book right now: *You can never take anything for granted. When you care for a patient, you are completely responsible for that care, you and you alone. You must be certain that everything is correct!*

My most time-demanding patient on the service was a patient with alcoholic cirrhosis (liver disease). I spent many hours plotting his electrolytes on graphs attempting to save his life, which I ended up doing. The doctors were very pleased with my care of the patient. Months later when my classmate, Bill D, was on the internal medicine rotation, he informed me about all the care he was giving to an alcoholic. When we passed the patient's bed, he informed me that's the patient. It was the exact same patient I had spent all that time with. I told Bill I was upset about it, but it certainly pointed our how very serous alcoholism is.

I had been assigned to cardiology. I went to see Dr. H, the chief of cardiology, a "high-powered" cardiologist. I informed him that since I planned on going into psychiatry, Gastroenterology might be a better choice for me. He was not pleased. He told me I was to learn about the heart, and he forbade me to say the word psychiatry in his presence.

One evening a few weeks later, I was working up a young, female executive who was in a very high-powered stressful position. I was convinced her problem was psychosomatic. I presented all my findings to Dr. H. I then told him what I believed and requested a transfer of the patient to the psychiatry service. He had a "meltdown." It is interesting that the next day I had learned that he did have the patient transferred.

I had an amusing experience while on cardiology. We had a major case presentation on one of our patients by a famous cardiologist. It was in the large auditorium area. I was late, because I had been doing a workup on a patient. When I walked in the front door, the room was packed with all the medical staff. Since I like to be "up front" where the action is, I went up in front of the patient's bed, directly across from the cardiologist. He was discussing the patient. He handed me the second attached stethoscope, and as he described all of the intricacies of the heart sounds, "of course" I shook my head in agreement. I received a lot of ribbing from my classmates about it later. They said, "You're a psychiatrist; you were putting on a big show for the cardiologist."

One evening when I was attending a social at the Moody Bible Church, they showed a very good film: *Daktar*. It was about a surgeon in Bangladesh. I got his book, entitled *Daktar*, by Dr. Viggo Olsen. It was about his experiences as a surgeon in developing Christian Memorial Hospital in Bangladesh. It was very inspiring. He is one of the greatest Christian surgeons on the earth.

He believes the whole patient should be treated; body, mind, and spirit. He believed by living a Christ-like life in Bangladesh, he drew people to Christ.

I completely agree with his notion of treatment. I have always used the complete holistic approach to my patients, the bio-psycho-social-spiritual model.

A famous medical missionary, Dr. Albert Schweitzer served in Africa and was a great inspiration for me, as was Dr. Tom Dooley, a young medical missionary who had worked in Laos. He died of cancer at age thirty-four. Before he died, he wanted to help achieve the dream of Anne Frank's which was, "Things will change, and men become good again, and these pitiless days will come to an end, and the world will know once again order, trust and peace." She had been the young girl who had written the *Diary of Anne Frank*. She met her fate at the hands of the Nazis.

My next five weeks of rotation was surgery. This was an extremely busy service. I also had to work nights and weekends. On the first day of the rotation, my classmates and I arrived on the service at the same time Dr. R C did. He asked me if I wanted to do the case in room two. I said, "Certainly." My classmates were shocked.

They asked me, "Are you going to do an operation?"

I told them, "Look, Dr. C looked at this group and realized there was only one 'surgeon' here who was capable of doing an operation, and that was 'Dr. Scarnati.'" Do you actually believe he was going to ask one of you bozos to do an operation?"

My classmates did get back on me on that one. They did a skit on me at our graduation party. Now before I terrify the public, into responding, "Oh my God, medical students are doing operations," be aware that I had completed an entire summer in a surgical clerkship assisting surgeons. The case was a circumcision on an eight-year-old. I was fully capable of doing that operation. I would have never done it if I believed I could not do it safely. At the time I was doing the operation, I had a surgical intern to the left of me and a surgical resident to the right of me. An anesthesiologist was also there. I did a successful operation without any complications.

One of the most impressive and inspiring physicians I had ever worked with was a surgeon, Dr. Vincent DiRito. I spent my first two weeks with him. He was a surgeon unable to do surgery. He had MS and could only move his head a little. His knowledge of surgery was "encyclopedic." I made rounds with him, pushing him in his wheelchair. I would work up the case in his presence, and he would go over it with me. The surgical resident would verify or refute my physical findings. I was also on Dr. L service, the chairman of the department of surgery. Since he was aware that I had done an entire summer at Illinois Central Community Hospital as a surgical clerk, I was permitted greater responsibilities, under very watchful supervision.

In July 1975, I joined the Chicago Council on Foreign Relations, an organization interested and involved in world events. They had "socials" that I enjoyed. A lawyer friend of mine, Al H, had suggested that I join the group. He and his wife, Jackie, liked to take advantage of the trips with the group. They have very good speakers.

From August 11 to September 14, I was on the obstetrics and gynecology service, which included night service in the emergency room. This was the most energy-demanding service I had been on.

We worked twelve to fourteen-hour days. The staff was very good. I enjoyed training under the interns, because they permitted me do procedures once I had been taught. My two favorite interns were Dr. James P and Dr. Allen S.

We had an extremely busy OB service, and we would be doing constant deliveries, working all night long. Even the emergency room was full all the time. I only had three days off in the whole five weeks on this service. The Gyne Clinic was very busy. I became very adept at diagnostics.

One afternoon, an OB doctor was making rounds with his nurse a few beds ahead of me. I examined a patient and informed the aide to move the patient to the labor area.

The doctor heard me and started barking at me, "Are you saying my nurse doesn't know what she is talking about?" I was surprised to hear that, because I had not said anything to them. I told him what the cervical dilation was, and I stuck to my findings.

He told his nurse, "Get me a glove." After he had examined the patient, he found I had been correct, and he had the patient moved.

One night working by myself, I had just finished examining my OB patient.

She called me over, "Doctor, move me to the delivery room. I am going to have my baby." I informed her I was not going to do that because of my exam.

She said, "How many babies have you had?" I informed her I was a male and could not have children.

She replied, I have had eight kids, and you mean to tell me I don't know when I am ready to have my baby?" I told her I was sorry, but she needed to wait. Just in a flash, she started to deliver. I rushed the gurney into the delivery room and transferred her to the delivery table. Just as I sat down, the baby popped out into my hands. At that second, who should walk into the delivery room, but the chief OB resident.

He said, "Scarnati, I know you think you're a hot OB 'doctor,' but can you get some assistance when you're doing deliveries?" She didn't say anything while he was there, because she knew I would get into trouble. As soon as he left, she said, "I told you, I was going to have my baby!" I informed her that whenever a multigravada woman told me that, I was certainly going to listen to her.

After I assisted in about forty deliveries, I did thirty deliveries and six episiotomies by myself under extremely close supervision. You can't imagine the thrill of doing a delivery.

The chairman of the OB department met with me, to encourage me to go into OB-GYNE. I informed him I was planning on going into psychiatry. He spent three hours with me, attempting to discourage me from doing that, because he did not believe that was in my best interest. I developed high skills on OB-GYNE and remained confident that I could help deliver a baby in an emergency someday if need be.

After all the care I gave in the E.R., my diagnostic skills became very much greater.

In August 1975, I had my first interview for a residency position in psychiatry at Loyola University. I had decided to apply to many programs and pick the best one.

I started to formulate ideas on how I might best treat the total patient. Even though I am in medicine, I am interested in my patients' spiritual well-being too.

I discovered the "super specialty" of psychiatry, logotherapy, when I read the book by Dr. Viktor Frankl, *The Doctor and the Soul*, published by Bantam Books. It is Existential Analysis.

Dr. Frankl believes that man lives in three dimensions: bodily, mentally, and spiritually. The spiritual dimension cannot be ignored. Man has a will to meaning. Logotherapy is medical ministry that can be applied by all doctors.

The goal of psychotherapy is to heal the soul and make it healthy. Logotherapy is education for personal responsibility. Psychotherapists have not spent enough time on the spiritual needs of man. There is much wisdom in Dr. Frankl's writings. I read all his writings that have been translated.

I had been so impressed with Dr. Frankl's writings that I desired to become a logotherapist upon graduation from medical school. I wrote to Dr. Frankl in Vienna, Austria, in hopes of going there and studying under him. He wrote back and told me to read as much as possible. Since I planned to be a psychiatrist, he believed it would be better for me to remain in the USA and take a standard program in psychiatry to enable me to obtain board certification. Logotherapy was too specialized to be the only area of study for a psychiatrist, and he believed I should have a broad foundation in psychiatry. He suggested that I might want to do an elective period with him in my last year of residency.

I obtained four hundred articles relating to logotherapy. The most inspiring of his books was *Man's Search for Meaning*, published by Pocket Books. I cried through most of the book, for it was a living nightmare. Dr. Frankl related his experiences in the Nazi concentration camps, where his young wife and most of his family had been exterminated. It was during these "hellish" years that he developed logotherapy. For me, Dr. Frankl represented the biblical story of Job. Gordon Allport had called logotherapy an introduction to the most significant psychological movement of our day.

In the camp, he was fond of quoting Nietzsche, "He who has a why to live, can bear with any how."

Dr. Frankl believed that love is our highest goal. The salvation of man is through love and in love. The way in which a man accepts his fate, suffering, and the way in he takes up cross, gives him ample opportunity even under the most difficult circumstances, to add a deeper meaning to his life.

In working with would-be suicides, he noted that their excuse was that they had nothing more to expect from life. He would help them realize that life was expecting something from them. We all have our mission in life to fulfill.

He is one of the greatest psychiatrists I have known. He had been in four Nazi concentration camps.

His latest book, *The Unconscious God*, is a combination of psychotherapy and theology.

Jesus and Logotherapy, by Dr. Robert Leslie, published by Abingdon Press, New York, is about the ministry of Jesus as interpreted through logotherapy. Leslie believes logo therapy is much in line with the Christian view of life.

On November 15, 1975, I began my ten-week rotation in the Family Medicine Clinics. I treated many diabetics and hypertensive patients. This was a very busy clinic. All our cases were supervised. I liked Dr. Wiley the best; he was also the medical student's physician.

Northwestern University had interviewed me as a potential psychiatry resident.

They have a very good program in community psychiatry. I was also interviewed at the Medical College of Wisconsin in Milwaukee, Wisconsin. I was also impressed with their program.

During the fall, I had joined the Analytical Psychology Club of Chicago. They study the works of Carl Jung, M. D. I had read much of his writings. He had worked with Freud but split off from him. I was interested in what Jung had studied, such as world religions, metaphysics, and philosophy. He had traveled throughout the world. He had also studied the occult. He believed religions were psychotherapeutic systems.

I found some of his writings difficult to interpret. Jung believed there were points very obscure about the *I Ching* (or the Book of Changes). It looked complicated to me; I have never had the time to spend on it.

I was surprised to discover his interest in the *Tibetan Book of the Dead* or the *Bardo Thodol, supposedly,* a guide for the dead man, a book on death and rebirth. Since Scripture doesn't accept reincarnation, I can't either. There was also astrology in the book, which is condemned by Scripture. I am surprised that Jung believed in this.

On September 21, 1975, for the first meeting of the Jung Analytical Psychology Club, we had a presentation entitled "The Dream Theater," put on by an experimental dance group, The Body Politic. This dance group would enact dreams. They were very talented.

On October 12, 1975, Dr. Elmer and Alyce Green from the Menninger Clinic spoke on Jung, yoga, and biofeedback training. They presented a film and slides about their trip to India. They found that some Yogis were able to simulate heart rate irregularities (arrhythmias). The Greens are experts in biofeedback research.

On November 24, I started my rotation in pediatrics, which lasted until December 21, 1975. I was supervised by pediatric residents and pediatricians. The pediatric clinic was always packed and as soon as the children saw us, they started crying. They knew they would get a "shot." We took a medical history, did a physical exam, and then presented the case to the pediatrician, who would then confirm or refute our diagnosis. Many times, the mothers had already made the diagnosis, such as chicken pox or measles. We always had "suckers" for the children, and they got a "sucker" after their "shot." I always saved the shot as the last part of the treatment. I also spent a week on the pediatric in-patient service and the neonatal intensive care unit. I was extremely impressed with the pediatric staff.

Assistant professor, Dr. Philip H was one of the best doctors I have ever worked with. When the pediatrics rotation was over, I went home for Christmas vacation.

From January 5, 1976 to February 8, 1976, I did my elective rotation in neuropsychiatry at Oak Forest Hospital. It was one of the electives I had helped set up.

I trained under Dr. Sherman Kaplitz, a neuropsychiatrist and a good friend of mine. I also rotated with Dr. M a clinical psychologist. I did neurological evaluations on patients.

I also spent time with the neurologist, who did evaluations on public school children. They had a team approach.

In January, I had an interview for a psychiatry residency position at the Chicago Medical School. They had been kind enough to offer me a position. I was also interviewed at the Illinois State Psychiatric Institute for a psychiatry residency position. I was very impressed with their program. They have one of the best research programs in the country.

From February 1 to February 3, I was interviewed for a psychiatry residency position at the Menninger Clinic in Topeka, Kansas. Even though I was extremely impressed with the Menninger Clinic, I decided I wanted to stay in Chicago. Being single, I didn't believe I would like it in Topeka.

On February 4, 1976, I accepted a psychiatric resident position to begin July 1, 1976, at the Illinois State Psychiatric Institute. This is not the typical "state hospital"; it's one of the top psychiatric research centers in the world. The other big advantage here was that we had consultant staff from other universities in the city, such as the University of Chicago. Several osteopathic physicians had completed this residency program and recommended it to me.

On February 9, 1976, I began my ten-week vacation period. But since our national board exams were the week of March 15–21, I spent my vacation in extremely heavy review of clinical medicine.

On Thursday, March 11, I attended the Chicago Council on Foreign Relations. I saw the film entitled, *The Triumph of the Will*. This was said to be the most effective propaganda film ever made. Hitler had himself commissioned Leni Riefenstahl to produce a record of the Sixth Annual Party Congress in Nuremberg. Hitler and Goebbels staged the largest propaganda rally the world had ever seen. It was a two-hour fanatical expression to the Fuehrer. It also showed the mob psychology of the Third Reich. There was a bomb scare at the center, and the police evacuated everyone. I had assumed that afterwards, the film would not be shown and I went home. Unfortunately, they did show the film, and I missed it at the time.

Since I was on vacation in March, I decided to grow a beard. I had never grown a beard before, and I wanted to see what I would look like with a beard. After several weeks, I looked like a hairy bear. I wanted to shave it off, but before I did that, I decided I would take a picture of myself and shave sections off with different beard styles. Since the Museum in Hyde Park had an automatic picture machine, I decided to go there and take a picture of me with my beard.

On March 17, St. Patrick's Day, after taking board exams, I went to the museum to take my picture. I parked my car, and there were a lot of school buses there. I assumed school children were on a field trip to the museum. I looked off into the distance, and I saw a young boy running off with a young man "hot on his tail."

I assumed that the boy was running away from his class, and the teacher was after him.

The kid was very fast; I didn't think the teacher was going to catch him. The teacher was yelling at him. The teacher had caught him by the hair and knocked him down. I stopped in my tracks to observe this, because I believed the teacher was a little rough on the kid. Even though I was far away, I could see everything. He started dragging the kid by the hair, and I assumed he was taking this kid back to the museum. The next thing I knew, he took the kid up to the school bus, threw open the back door, and threw the kid down against the steel steps. At that point, I took off running toward the bus yelling for the man to stop, but he didn't hear me. He had thrown the boy into the seat and was punching him.

I was yelling at the top of my lungs and was red with rage. At that point, he saw me and opened the bus window and told me to mind my business. Just then, a young couple ran up, and they were yelling at the guy, too. Fortunately, just then, I saw a police truck off in the distance, and I called them. They came to the scene. We told the police what happened.

I told the police I wanted to press charges against the guy, and the young couple also wanted to do this too. We went to the district station on the South Side of Chicago.

I learned that the child's name was Louis. The young couple's names were Alan and Beverly. Beverly happened to be an RN at Skokie Valley Community Hospital. I checked the boy, and she did also. I saw a bruise on the boy's leg. I told the police to take the child to a hospital to be examined. They told me they would take him to Jackson Park Hospital. I signed a complaint. The police said it wasn't necessary for the couple to sign the complaint. The hearing was set for the thirty-first of March. I decided that when the hearing came up, I would be present for it. Alan and Beverly said they planned to be there, also. After that I went back to my apartment.

I received a call that evening from a police lieutenant who was the watch commander from the Third Police District. He told me that it wouldn't be necessary for me to attend the hearing, that the charges had been dropped. I couldn't believe it. The next day, I called the director of the police department to have this checked out. I believed someone had received a "payoff" because I had signed a complaint and I had not dropped the charges. He told me the charges had been dropped by the Illinois State Attorney's Office.

I decided to investigate this case myself. Since I was on vacation, and national board exams were over, I would have time to look into this case. I discovered that the boy lived at a home for orphans. I called the director of the school and told him what had happened. I told him I was concerned about Louis and wanted to see the school and the boy. Fortunately, he gave me permission to do that. We set up an appointment. I discovered that the guy who attacked fourteen-year-old Louis was a schoolteacher in the public school next to the orphanage where the children attended classes.

I was not impressed with the orphanage or the director. Louis informed me that the staff would beat them at times. I wanted the place investigated. I called the school nurse that worked at the orphanage. She told me that Louis had chronic kidney problems. I was much more concerned, because I knew that if he was beat all the time, he might die.

Since I was a medical student and had completed the emergency room rotation, I knew "battered child" signs. Also, in most places, it's a misdemeanor against the doctor if he fails to report such cases. The signs one looks for in a "battered child" is general neglect, poor skin hygiene, malnutrition, bruises, abrasions, soft tissue swellings, and hematomas. On X-rays, one will see subperiosteal hematomas, epiphyseal separations, periosteal shearing, metaphyseal fragmentation, or squaring of the metaphysics. These are all bone changes that one can see on X-rays.

I asked the director of the school, to have X-rays taken. Louis was treated at Lutheran General Hospital for his kidney problems. I knew that if X-rays were taken and the signs of "battering" were there, the doctor would be legally bound to report this. I believed I could then have the case reopened. However, this was not done. I was very angry about the whole thing. I decided to go down to the Illinois State's Attorney's Office myself and look into the case. All that department did was give me the "runaround."

I contacted J. Terrence B of the Better Government Association. He was a lawyer who had given a talk at the Fourth Presbyterian Church social group that I had attended. I believed he might be able to help me look into this case. I told him the story; he told me he would find out who the State's Attorney was who dropped the case, and why, and get back to me.

I was called by the assistant state's attorney who was responsible for having the decision dropped. I was told that the child had actually assaulted the teacher before he ran out of the museum. I still didn't believe that it was justified for the teacher to attempt to "kill" the boy. I found out later that the legal guardian of the child was the Illinois Department of Children and Family Services. I went there and met with two directors, who told me they would start an investigation of the case and would ask me to serve as a witness, which I agreed to do.

On April 9, I did see the film, *The Triumph of the Will*, a record of the Sixth Annual Party Congress in Nuremberg. It was one of the most extraordinary films I have ever seen. I was very surprised at the "magnetism" that Hitler projected. I believe the feelings projected in the film were real. I was overwhelmed by it. It was as if the Nazis looked upon Hitler as God. One could certainly see the power of a dictator in this film. I had been in a lot of Army marches and parades but nothing as spectacular as this.

On April 26, I began my last senior rotation in the department of medicine. It was an extremely demanding service. We also attended seminars that began at 7:30 a.m. three mornings a week.

On May 15, I was notified that I had won second prize in special category in the 75–76 Student Medical Writing Contest, sponsored by the American Osteopathic Association and Marion Pharmaceutical Laboratories. My paper entitled, "The Application of Logotherapy in Osteopathic Medicine," was one of the most extensive papers I had ever written. My bibliography consisted of 181 references.

I made plans to move to the "Near North" of Chicago, which was near "Rush Street," the "in-place" for singles. I moved into a brand new high-rise, the Elm Street Plaza. It hadn't even been completed when I moved in. My studio apartment faced the lake, and I had a very good view of the city. I purchased very nice furniture at this time.

On June 5th, I attended the Graduation Ball. At the special awards part, I received a writing award.

On June 6 at 3:00 p.m., I attended commencement exercises at the University of Chicago's Rockefeller Memorial Chapel. When it came time to receive my degree, I was in the back stage waiting for my name to be called. I look up and saw a *heavenly host*. It was extremely beautiful. The next thing I experienced was Dr.

Strakan shaking me, telling me they were waiting for me to receive my degree.

I had finally achieved my dream. I had completed the grandest of all professions, the highest of all priesthoods, that of medicine. I was now a physician. I was awarded the degree, Doctor of Osteopathy (D.O.). It was one of the greatest moments of my entire life. I was so happy. I had worked harder for that degree than anything I had ever done before. Without the support of my shepherd Jesus Christ and the *firepower* of the Holy Spirit, I could have never realized such a wonderful accomplishment. With Christ, I had achieved the impossible. I also felt very humble at the time, for I knew the very grave responsibility of being a physician that lay before me.

My four-year class average was 80.2, and my class standing was 76 in a class of 92.

On graduation I took the Osteopathic Oath:

> I do hereby affirm my loyalty to the profession I am about to enter.
>
> I will be mindful always of my great responsibility to preserve the health and the life of my patients, to retain their confidence and respect both as a physician and a friend who will guard their secrets with scrupulous honor and fidelity, to perform faithfully my professional duties, to employ only those recognized methods of treatment consistent with good judgment and with my skill and ability, keeping in mind always nature's laws and the body's inherent capacity for recovery.
>
> I will be ever vigilant in aiding in the general welfare of the community, sustaining its laws and institutions, not engaging in those practices which will in any way bring shame or discredit upon myself or my profession. I will give no drugs for deadly purposes to any person, though it may be asked of me.
>
> I will endeavor to work in accord with my colleagues in a spirit of progressive cooperation and never by word or by act cast imputations upon them or their rightful practices.
>
> I will look with respect and esteem upon all those who have taught me my art.

To my college I will be loyal and strive always for its best interests and for the interests of the students who will come after me

I will be ever alert to further the application of basic biologic truths to the healing arts and to develop the principles of osteopathy, which were first enunciated by Andrew Taylor Still.

Since I was going to go into an AMA-approved residency, the AOA would not permit me to take part three of national boards, because the American Osteopathic Association (AOA) requires one to do an AOA-approved rotating internship.

Since I was not eligible to take part three of national boards, I would not be able to obtain a medical license. The only route that was open for me was to take the FLEX exam, the Federal Licensure Examination given by the Federation of the State Medical Boards of the U.S.A. Most states accept this exam and will give one a medical license, if they have passed this test. I had studied extremely hard in medical school and believed I was prepared to take the FLEX exam. On June 15, 16, and 17, I took it in Baltimore, Maryland, because I was on vacation the month of June and knew I would be visiting with my brother in Washington, D.C. This was the most difficult exam I had ever taken. After the first day, I was "in shock." The second day was somewhat better. On the third day, we had cases to diagnose, and I was confident that I had made the correct diagnoses. Thanks to God, I did pass the FLEX exam, and I received a license as a physician and surgeon in the State of Maryland. The State of Illinois doesn't issue a medical license until a doctor has completed one year of postgraduate medical training.

Psychiatry Residency Years

After spending some time at home with my family, I began my first year of residency in psychiatry at the Illinois State Psychiatric Hospital. I was assigned to a psychiatric impatient ward, Ward 8 East. There were about thirty patients on our ward.

My first day was extremely eventful. I had never seen a psychotic patient before. I was sitting in the staff open area and patients were running around screaming and staff were running after them attempting to subdue them for placement in restraints. I was shocked. I thought to myself, *Oh my God, what did I get myself into?*

I met with Dr. Richard L, my psychiatrist supervisor, and informed him I had made a mistake in my choice of psychiatry and was going to transfer to internal medicine. He informed me he had just begun that day and requested that I at least stay on with him for a month. If after that I did not want to stay, he would let me out of my contract, and also provide a reference for me.

My first patient, an elderly lady with Schizophrenia, had been brought to the hospital by her sister. Her sister informed me she had not wanted to bring her to the hospital but had to, because she had been starving herself.

Dr. L asked me what medicine I was planning on giving the patient. I informed him I was not going to medicate her, because I was going to do Rogerian therapy on her. He told me he expected to see great things that day. He, of course, was being facetious, because he knew the patient would not get better without meds. Two hours later, he asked me how the therapy was progressing. I informed him I was not getting anywhere with the patient. He reminded me that I still had a few admissions to work up before the end of the day. I asked him what he recommended for the patient. He recommended I order IM Haldol 5mgs/hr until calm for the patient. I did that. I then did the admission workups on my other patients.

The next morning when I arrived on the ward, my patient was in a clean dress, sweeping the floor for the nurse. I was in total amazement. I had never seen anything like it. I couldn't believe that a medication was capable of changing the way a person thought and acted. I was so impressed! When her sister arrived on the ward, she could not believe the complete change in her sister. She was regretful that she had not brought her sister for treatment sooner. After that experience, I, too, used meds for all my patients.

I had an average of about eight patients. There was a team approach in the treatment of patients, with collaboration with a rehabilitation therapist, psychologist, activity therapist, occupational therapist, nurses, and a social worker. I participated in family therapy with a social worker. I also did comprehensive evaluations on adolescents and children. I taught medical and nursing students that rotated with me on the ward.

I had assigned courses that I took during the day. In July, we had Psychology, Psychopathology, Therapeutics, a crash course in handling Psychiatric Emergencies, and Basics of Psychopharmacology. I was also on emergency call, which meant that I was the "psychiatrist" for the entire hospital and was responsible for admitting psychiatric emergencies.

The academic and clinical work was extremely demanding. Most of my inpatients had severe depression, manic-depressive psychosis, schizophrenia, and character disorders. I was astonished at the effects the major tranquilizers, such as Thorazine, had on my psychotic patients. Patients who, on admission, had been acting extremely bizarre, hearing voices, seeing visions, having delusions, and unable to relate with me, were within a few days able to relate to reality because of medication. There was a considerable amount of research going on in this institute.

I received a very intense introduction to psychiatric research. Emergency call was very demanding. Since our patient catchment area covered several inner city police districts in Chicago, we received very violent patients from time to time. When I was on call, I was up all night. When I had weekday call, I might be up for over thirty-five hours at a stretch.

I received my initiation in emergency psychiatry the first night I was on call.

In the middle of the night, six policemen brought in a very large, tall, psychotic lady. The best way to describe her was that she appeared as a lumberjack. She had hand and leg chains and was howling. I was very shocked to see her in chains and identifying myself with Dr. Philippe Pinel, an early psychiatrist who had removed patients from chains, I demanded that her chains be removed at once! The police appeared very startled, as did the patient, but they removed her chains. I believed that possibly, the police were frightening for the patient. I asked them to wait at the desk, and the patient and I went to a bench at the end of the hall. I had my notepad and was a bit groggy from lack of sleep. We sat down together, and I asked the patient what her problem was. She grabbed my notebook and ripped it up, and then put her arm around my neck in a hammerlock. I was suddenly wide awake. The police were running down the hall toward us to my rescue. She jumped up and grabbed a large ashtray connected to a large base filled with sand. She swung this around as if she was doing an Olympic Shot Put and let it fly through the air. Sand went flying everywhere. Finally, after much effort, she was subdued and put back in chains. She was taken to the ward and placed in full leather restraints and tranquilized with medication. I realized that the police knew more about who should be restrained at that point than I did. The next day, the patient was calm enough so that her restraints could be removed. Some patients need restraints to protect themselves and others from harm. Even though restraints may appear a bit barbaric, restraint was done under very humane procedures, and the patient was removed from restraints as soon as she was calm.

We were given a reading list, and I did a tremendous amount of reading. I read most of, the classical readings in psychiatry. Since we had one of the most comprehensive psychiatry libraries in the country, I spent as much time in the library as possible. Daily, I skimmed all of the psychiatry journals during lunch break.

Actually, I had read a lot of the readings when I had been a medical student.

Some of the major works I read were: *The History of Psychiatry* by Franz Alexander, a good introduction to psychiatry. *Psychiatric Diagnosis* by Woodruff, Goodwin, and Guze a good, concise introduction to the major psychiatric syndromes; *Interviewing the Patient* by Engel and Morgan. *The Psychiatric Interview* by Harry Stack Sullivan, the residents' "bible" for patient interviews; Frieda Fromm-Reichmann's *Principles of Intensive Psychotherapy; Behavioral*

Neurology by Pincus and Tucker; *Contemporary Psychiatry* by Snow; *Psychosomatic Medicine* by Franz Alexander; *Fish's Clinical Psychopathology*; Nemiah's *Foundations of Psychopathology*, and others.

Many books by Piaget were required because one of our instructors, Dr. Terry B, had studied with him in France; Tarachow's *An Introduction to Psychotherapy*, *Schizophrenia* by Frank Fish; *An Elementary Textbook of Psychoanalysis* by Charles Brenner, probably the best introduction to psychoanalysis available; *Clinical Psychopathology* by Kurt Schneider; Karl Jaspers' *General Psychopathology*, my psychopathology bible; *Asylums* by Erving Goffman, a book that tells what inpatient psychiatry is all about, a must for inpatient staff: and Henderson and Gillespie's *Textbook of Psychiatry*.

I had also read a lot of pop psychology. Among my favorites are the following:

Carl Rogers' *Client-Centered Therapy*, a very warm, humanistic approach to patients; The Practice of Behavior Therapy by Joseph Wolpe, a classic on behavior modification; *Reality Therapy* by William Glasser, his new approach to psychiatry offers provocative insights; *The Primal Scream* by Arthur Janov, great for "letting it all out"; *Psychotherapy East and West* by Alan Watts; I don't agree with everything Alan has to say, but he did a good on comparing psychotherapy with Eastern thought.

The basic handbook of transactional analysis, *Games People Play*, by Eric Berne is a great analysis of the games of life. Along the line of life scripts, Thomas Harris's book, *I'm Okay—You're Okay*. Maxwell Maltz's *Psychocybernetics and Self-Fulfillment* is loaded with positive suggestions.

By August, I knew most of the residents. The professional staff had a party for us, and we also had our own picnic.

In September, we began our formal fall quarter seminar schedule. Our seminars were: Psychology; inpatient seminar, and treatment resistant cases; Dr. C, an English psychiatrist, was our instructor. He was one of the best psychiatrists I have ever studied under. Dr. R, a psychoanalyst, was our professor for inpatient seminar, Psychodynamic Issues. We did adolescent comprehensive evaluations under the supervision of Dr. T. He is one of the best adolescent psychiatrists that I have ever known. We did adolescent interviews under supervision. This was one of the best evaluation systems I have seen.

The child development seminar was at the University of Illinois, Lawrence Armour Day Care Center, where we had interaction with children. Dr. T, a child psychiatrist and D.O., supervised the program. Dr. L, my ward chief, was the instructor for the inpatient seminar, Diagnostic Issues. In this course after watching Dr. L do psychiatric interviews, we did them under his supervision. Drs. M and G held the family therapy seminar. Dr. G was one of the brightest psychologists I have ever worked with. We learned family systems theory, diagnosis, and family marital treatment technique. We also had live and videotape demonstrations of family interviews by experts in the field. We also studied resident group interactions.

Dr. G held the inpatient seminar, Somatic Treatment. We learned the theoretical foundations of psychopharmacology. Dr. C also taught Clinical Psychopathology. Dr. John D, one of the top researchers in the world, was a big help to me on my treatment resistant cases.

In studying stress, I looked into TM (Transcendental Meditation). I first heard of TM when the Beatles were doing it. When I was in college, I had several friends who practiced TM, but I was not interested in it at that time. In medical school, many of my classmates took the course and urged me to do so because of its "great benefits." I still declined to do so at that time. I now was perusing articles about TM in medical journals and was so impressed with the findings that I believed I had a responsibility to look into it, not only for myself but as possible therapy for my patients. I completed a computer search on meditation and obtained about two hundred professional articles. I was astonished to learn that the effects of TM had been reported in all of the professional fields, not only medicine and psychiatry, but also psychology, sociology, business, law, religion, education, the military, and politics. All of the reports were very positive in regards to the effects of TM.

I read Maharishi Mahesh Yogi's *Transcendental Meditation*. Maharishi had lived as an ascetic Hindu monk in the Himalayas. He had a teacher, Guru Dev. He wanted to bring TM to the world. I read other books on TM: *Maharishi, The Founder of Transcendental Meditation*, edited by Martin Ebon; Denise Denniston and Peter McWilliams, *The TM Book*; Dr. Harold Bloomfield's extensive book on TM, *Happiness: The TM Program, Psychiatry, and Enlightenment*. I considered encouraging my patients to take TM. I also thought about doing research in TM with my psychiatric patients. I encouraged my family to take TM.

From all the reading I did on TM, I got the impression that through this technique, one may transcend consciousness and reach the source of being. In August of 1976, I contacted the TM Center in Chicago and was scheduled for the introductory lecture. After that, I attended the preparatory lecture and was then scheduled for a personal interview. I had made up my mind that I definitely wanted to take the course. I was scheduled for what I was told was to be "personal instruction" for September 11, 1976.

I was told to bring six flowers, three fresh fruits, and a new, white handkerchief for a ceremony, and I did. I was not told this was to be a religious ceremony. When I arrived there, I was taken into a room by an attractive young girl, who was my instructor. There was an altar there with a picture of someone, and there were candles and incense. I stood at the side while this young girl did some chanting and at the end, she told me my mantra. Being a Christian, I was extremely upset about the ceremony that I believed was religious. I had been told that TM was not a religion beforehand. However, I believed that since I was a Christian and did not recognize the picture the young girl was chanting to and had been told my mantra was a meaningless sound, I believed no harm could come about by completing the program. I did want to experience all the benefits that TM supposedly had to offer. I was then told to do my mantra in my mind twenty minutes, twice a day. Then I was scheduled for follow-up "checking" to make sure I remembered my mantra and to discuss any problems about my practice of TM. I was told not to tell anyone about the ceremony or to tell anyone my mantra. I later asked my instructor what language she had used. She told me it was Sanskrit. I did my mantra religiously. I would get up early before work and do it for twenty minutes and then again at around 6:00 p.m. I was told to think my mantra over and over in my mind while relaxed and with my eyes closed, which I did. I was told to be very passive and not to fight against thoughts but only concentrate on my mantra which I did each day.

I continued to treat all my patients each day. I also participated in group therapy for the patients on the ward.

One night when I was on call, a young heroin addict came in the psychiatric ER. She was in withdrawal. I informed her that instead of sending her to the University of Illinois Medical Center, I was going to admit her and detox her with Lithium. She was in considerable distress, and she started yelling at me, "You're a crazy doctor! Can't you see am in withdrawal?" "Get me a doctor who is going to help me!" After a time, I did get her calmed down. I encouraged her to try the Lithium, which I believed would be effective. It was, and I had her case published:

"The Use of Lithium Carbonate in Heroin Withdrawal: A Case Report."

Lithium carbonate has been reported to be of benefit to heroin addicts in heroin withdrawal. A case describing the successful use of lithium carbonate in heroin withdrawal is reported. While on lithium carbonate, the craving for heroin is not experienced. A heroin addict on lithium carbonate will not achieve a euphoric high, and this is seen as substantial prevention of heroin addiction. Because of the beneficial effects of lithium carbonate in heroin withdrawal and its elimination of the addict's craving for heroin, it is recommended that further studies be carried out, especially in drug treatment centers by experienced psychiatrists.

Background Information

The use of lithium carbonate in heroin addiction appears to be another possibility for the use of lithium. This psychiatrist first learned of its use in an article in *Psychiatric News*[1] *and* fortunately had received a heroin addict a short time later for whom lithium was used for withdrawal symptoms secondary to the use of heroin. It has been reported that lithium carbonate was found to block the craving for heroin in certain addicts, and thus prevent their addiction or post-detoxification re-addiction[1]. The investigators were encouraged by their results and suggested "the advisability of further investigation of this modality of treatment." It was also noted that underlying affective disorder symptoms were brought under control. The patient's craving for heroin vanished with serum levels of 0.5 to 0.8 meq./L. One case reported loss of craving for heroin on only 900 mg, of lithium per day. On a dose of 1200 mg per day, the patient had reported she hadn't wanted to do dope at all, "It turns me off completely." An earlier report of lithium carbonate seen as help in heroin withdrawal was also noted.[1] It has been found that lithium significantly reduces the ability of the addict to achieve the euphoric "high" stimulated by heroin consumption. Heroin hunger was greatly reduced on a dose of lithium carbonate 300 mg, Three Times a Day, and physical symptoms of heroin withdrawal were much relieved. It is also suggested that a mild tranquilizer and/or tranquilizing antidepressant such as Valium, or Sinequan, etc. may assist the anti-opiate effect of lithium carbonate.[2]

An earlier report by Dr. Scher[3] deals with the remarkable effect of lithium on a composer who was manic and a Darvon addict. From the first day of the use of lithium, the patient spontaneously reported that he lost the need for Darvon. Lithium Carbonate had had striking effects and they were almost immediately noticeable. Lithium was reported to have the capacity to reduce opiate hunger quickly, and reduce or ameliorate the agitation, sleeplessness, nausea, and other effects of withdrawal, including the terror of withdrawal itself. The author believed the results deserved considerable more investigation and trial with patients.

Altamura reported in his study of young drug addicts that no patient went back on drugs as long as he was taking lithium carbonate. All recurrences of drug usage took place after discontinuation of lithium therapy.[4]

Flemenbaum had also reported on the use of lithium for alcohol and drug addiction.[5] He believed that there is the possibility that some patients may well respond to prophylactic treatment with lithium for their alcoholism or drug dependency.

Case Report

The patient was a 31-year-old Mexican female, separated, mother of four children. She was a voluntary admission to Illinois State Psychiatric Institute on March 2, 1977, after being transferred from the Emergency Room at the University of Illinois. She had cut both forearms in a suicide attempt. Her chief complaint on admission was "I am feeling depressed and I want to kill myself," She had lost custody of her children, who were living with her mother in Texas, and was "tired" of being a prostitute and a junkie. She was very depressed, disheveled, experiencing visual and verbal hallucinations.

Admitting diagnosis was Reactive Depression with attempted suicide and heroin addiction. Her mother did not want her to return home as long as she was an addict. The patient also admitted to long-term use of alcohol.

Physical exam was remarkable for needle marks and various tattoos.

Regarding the heroin abstinence syndrome,[6] the patient had the following behaviors; drug craving, increased respiratory rate, sweating, lacrimation, yawning rhino rhea, piloerection, tremor, anorexia, irritability, dilated pupils, insomnia, nausea, weakness, abdominal cramps, tachycardia, and involuntary muscle spasms.

The patient reported having used four $20 bags of heroin per day for the last four years. She had failed three methadone programs, one each in Texas, Indiana, and Illinois. There was no reported family history of mental disorders except for the patient's mother's history of alcoholism. She stated that her mother hated her. The patient was the 3rd sibling in a sibship of six. The parents were reported as not really caring for the children. The patient had obtained only an 8th grade education. She was married at age 16. From age 17 to 21 she worked in the fields. Age 21 to 23 she did packing work in a factory. For a year she worked as a waitress and a go-go girl.

When she first came to Chicago, she did factory work for four months. She had four children and four abortions. She had been a heroin addict and a prostitute for the last four years. Her first hospitalization was in Texas for depression. She had slashed her arms. She was in the hospital for one month, given ECT and her illness remitted. She was twenty-six at the time. In the same year she was again at the same hospital for extreme nervousness. She remised after three weeks. There were no other psychiatric hospitalizations until the present.

In describing her personality before illness, she characterized herself as shy, timid and sensitive. She was suspicious at times, very resentful and very quarrelsome. She believed she was very rigid. She had had morals and was very religious. She had hated herself for being born, and did not feel good about her health or her body, but her goal was to have a good life. She said her energy had been good but she had trouble making decisions. She day-dreamed a lot but could not remember the contents. She had always had poor eating habits. There were no problems with sleeping or excretory functions.

Present illness revealed a rapid onset of one week's duration. She stated that her mother had made her very depressed and that she was tired of being a "whore" and a "junkie." She displayed decreased psychomotor activity, and had suicidal plans. There were no homicidal plans. Her speech content was centered on death wishes. She felt depressed and hopeless, and worthless. She heard voices calling her at times. There were no ideas of reference, no illusions, or experience of depersonalization. She reported a fugue state at times. No conversion symptoms or phobias were noted, and obsessions were questionable. Mental status showed that the patient's general behavior was appropriate. She was in touch with her surroundings in general and in particular. Her relations with others at that time were good. No waxy flexibility or automatic movements were noted. She had a clean appearance.

She said little and was not spontaneous in speech but did answer questions. She was prompt and to the point. She was coherent. There were no interruptions or sudden silences, no changing of topics, no use of strange words, syntax, rhymes or puns. Her form of speech varied appropriately with the subject at hand. She was oriented to time, person, place, and situation. Her intelligence could not be adequately evaluated because of her poor attention and concentration but it was believed that it was probably decreased. Insight and judgment appeared to be good at times.

Hospital Course and Treatment

(a) Immediate management: On admission the patient was placed on suicide precaution and received supportive individual psychotherapy. For emergency inpatient treatment it was decided to detoxify her with codeine since methadone was not available. She was placed on codeine 60 mg P.O. Q 4hrs. She also received valium for anxiety because she had reported favorable response to this medication. Appropriate lab tests and X-rays were ordered. Her forearm cuts were observed daily, dressings changed, and sutures removed. Since the patient had an extreme desire to return to Texas, it was believed that as soon as she was detoxified and the acute crisis was over, she would probably be sent back to Texas to be followed up in a drug treatment program there. Plans were made to have the social worker contact her family as soon as possible to discuss the possibilities that were open for this patient.

Treatment

The patient was started on a daily dose of codeine of 210 mg/day to be decreased on each successive day by 30 mg until her withdrawal symptoms abated. She was taken off of suicide precaution and was placed on nursing observation. On the third day patient still reported having various withdrawal symptoms. She was also started on a PRN of Chloral Hydrate 500 mg at U.S. for sleep. On the 4th day, patient was placed on lithium carbonate 300 mg TID P.O. On the 5th day, she reported complete loss of craving for heroin and did not even think of heroin. She believed, however, that she might go back on heroin if placed back with her "drug" friends in the community. She reported having a good appetite. She was irritable at times, and was still having insomnia. All of the other symptoms listed in the previous heroin abstinence syndrome were gone, and this had occurred on only 900 mg of lithium carbonate per day. Since the patient was still depressed and affect was labile, it was decided to titrate her up on lithium carbonate to 300 mg Four Times a Day, by mouth. On the 7th day, even though she no longer had the heroin withdrawal syndrome, Darvon #65 2 tabs Q 6 hrs PRN had to be instituted, as recommended by the dentist, since she was having extensive dental work done, and Tylenol was not very effective in decreasing her pain. Her serum lithium level was reported at 0.8 meq./L. On day 11, her lithium carbonate was increased to 1500 mg/day in divided doses. On the 12th day, Darvon was discontinued.

On day 14, her lithium was increased to 1800 mg/ day.

On the 15th day, the patient stated that she believed the lithium was a tremendous help to her. She had had an opportunity to have a "free fix" over the weekend when she was on pass but she didn't feel like taking it. It was also noted that her mood, even though being labile at times, was very much more stabilized. She was having fine tremors of the hands, due to the lithium, and another serum lithium level was ordered. She also made a very noteworthy statement that she believed methadone was also a habit. She said if she only missed one day of methadone, she would get sick and need a fix. She believed it was worse than heroin. She believed that being on lithium instead of methadone gave her a sense of worth.

On day 19, she went on an unauthorized absence, and I notified police to bring her back to the hospital. When they found her and brought her back to the hospital on day 23, she had been drinking and cut her arm in a suicide gesture, and had to be placed in full leather restraints for her protection. She was given 10 mg. of Valium I.M. to help calm her. On day 24, she stated that she would not take her lithium. It was believed that she now wanted to use this as a tool to manipulate staff. After psychotherapy, she again agreed to stay on lithium. On day 25 she cut her wrist because she had not been given a pass. On day 28 she was placed in full leather restraints for fighting with another patient.

It was believed that her depression was more of a reactive nature, and even though her mood had been much stabilized on lithium, a decrease in lithium was now started. On day 44, her serum lithium level was 1.0 meq/L. The patient now stated she had no desire to ever go back into the drug culture, and she believed this hospitalization had been a great help to her. She wanted to stay in Chicago, get a job, a place to live, and then send for her children.

On day 45, her case was presented at a case conference to Dr. Phil Holzman, a visiting consultant from the University of Chicago. It was suggested that a living place should be obtained for patient, and that she should be followed up at our outpost for psychotherapy. It was also suggested that she be continued on lithium and that this interesting effect of lithium continue to be studied.

On day 46, the patient voiced much happiness about the help she was receiving and went on a visit to the outpost. Her lithium was now decreased to 1200 mg/day in divided doses, and it was planned to maintain her on this dosage. On day 50, her serum lithium level was 0.45 meq/L. On day 51, plans were being made for discharge, and she was given a pass to look for work.

I spoke with the physician at the outpost and he believed that the use of lithium in this patient was probably of a "research" nature, and suggested that if this patient was to be continued on lithium, I would need to take the responsibility for this. I was happy to do this, and went to see the outpatient director and made arrangements to follow her as an outpatient. On day 53, she was discharged.

Discussion

It appears that lithium may be of great use in treating opiate detoxification, and may also be used as a prophylactic treatment for drug dependency. Lithium carbonate did appear to have a mood stabilizing effect on this patient.

Since one of the studies reported[4] that no patient went back on drugs as long as he or she was taking lithium carbonate, long term studies should be established. The low dosage of lithium carbonate previously reported[3] as 300 mg. Three Times a Day, by mouth, would probably indicate less possibility of toxicity at such low dose and greater compliance. The same results were seen in the case presented. Also, the effects were almost immediately noticeable and striking, as had been reported in previous studies.[3] Since lithium carbonate appears to have such rapid effects as the reported quality of reducing heroin (opiate) hunger quickly, reducing or ameliorating the agitation, sleeplessness, nausea and other effects of withdrawal, including the terror of withdrawal itself, it may be of use in acute treatment in the practice of Emergency Medicine.

It was noteworthy that in this particular case the patient had reported failing three methadone programs, and yet she appeared to be willing to take lithium and it gave her a "sense of worth." This experience certainly is worthy of further investigation.

Might it also be that, if lithium is successful in treating drug addicts, the cost would be extremely reduced in that methadone may no longer be used, nor would excessive "red tape" have to be worked through, in order for a patient to receive lithium at any hospital or clinic as may be the case for methadone.

It is important that only experienced physicians such as psychiatrists treat such patients. Lithium carbonate can be very toxic and potentially fatal if the serum or platelet level is not carefully monitored. This is especially true in an impulsive addict with suicidal tendencies and an underlying personality disorder, because the therapeutic/lethality ratio with lithium is small.

If an addiction is secondary to bipolar affective illness or schizoaffective illness, lithium could possibly be considered for therapy here, too. One must also be made aware of the fact that lithium carbonate is usually not the treatment of choice for a reactive depression, but was considered for this patient for treatment of heroin withdrawal symptoms and potential heroin craving.

Although the exact mechanisms by which lithium carbonate acts in the long term management of addiction to heroin are at present unknown, Singer and Rotenberg[7] believe that there are at least two mechanisms by which lithium might act within the central nervous system: ion substitution in a critical cation transport process; and alteration of the microenvironment for a critical hormonal or metabolic process in the nervous system.

Bozarth and Wise[8] have noted that heroin reward is dependent on a dopaminergic substrate. This was noted when they blocked the rewarding property of heroin by pretreatment with either nalaxone or pimozide, suggesting that this opiate-receptor mediated effect is dependent on a dopaminergic substrate.

It has also been shown that opiate self-administration is attenuated by neuroleptics that block dopamine receptors.

Heroin, (diacetyl morphine), is a semi synthetic derivative

of morphine, which, owing to its greater lipid solubility than that of morphine, crosses the blood brain barrier in considerable amounts. In the brain, heroin is rapidly de-acetylated to 6-monoacetyl-morphine and to morphine; in this sense, heroin carries morphine rapidly into the brain.[9] A decrease in brain dopamine has been found in morphine withdrawal.[10]

An increase in levels of homovanillic acid deaminated-o-methylated metabolite of dopamine in the CSF has been observed in patients during treatment with lithium, and urinary excretion of dopamine has been noted to be decreased during treatment with lithium,[11] A role in central mediation of reward perception is suggested for dopamine.[12] Therefore, the increase in dopamine by lithium may hold significance in a support for continuation of "reward" in the reward center.

As I revise this paper for publication, I reflect that with my present knowledge, I would not have given this patient Valium. Because of the disinhibiting effect of Valium on behavior, one is prone to act out impulsively. Valium has been shown to elicit increased hostility in normal subjects and this could be considered a form of disinhibition.[13]

It has also been reported that patients on Valium and other disinhibiting drugs can develop suicidal ideas and severe emotional upsets.[13] Dr. Hollister believes that anyone who has substance abuse such as alcohol, heroin, or hallucinogens is a poor candidate for benzodiazepines.[14] Valium also has an adverse effect on the normal sleep cycle.

Benzodiazepines reduce REM (dream sleep) and the deep stages of sleep especially stage 4.[15] REM sleep is believed to provide psychological benefits, and stages 3 and 4 of sleep are believed to be associated with the physically restorative aspects of sleep.[16] In addition, patients who have been on benzodiazepines for a long period of time may have withdrawal.[17] Therefore, it may be more prudent not to put patients on these medications in the first place.

In reference to the hypnotic that was used for this patient for sleep, at present, I would have used L-Tryptophan, an essential amino acid which is a precursor of serotonin, a "natural hypnotic."[18] It has been reported that chloral hydrate has been used for kicks,[19] and therefore, should probably not be given to patients who are prone to drug abuse.

Because of the additional questions that may be raised in

light of current information, I would highly recommend that
controlled studies be initiated to validate this preliminary report.

In November I was fortunate to have another of my
articles published: "Psychologic Problems of the Physically
Handicapped"

On Monday, November 22, I attended a very interesting program by
the Institute for the Study of Human Knowledge and the Institute
of Psychiatry at Northwestern University, who presented Robert
Ornstein lecturing on the Mind Field.

I had also read several of his books. *On the Experience of Time*
he gives a history of theories on time perception and analysis of
theories and experiments on time perception. In his *The Psychology
of Consciousness*, he explores the consciousness of the traditional and
esoteric psychologies, along with an extended concept of man.

I had been doing TM for several months. During the early sessions, I experienced altered states of consciousness. It is not possible
for me to describe this adequately, because there are no words to
describe what I had experienced. It was as if I was traveling at a
speed beyond light, through the universe or time. I would feel very,
very light at times, almost as if I could float away.

During the first few weeks, I experienced hostility, and my anxiety increased. I was quite concerned because this was not my usual
self. I even considered dropping TM, because I believed it was having an adverse effect on me. I informed the TM instructor, and
she encouraged me to go on. I think my sleep may have improved
somewhat during the two months that I did TM. Two months after
starting TM, I began to notice that my cognitive ability was actually
"dulled." I was very concerned about this. Also, my body weight had
increased to the heaviest weight I had ever been.

I came to believe that my mantra was the name of a deity. I quit
doing TM on November 27, for the main reason of a feeling of a
great evil around me. Also, when I would pray, I had a very difficult

time visualizing Christ as I do in my prayers; instead, there seemed to be a hideous form in my mind.

I had done a tremendous amount of reading on meditation. One of the best overviews was *On the Psychology of Meditation* by Claudio Naranjo and Robert Ornstein. I learned every deity has a mantra, and every mantra a deity. This confirmed my belief that I was saying the name of a deity.

A so-called Christian mystic, Heiler, talking about contemplation, said when it is directed toward the ultimate, highest, absolute, toward God that all concrete conceptions, and imaginings are left far behind, such as the humanity of the Son of God, the Child in the manger, the Sufferer on the Cross. As far as I am concerned, this is not true, because it would imply that Jesus is not God, which is not the case. In this respect, Heiler cannot really be considered a Christian.

Two of the greatest Christian mystics I have studied are St. John of the Cross and St. Teresa of Avila. In *The Mystical Doctrine* of Saint John of the Cross, he believes we should abandon meditation for spiritual contemplation. St. John believes the soul longs for divine wisdom. Saint Teresa, in *The Interior Castle*, said that to be really spiritual, we must be slaves of God and branded with His sign, the sign of the cross. In Luke, chapter 9, verse 23, Jesus said, "If anyone wants to be a follower of mine, let him renounce himself and take up his cross every day and follow me."

One needs to have a firm foundation in absolute truth. For me, it is Scripture, the Word of God.

Two good cases were reported regarding automatic writing. A chemistry professor, Dr. Ludwig Staudenmeier, had experimented with this. He believed he was a medium for spirits who performed the automatic writing. One reply he received from the spirits was that they were evil spirits that were obliged to stay near him. It goes to show us that if we are going to play with fire, we are going to be burnt.

Even though we may do scientific exploring in parapsychology, we may, in fact, be fascinated with the beauty, structure, and workings of the "web." When we do discover the real substance behind it all, we may find ourselves in the fatal hold of the "spider."

Scientist Emanuel Swedenborg had had a great interest in automatic writing . I had read his book *Heaven and Hell*, which supposedly was based on spiritual realm. It was one of the most boring books I have ever read.

He was a prophet of a "New Church." The blind Helen Keller was inspired by him. He rejected the notion that Jesus died on the cross to redeem us from original sin. Emanuel could not have been inspired by God, for Jesus died for sinners. He also said angels could not speak a single word of the human language. How, then, is he is to explain the annunciation of the angel Gabriel to Mary in Luke, chapter I, verse 30:"...the angel said to her, Mary, do not be afraid; you have won God's favor." He also denies the existence of Satan, although Satan is mentioned in both the Old and New Testament.

I spent Thanksgiving with Sister Oliva at the Sisters of Mercy Convent in South Chicago. She had been my Organic Chemistry Professor at Saint Xavier College the year before, when I was taking my premed courses. They had a Ugandan minister couple visiting. I do not remember their names. I had been talking with them for a while. When they informed me they were going back to Uganda, I was very concerned. I told them they could not do that, because the Ugandan leader Idi Amin was a monster.

She got very angry at me and said, "We don't care about him. We must care for our people." I had a very bad feeling. I was sure they would be murdered. It was Thanksgiving. I gave thanks that we had blazing spirits like them. They were not black; they were pure gold! A long time later, I saw a picture of them in a newspaper. They had been chained to a pole and shot.

On December 24, I saw an advertisement in a popular Chicago newspaper titled the "Reader." It was about Maharishi Mahesh Yogi.

It stated that for accurate information on TM and other "New Age" groups and gurus, examined from a biblical perspective, one should write to:

Spiritual Counterfeit Project Department M Post Office Box 4308 Berkeley, California 94704

I wrote to them and was placed on their mailing list. The spiritual counterfeits project newsletter raised some very interesting points. It was stated that since TM was not acknowledging the fact that it is religious, TM may be engaged in consumer fraud. I certainly think this is the case.

The essence of his book, *Transcendental Meditation*, is "religious." To say that TM is not "religious" is absurd.

I was very surprised to note, that in the August 1976 Spiritual Counterfeits Project Newsletter, Mr. Richard D. Scott had volunteered his testimony for the benefit of a TM lawsuit. He had been a teacher of TM and had a strong inkling that his mantra and others were not meaningless sounds. He had read the book *Tantra Asona* and discovered that his mantra did have a meaning. His final mantra, he discovered, could be translated as, "Oh, most beautiful Aaing, I bow down to you." I found this quite upsetting and hoped that my mantra was not the name of a deity.

I noted in Martin Ebon's book on Maharishi that most mantras are in Sanskrit. According to a universal Hindu belief, shared by Patanjali, as well as Ramakrishna, mantra is an active symbol of a particular deity, even if the name of the deity represents only one aspect of the absolute, a symbol of one of his visible forms. Therefore, if a worshipper repeats a mantra a hundred or a thousand times, making a constant effort to identify himself with it, the power of that which the mantra represents, comes, as it were, to him. Sutra 44 states, "By repetition of the mantra comes the realization of the intended deity."

In Deuteronomy, chapter 5, verse 7, the first commandment states, "You shall have no gods except me." Therefore, it doesn't appear that Christians should be saying mantras.

Maharishi has also spoken about reincarnation, but in the Bible, Hebrews, chapter 9, verse 27 states, "... men only die once ..."

It was reported in Martin Ebon's book *Maharishi* that a man had asked Maharishi, "What is your answer to the noble sacrifice that Christ made at the Crucifixion?"

He replied, "Christ did not volunteer for the Crucifixion. He had much help getting up on the Cross." Scripture certainly doesn't substantiate what Maharishi stated about Christ not volunteering for the Crucifixion. John, chapter 12, verses 27–28 states, "What shall I say: Father, save me from this hour? But it was for this very reason that I have come to this hour. Father, glorify Your Name!" And Mark 10:45 stated, .."the Son of man himself did not come to be served but to serve, and give his life a ransom for many." I believe that the extremely positive aspect of TM has been that it has shown society that professionals from every profession may do "professional studies" on such phenomenon. Put their "professional label of creditability" on such a technique, without really realizing that such phenomena may not be fully objectified by the limitations of science. Second John 1:9 is appropriate here: "If anybody does not keep within the teaching of Christ but goes beyond it, he cannot have God with him ..."

My experiences with TM were published:

"Transcendental Meditation: A Case Report of a Physician's Response, to Transcendental Meditation"

Dr. Herbert Benson in *The Relaxation Response*, stated it was not necessary to use TM to obtain the beneficial effects of meditation. Tests at the Thorndike Memorial Laboratory of Harvard showed that similar techniques could produce the same physiologic changes.

Martin Ebon's book, *The Relaxation Controversy,* compares the relaxation response and TM but does not realize the spiritual or psychological dangers of these techniques.

Hans Selye, in *Stress Without Distress,* tells how to use stress as a positive force to achieve a rewarding lifestyle.

The Spiritual Counterfeits Project, a ministry of the Berkeley Christian Coalition, has looked into TM, Werner Erhard and EST, UFOs, holistic health, Sun Myung Moon and the Unification Church, and many other "cult" movements.

A book by R. D. Clements, *God and the Gurus,* published by InterVarsity Press, Downers Grove, Illinois 60515, is excellent for practical advice to persons who want to know more about Eastern religions, the Divine Light Mission, the Hare Krishna Movement, and TM from a Christian perspective.

The winter quarter seminar schedule was almost the same as the fall quarter. I was now assigned to a different inpatient ward, Ward 10 East.

On January 8, 1977, I met Alice through Visual Dates. She was an ex-nun who was working on a doctorate degree in education at Loyola. She has become a lifelong friend. She was into EST and wanted me to take the EST training. She believed it had been a great influence on her life. I believed EST was probably another cult, but I decided to read about it.

Robert A. Hargrove, a journalist, wrote about his experiences EST, and EST's founder, Werner Erhard in *EST: Making Life Work.* There are good points about the book, such as taking responsibility for one's life. I was concerned about trainee's revelations, such as one girl reported leaving her psychiatrist; another had been very, very depressed. I don't know if they believed EST was the answer to their problems, but it would be interesting to explore follow-up experiences of these women.

I believed the technique might be too confrontational. I was concerned about the effect of such confrontation on someone with poor ego strengths and ego boundaries. One woman admitted to being so depressed that she was near suicide. Nothing was said about if and how she was helped. There did appear to be some cathartic effects that were probably due to intimate sharing of problems with a large number of people. It would be interesting to follow these cases up to see if the effects are lasting and have led to change in the trainees.

William Greene's book, *EST: 4 Days to Make Your Life Work*, gives a description of EST, a glossary of terms, seminars, and the experience of training. Again, I was concerned about the number of people having depression and feeling suicidal. I don't agree that beliefs prevent an individual from experiencing life. My belief in God has added much to my life. The concept that, "Your belief systems are all wrong," doesn't make any sense to me. That only experience is the truth is not my truth. The EST training statement, "You are God," is complete nonsense.

James Kettle's *The EST Experience* is about his experience with EST and for him, Werner is an instant savior.

My savior, Jesus Christ, has always been around and will always be around. You can have the "instants." I prefer to stick with the real thing!

For me, God is all. Mark Brewer's article on Erhard Seminar's Training (EST) in August 1975 *Psychology Today*, "We're Gonna Tear You Down and Put You Back Together" is an excellent evaluation of EST.

My concerns about adverse psychological effects are well grounded. An article in *Human Behavior*, September 1977, pp. 46–47, entitled "EST's Edge of Madness," reveals several cases of severe after-effects of EST.

Since I have always had a great interest in parapsychology and the psychic realm, I joined the Illinois Society for Psychic Research. On February 22, I attended a lecture on "The Science of the Pyramids." Pyramids are said to focus "life force." Science needs to study this phenomenon to see if it's really real.

Uri Geller is one of the most popular person's people with psychic powers. I was very fascinated by his book, *My Story*. He claims spectra, a force in outer space, may be helping our world.

In a more scientific vein, two articles regarding Geller's claims of paranormal powers were published in *Nature*, Vol. 251, Oct. 18, 1974 and Vol. 254, April 10, 1975. Appropriate scientific critical remarks regarding investigating the paranormal were published in "Investigating the Paranormal," *Nature*, Vol. 251, Oct. 18, 1974.

Since I have always been interested in being a channel for God's work, I read *The Gift Within*, about the experiences of a "spiritual medium," James H. P. Wilkie. However, he was not a medium for God but Rama, a so-called spirit guide. I believe we are really asking for trouble by letting spirits take possession of us. The psychic Bishop Pike certainly met a bizarre death.

Of all the psychics I read about, the one I believe may have been a channel of God's grace was JoAnne Chase. Her book, *You Can Change Your Life Through Psychic Power*, is very interesting. There has been an information explosion on parapsychology. Again, we must be careful not to get trapped in a web. I have spent many years researching psychic phenomena. Science should explore these areas; however, this phenomenon may be beyond objectivity.

The winter quarter seminar schedule was quite heavy. One Friday evening when I was on call, a main water line broke and set off the entire fire alarm system in the hospital. Many fire companies came to the hospital. We had to transfer patients to other wards. The medical director gave me a letter of appreciation for the way I handled the problem. I was also assigned to Ward 10 East, one of the busiest wards in the institute.

In April, I started the spring quarter seminar schedule, the last quarter of my residency.

Even though I was in psychiatry, I made good medical diagnosis. I diagnosed a collapsed lung on a patient in the jail-unit of the institute. A challenge occurred on the adolescent ward one night. A lot of teens had the flu on the unit. I always examine patients before giving medicines. One teen had abdominal complaints. When I was examining him, he had "guarding" that made me feel uneasy. I asked him if I gave him some money, if he would like to go to the movie.

He said yes. Usually, a patient that has an "acute abdomen" would have no such desire. Well, since I had an "inner uneasiness" and the child had schizophrenia, I decided to send him to the University of Illinois Emergency Room. His diagnosis was acute appendicitis, and he was taken to surgery. There are many times when even though we know how to make a diagnosis based on signs and symptoms, we have to give in to inner feelings. A computer would not have diagnosed this child.

In the spring, I decided that I didn't want to stay in Chicago any longer. The winters were too cold. I wanted to be closer to home.

I had wanted to complete my last two years of psychiatry residency in the Washington, D.C. area, but unfortunately, they did not have any second-year psychiatry residence positions open. I applied to the Medical College of Virginia in Richmond, Virginia; Eastern Virginia Medical School Affiliated Hospitals in Norfolk, Va. area; and the University of Virginia in Charlottesville, Virginia.

During the third week in May, I went for interviews, and decided to go to the Medical College of Virginia in Richmond, Virginia.

I gave my notice at the Illinois State Psychiatric Institute. My psychiatry resident's classmates attempted to talk me into staying there, but I wanted a change. I received a certificate for my year of residency in psychiatry at the institute.

After spending a week in Pittsburgh with my family, I moved to Richmond, Virginia.

I moved into the River Towers Apartments across the James River close to the Medical College of Virginia.

For the first six months of my residency, I was assigned to the McGuire VA Hospital. Since they were short of staff there, I worked very hard. I treated inpatients and outpatients and did emergency consultations throughout the hospital when requested to do so. The one advantage was that I could take "call" at home, but I usually went in to see the patient when I was called.

After being in Richmond a few weeks, I realized that it did not offer the social potential for me that Chicago did. I had believed that I would be able to go to Washington, D.C. fairly often, since it is only about a hundred miles away, but I really didn't have much time to be driving back and forth.

I joined the Washington, D.C. Catholic Alumni Club and the Tidewater Catholic Alumni Club in Virginia Beach. Virginia Beach and the ocean are over a hundred miles east of Richmond. I did visit the Shenandoah National Park in the fall, and the mountain ranges are very colorful and beautiful. It's about eighty miles west of Richmond. There are good museums in Richmond, such as the Edgar Allen Poe Museum. I did go to Kings Dominion a few times with my brother and sisters, twenty miles north of Richmond. I enjoyed the monorail ride through Lion Country, where they have a lot of wild animals.

I went to my first steamed crab fest in July. The psychiatry residents do it once a year for the new residents. It was a great feast!

Socially, Chicago was the best place for me, but I love San Francisco the best.

In Virginia Beach, I visited the Edgar Cayce Foundation, the Association for Research and Enlightenment. It probably has the most extensive "psychic" libraries in the country. I do not believe that Edgar Cayce got his "powers" from God.

When I had applied to the University of Virginia, I had hoped on meeting Dr. Ian Stevenson, who was a past chairman of the department of psychiatry, but he was doing a study in South America. He has been engaged in psychical research for a number of years, especially reincarnation. *Twenty Cases Suggestive of Reincarnation*, through the University Press of Virginia in Charlottesville, doesn't claim that the cases he has studied offer positive proof of reincarnation but are only suggestive. He does take a look at possible phenomenon at the end of his book, which may help to explain the so-called reincarnation. As a Christian, I do not accept reincarnation as a fact but believe phenomenon such as possession states may explain this experience.

Another popular writer from the University of Virginia who had studied psychiatry is Dr. Raymond A. Moody, Jr. His book of case histories of people who have experienced "clinical death" is extremely fascinating, *Life After Life*, published by Bantam Books.

Be aware, however, that these are "clinical death" experiences, not actual death, which may be completely different. This is an area doctors should be exploring with patients. It helps us to have a greater knowledge of the profound depth of existence.

Dr. Elisabeth Kubler-Ross had written the foreword to Dr. Moody's book. She has a very remarkable book published by the Macmillan Company, *On Death and Dying*. She is a pioneer in "doctoring" the dying patient. She has helped us to gain a deeper understanding of the care of the dying patient. Dr. Kubler-Ross has also been interested in the paranormal. According to an article in September 1977 *Human Behavior* entitled "The Miracle of Kubler-Ross by Ann Nietzke," she had out-of-body experiences and communicates with "spiritual guides."

An evaluation of this phenomena from a biblical perspective is given in a seven-page article entitled, "Thanatology: Death and Dying" in the April 1977 *Journal of the Spiritual Counterfeits Project*, published by the Spiritual Counterfeits Project, Box 4308, Berkeley, California 94704. They believe the entire subject is a prime candidate for satanic meddling.

I was very fascinated by Dr. John C. Lilly's book, *The Center of the Cyclone*. He is a qualified psychoanalyst who has spent many years studying dolphin-human relationships. He has done isolation experiments and "controlled" LSD experiments. I am very interested in doing research on altered states of consciousness but not in LSD experiments. That drug is too unpredictable in its effects. I have met too many people who have had bad trips. One of the best examples of bad trips is the drug-induced vision of Castaneda's initiation into sorcery as reported in *Tales of Power*.

On November 4, 1977, I went into psychoanalysis. I believed it would help me to become a better psychiatrist, if I could learn more about myself.

I volunteered to be on call Thanksgiving and that weekend, in hopes of getting a weeks vacation at Christmas. I did get my week vacation at Christmas and spent a few days in Pittsburgh with my family.

My brother, Gil, had taken dance for several years and on December 30, I attended the Washington Ballet in Tchaikovsky's "The Nutcracker." He was fortunate to have two parts, one as one of the guests and also as one of the rats. I really enjoyed the performance.

December was my last month at the McGuire VA Hospital

I was assigned to the Medical College of Virginia psychiatric outpatient department for the next six months. I was assigned three supervisors. I was permitted to keep Dr. Bob B, a VA hospital psychiatrist, who was an excellent supervisor. Dr. John Mullaney, a forensic psychiatrist and also the residency training director, gave me supervision. I was pleased about this, because I was interested in becoming a prison psychiatrist. Dr. George Kriegman, my other supervisor, was a psychoanalyst who had studied under Harry Stack Sullivan. He was also the director of the Virginia Psychoanalytic Association. I was very happy to have Dr. Kriegman, because of my interest in psychoanalysis. Since I was in psychoanalysis, I was considering going on into psychoanalytic training once my residency in psychiatry was over.

Harry Stack Sullivan's works had an influence on my clinical thinking.

I had also joined the Carl Jung Analytical Center in Washington, D.C. and had the great experience of meeting Jungian analyst Elined Kotschnig, who had studied with Carl Jung in Zurich.

I had read Wilhelm Reich's book, *Character Analysis*, a classic in psychoanalysis; *Sex Pol*, which includes a lot of his political ideas; *The Murder of Christ*, which examines problems in living; and *The Function of the Orgasm*, a study of sexuality. There is wisdom in Reich's writings, but he has contradictions in *The Murder of Christ* with Scripture. For example, he doesn't accept the real meaning of the crucifixion as an act of love and a means of salvation. I got the impression that he believed Christ may have been a myth.

I am very impressed with Sigmund Freud. His contribution to the understanding of man was genius, especially in regards to dynamics. I am very impressed with his ability to change his theories when he discovered a better explanation for the phenomenon he was studying. He was a real scientist. He was a bit too dogmatic at times and may not have been as flexible as he probably should have been regarding the ideas of others. Some of his early associates departed from him, such as Jung and Reich. I do not hold his views on religion because I got the impression he believed God was a myth.

Erik H. Erikson's *Childhood and Society* is one of the best books I have read on childhood.

The most profound case history I have ever read was Erikson's *Gandhi's Truth*. It is unique, being the first instance where a psychoanalyst has done a dynamic study of a religious leader who has affected millions of people. It is one of the most beautiful books I have read.

I enjoyed Irving Stone's *The Passions of the Mind*, about Sigmund Freud. It gave me an understanding for the times Freud lived in.

Theodor Reik one of Freud's students had shown much wisdom in *Of Love and Lust* and *The Need To Be Loved*.

I have also been heavily influenced by the Catholic psychoanalyst, Ignace Lepp. A Christian approach to psychoanalysis is *The*

Depths of the Soul. In *Health of Mind and Soul,* he probes into the basis of psychic disorder, gives principles of prevention and offers realistic, mature solutions.

The most colorful analyst and founder of Gestalt Therapy, Fritz Perls had a great book, *In and Out of the Garbage Pail.* I wish he were still alive; I would have enjoyed being in one of his group sessions. He looks like Santa Claus.

Karl Menninger's *Whatever Became of Sin?* and *The Crime of Punishment* is full of wisdom. I was very impressed with his analysis of our penal system. His ideas were very helpful to me when I was employed as a prison psychiatrist.

A number of philosophers have had a great influence on my thinking, such as Karl Jaspers, Martin Heidegger, William James, Kahlil Gibran, and Rollo May. Actually, Rollo May is a psychologist with a very good philosophy. In *Love and Will,* he reasserts the importance of feeling values in sex rather than just techniques. His *Meaning of Anxiety* gave me a deep insight into all aspects of anxiety.

I love Gibran's writings; they are so filled with spiritual beauty.

William James' *The Varieties of Religious Experience* is a classic on the psychology of religion.

Alan Watts's writings are rather philosophical, especially his comparison of eastern thought with western psychotherapy in *Psychotherapy East and West.* There were some very good points in Sheldon B. Kopp's *If You Meet the Buddha On the Road, Kill Him!* I did enjoy reviewing his presentation of the myths of Gilgamesh and Siddhartha.

R.D. Lang and Anti-Psychiatry, edited by Robert Boyers and Robert Orrill, is a deep analysis of mental illness stemming from poor interpersonal relationships, and explores some of Laing's views on the subject.

The Myth of Mental Illness, by Thomas S. Szasz, raises for us in the profession moral implications that are important for us to be aware of. I don't like to label patients with a diagnosis of schizophrenia, but we need labels for treatment and research. I wish that mental illness was a myth, but it is not.

I enjoyed working in the outpatient department. Unfortunately, during most of the time I was there, we did not have a psychiatric director. I filled in when prescriptions needed to be given to patients that were not mine. I had long-term psychotherapy cases, and many more patients that I maintained on psychotropic medications. One day a week I had Walk-In Clinic, which meant that I would see all of the patients who came to Walk-In Clinic that day. I also supervised and taught medical students. I gave lectures to medical students and would supervise interviews done by them.

I now had time to attend seminars that were outstanding. I had been attending a two-hour psychotherapy case seminar with analyst, Dr. McDonough, for two hours every Tuesday morning. We had a residents' meeting every Wednesday from 12:00–1:00 p.m., where we would discuss problems.

I attended Dr. Kriegman's Personality Development Seminar on Wednesday afternoon. Every Wednesday from 5:00–6:00 p.m., we had a literature seminar that was supervised by Dr. N. We would review important papers in the field at this seminar.

One of the most important courses was the Interview Technique Course that Dr. Kriegman, an analyst, gave on Thursday afternoons. One resident would interview a patient in a room that had a one-way mirror and would be observed by Dr. Kriegman and other residents. Dr. Kriegman would take over the interview when he felt we weren't getting anywhere with the patient.

On Fridays, we would attend Grand Rounds. Noted authorities from across the country would give us presentations on various subjects. On Friday afternoons, we were fortunate to have a child analyst from Washington, D.C., Dr. Virginia Clower, give a child development seminar. We would review most of the important literature in the field, studying development theories of Anna Freud, Sigmund Freud, Piaget, Mahler, Erik Erikson, and Kernberg.

I did a tremendous amount of reading during this time, as I usually do. *The Patient and the Analyst* by Sandler, Dare, and Holder was a book on the basis of the psychoanalytic process. It was our textbook for the psychotherapy case seminar. The two volumes on *The Technique of Psychoanalytical Psychotherapy* by Robert Lang helped me very much in doing psychoanalytic psychotherapy with patients. I also used Hilde Bruch's *Learning Psychotherapy* and the classic, *Principles of Intensive Psychotherapy*, by Frieda Fromm-Reichmann.

From time to time, I attended the Richmond Teilhard Society at the Southminster Presbyterian Church. I had been greatly impressed with Teirhard De Chardin's writings.

He was a Jesuit and a professor of geology. He discovered the skull of "Peking Man." I was very fascinated by his theory of spiritual evolution.

Another theologian I have been impressed with is Paul Tirrich. His *Biblical Religion and the Search for Ultimate Reality* shows the function of philosophy in religious thought. His definition of faith was full of wisdom.

Martin Buber, the Jewish theologian, had a profound affect on me.

His insight into the human encounter is wisdom of the highest degree, and is seen in his *I and Thou*.

Years ago when I was sixteen, I would visit Dr. Jonstantin Jaroshezich, the Christian minister who had helped me so very much. He had studied revelation all of his life. He had a time map about biblical history. He told me that my eyes would see the nightmarish things at the end of the world by the antichrist, the beast, and the false prophet. I would live in the time of the battle of Armageddon. He said he would not see this, for he and his wife were elderly and indeed, they have died since. He also said that since I had aligned myself to Christ, and would not accept the brand of the beast on my right hand or forehead, I might survive with the grace of God, even though I would be living in such a hellish nightmare.

I would witness the return of my Master and Lord, Jesus Christ. And the thought of this would help me endure the nightmare that we are to pass through.

We are living in time when all of these things will come to pass. People should be reading their Bible so that they will have some idea of what to expect, and changing their lives. Unless each of us has accepted Jesus Christ as our personal Lord and Savior, there will be no hope for us.

There are four excellent books I have read concerning these events, Hal Lindsey's: *The Late, Great Planet Earth, Satan Is Alive and Well On Planet Earth*, and *There's a New World Coming. Satan in the Sanctuary* is by Thomas S. McCall and Zola Levitt.

If there is such a thing as the rapture where all faithful Christians are taken up to God before experiencing all of the terrible nightmares which are to happen, I would certainly love to be among them. I don't look forward to all of these terrible things. If I am given a choice, I should probably remain here. I am a doctor. I care about people and I know the Word of God. I should probably stay behind, in hopes that I may be able to save others. I wouldn't feel comfortable about leaving. It's analogous to a captain who abandons his sinking ship.

If I am fortunate to enter into eternal life, I will always be troubled that there is a hell and creatures suffer there. I have a very difficult time accepting failure. I wish there was someway the devil and his angels could be rehabilitated. He had so much wisdom at one time.

Since God is love, I wonder how He must feel about His fallen angel. In Revelation 12:4, it speaks of the dragon, Satan, and that he dragged a third of the stars, which I assume are angels that sided with him, from heaven, and dropped them to the earth.

It is extraordinary, that Lucifer could attract a third of God's angels who were in the presence of God. I assume that this angel must have had some very powerful attractive qualities to have a third of God's angels side with him. I would think that God must love this angel very much and suffer about what has happened. I believe my theory is substantiated in Ezekiel 33:11, "... I take pleasure, not in the death of a wicked man, but in the turning back of a wicked man who changes his ways to win life" Is it possible that Lucifer is included? And further, Luke 15:7, "... there will be more rejoicing in heaven over one repentant sinner than over ninety-nine virtuous men who have no need of repentance."

Would God rejoice if Satan repented? And in Luke, 15:11–32, there was joy over the return of the lost son.

Since in Luke 6:27, we are told to love our enemies, then I assume God must love His enemy. And in Luke 15:11–32, we find a father rejoicing over the return of his prodigal son. Would God too rejoice over the return of his prodigal angel?

From the above, I have developed a theory. Since God is love, the creation of man may have been the most incomprehensible act of love imaginable. Since God had already created angels, then of what use was it to create man? Could it be that all God wanted to do was to show His angel that He could create another life form and even in His own image. He would give the life form a total free will and create so many that it would not be possible for His angel to count them all. And further, not only would He give man free will, but also He would take total responsibility upon Himself for His creatures' wrongdoing; in the end, sacrificing Himself for the wrongdoing by permitting man to commit a crime beyond comprehension, the murder of God. And, by another incomprehensible act of love, He would forgive man.

Could it be that all God wanted to do was to say to His angel, by all of this, "Look, I have created man. He murdered Me, and I forgave him." I truly believe that if Lucifer and his angels were to repent, that God would offer them back with open arms. Just think how wonderful this would be if it could happen.

I can't get over how great God's love is. I have read many great books but have never found a greater book than the Bible. I can't get over the fact that many people have not read it or have not had the desire to do so. The Word of God is so profound! I have read the entire Bible several times now.

One of my all-time favorite TV programs is *In Touch Ministries* by Dr. Charles Stanley. I love his presentations on Scripture.

Love is so great that we could probe all existence, past, present, and future of all creation and never come up with anything greater than love. It isn't just the environment. Adam and Eve had the perfect environment but they disobeyed God. Man must change himself to make things better. The greatest war we will ever fight is with ourselves.

Since I heard that some Transcendental Meditation adherents could fly, levitate, and dematerialize, I decided to see the levitation film at the Richmond International Meditation Society. I saw people levitating on the film, which I believed was pretty incredible, but they wouldn't do it for me in person. I am rather concerned about them; for I do not believe their power to do this comes from God, if indeed they can do it. I am more interested in saving my soul than flying.

Since my experience in the outpatient department had been such a positive one, I extended my rotation another three months there. I took a week vacation in June and went home to see my family.

On the Fourth of July, I decided to attend a Mormon picnic. I have had a few friends who were Mormons. I have even read parts of *The Book of Mormon. The Bible, the Christian, and Latter-Day Saints* by Gordon R. Lewis, published by the Presbyterian and Reformed Publishing Company, Box 185, Nutley, N.J. 07110, presents a good evaluation of the Mormon Faith in comparison with Christianity.

In August, I had received an Astral Sounds tape from the American Research Team in Beverly Hills, California. The tape was supposed to trigger out-of-the-body experiences. I had ordered the tape through an ad in *Human Behavior*, the newsmagazine of the social sciences. I had played the tape several times. I did not achieve an out-of-body experience, but I experienced a very high degree of tension. I felt as if I was in hell and was surrounded by devils. It is the most irritating, bizarre sound I have ever heard. I have serious questions as to whether such a tape should even be sold to the public. I had such terrible evil vibrations around me when I was playing this tape. If I had an out-of-body experience, could a demon enter my body? I don't think I want to find out.

In August, I joined Amnesty International, According to the Richmond U.S. Group 134, Amnesty International is a worldwide human rights movement that works impartially for the release of prisoners of conscience; men and women detained anywhere for their beliefs, color, ethnic origin, sex, religion, or language, provided they have neither used nor advocated violence. Amnesty International opposes torture and the death penalty in all cases without reservation and advocates fair and prompt trials for all political prisoners.

Amnesty International is independent of all governments, political factions, ideologies, economic interests, and religious creeds. It has consultative status with the United Nations (ECOSOC), UNESCO and the Council of Europe, has cooperative relations with the Inter-American Commission on Human Rights of the Organization of American States, and has observer status with the Organization of African Unity (Bureau for the Placement and Education of African Refugees). Amnesty International was the recipient of the 1977 Nobel Prize for Peace.

Before I joined A.I., I had written letters for prisoners of conscience through the American Psychiatric Association Newspaper requests. During residency, I was a member-in-training of the American Psychiatric Association. When I learned of A.I. through one of my professors in psychiatry, Dr. Ken Solomon, I decided to join. I believe it's extremely worth my time and energy. I helped write letters and have gotten results. I think it's wonderful when letters can prevent torture and help the release of some poor person to his family.

I feel real good about being a member of A.I. I believe that as a doctor and psychiatrist, I have an extremely important responsibility toward my fellow man. I believe A.I. is a place where a lot of good can be accomplished. I am also brought to bear of my responsibility in Luke 12:48, which states: "When a man has had a great deal given him, a great deal will be demanded of him; when a man has had a great deal given him on trust, even more will be expected of him." And since I am of the latter, I hope I will meet the expectations.

When I think of my ethical responsibility as a Christian, Dietrich Bonheoffer comes to mind. His *Ethics* is one of the most powerful books I have ever read. He is a great inspiration for me. Unfortunately, parts of his book are not complete, for the Gestapo seized parts of his book. The Nazis didn't appreciate his writings, and they hung him with a piano wire, naked, in April 1945. What a horrible way to die, but think of the music he made entering Paradise!

I have read *Auschwitz*, Dr. Miklos Nyiszli's eyewitness account of his experiences there. I hope that if I am ever in the same situation that God will help me to act professionally and not adopt the business-as-usual attitude that enabled Dr. Nyiszli to help the SS as a doctor.

Since I have been in Amnesty International, I have been learning about current laws and practices of various governments, especially Russia. I have read *The Communist Manifesto* by Karl Marx and Friedrich Engels. Since it appears that religion and morality do not appear to be accepted by communism, I could never be a part of it. I value my freedom too much. I prefer, *better dead than red!*

As a member of Amnesty International, I would like to invite you, the reader, to join. The address is:

Amnesty International
2112 Broadway
New York, New York 10023

Membership fee is tax-deductible. It will give you an opportunity to meet new people and do something very worthwhile for your fellow man.

Albert Speer, Hitler's architect's book, *Spandau the Secret Diaries*, is one of the most powerful personal analyses that I have ever read. This book was written during the twenty years that Speer spent in prison as a Nazi war criminal. Speer was given the opportunity to experience some of the pain that the Nazi victims had experienced but not on such a high degree that they had suffered; the loneliness, depression, apathy, bodily symptoms, violent emotions, despair, nightmares, and the hopes about release from time-to-time over the years, only to have his hopes dashed. The poor concentration camp Jew experienced this but so much more. Speer could only see his family members once a year and could not have physical contact with them, only a touch of salt compared to the crimes committed against Jewish families. It is fascinating to see how he analyzed Hitler and his relationship with him. Over the years, he came to see the moral responsibility he had to bear for his association with Hitler. He came to realize Hitler's pathology in all its aspects. His book shows the pathology of the prison system and the adverse effect on the guards and administrators of the system. He came to know the pain of having "nervous breakdowns." His insightful, personal confrontations, constructive use of his time through academic pursuits, and how this affected his thinking showed character development. It also appeared that he had development of a deeper relationship with God.

In October and November, I did a rotation in child psychiatry at the Virginia Treatment Center for children. It's very challenging working with children. I had worked with children for years as a physical therapist, but this was so much more challenging.

My first patient was a "battered" four-year old. His father had even tried to kill him. In normal conversation, the child was unable to tell me about this. In fact, he said his dad was okay. However, in fantasy play, it all came out. We have a toy house with toy people in it. Since he liked to draw, I asked him to draw for me. He drew a ghost and told me all about him. The ghost, of course, was the father. Fantasy play is very important in child psychiatry. You learn so much about the home and family interactions just watching the child play with the toy house and toy people and by asking questions about the play. I enjoyed working with the children and teens. I got as much out of the experience as I could get in the two months I was there.

I would have preferred a longer stay there, but the psychiatry department only assigned me there for two months. After I had been there only for a few weeks, Dr. Draper, the director, told me that they would like me do a fellowship in child psychiatry there. It was quite a compliment, since I had only been there for a short time. My other supervisor Dr. Walter Hauser supervised my cases. A child psychiatry consultant would do case evaluations for us every Tuesday morning, a Dr. Lillian L. She had also been trained in pediatrics. I was extremely impressed with these child psychiatrists. They were three of the best teachers I have ever had.

In October, I decided to join MENSA, an international social club. You must have an I.Q. above 135. I decided to take the test and fortunately, I got a score of 137 and joined MENSA.

There are so many things I have been interested in. I have always had a great interest in UFOs. I would very much like to meet superior life forms from another world. *The Interrupted Journey* by John G. Fuller certainly gives one the feeling that UFOs do exist. It was a story of a husband and wife who revealed, under hypnosis, their time of two hours spent in a flying saucer.

I found Erich Von Daniken's *Chariots of the Gods?* as fascinating as the movie. Could it be that God was an astronaut or a superior intelligence from another world?

A view that UFOs may be due to activities of fallen spirits, or another aspect of demonology is presented in a most interesting article entitled: "UFO's: Is Science Fiction Coming True?" in the August 1977 *Spiritual Counterfeits Project Journal*. It was believed that UFOs are the means through which man's concepts are being rearranged.

The Bermuda Triangle raises a lot of interesting questions.

Bizarre phenomena were reported in Charles Fort's *The Book of the Damned*, which is about strange events that supposedly have stumped science.

Scientists are more interested in investigating the claims of the paranormal. A committee of scientists investigating unusual phenomena are publishing their findings in *The Skeptical Inquirer (The Zetetic)*.

From December through March, I rotated in the Psychiatry Consultation-Liaison Service. It had been a very good learning experience, and I had been helping a lot of patients. I was fortunate to be with the Chief of the Consultation-Liaison Service, Dr. Joel S combination internist-psychiatrist. He is now and has been the chairman of psychiatry for years.

This is an ideal situation for other doctors to learn about psychiatry. When I did consultative evaluation on their patients, they had the opportunity to see what psychiatry can do for their patients, and they become, more knowledgeable about psychiatry. After observing the way I interact with patients, they learn to become less anxious in working with patients with "psych" problems. Consultative-Liaison Psychiatry is a great way to teach psychiatry to other medical staff.

It is interesting to observe how the hospital environment is stressful on the patients, the stress of the patient's medical condition, and how one copes with the stress. I have come to learn the role of intrapsychic conflicts in the causation of medical illness. Emotional factors are very powerful in complicating medical disease. I worked with the staff in trying to promote desirable changes in patient care to help them become more "in tune" with the patient's needs.

There are a lot of drug-drug interactions that one needs to be aware of. There are many medical drugs that may cause psychic side effects, such as confusion or psychosis in susceptible patients that we need to be aware of. There are certain drugs that are harmful in certain disease states.

If one had liver disease and a drug that we want to use is metabolized in the liver, then we would probably use a substitute drug that is excreted in the kidney, so that we do not further complicate the patient's illness.

From time to time, I helped the medical staff deal with their unconscious attitudes toward patients, such as their unconscious feelings of inadequacy in dealing with medical patients having "psych" problems.

This service is one of the best ways to help change staff attitudes toward psychiatry. For example, on one ward, it was believed that a patient absolutely needed to be transferred to psychiatry because of his combativeness. But once the patient was adequately medicated with a major tranquilizer, he was able to be maintained on his medical ward, where he could be adequately treated for his severe medical problems. Another responsibility is helping the other doctors recognize emotional problems or "psych" problems in their patients, and this comes about by dealing with their problem cases and going over the case with them. Over a period of time, they have become more comfortable in working with patients, and better able to recognize when patients need to be referred to psychiatry. The challenges are unlimited. I have had a wide variety of interesting patients. For example, I had to help a sixteen-year-old female alcoholic cope with cancer. She had had a "wart" removed from her arm and it turned out to be cancer and she had to have a considerable amount of surgery.

Another young female on the OB service, who had been carrying a dead fetus for a week, had to be helped to realize that her baby was dead. At delivery, she had to be shown her dead baby, so that she would not deny the reality that her baby was dead. And even after, when she did deny that her child was dead, she was helped through the very difficult process of going to the morgue to see her dead baby, to bring home the reality that she could not take the baby home. My patient suffered very greatly; she cried, and I cried with her. I told her I didn't have a "magic pill" to plop in her mouth to make all the hurt go away. I helped her realize the death of her child, accept it, and work through grief. No, psychiatry isn't a "bowl of cherries." It's not sitting around having a gab session. It's walking hand in-hand with the patient down the long road of mental pain and helping one recognize the pain, deal with it, and work through it.

Psychiatry is very hard work. I never come out unscathed. I care about my patients and empathise their pain. With the knowledge of my profession and the help of my God, I help to make them whole again.

A Catholic alumni club developed in Richmond. Since I had been in other Catholic alumni clubs for about thirteen years at that time, I started the ball rolling by being the first to join the new group.

The Bible is the greatest book I have ever read, and yet even I do not understand everything that is contained therein.

Some of the enigmas for me have been humans seeing God face to face. For example, in Genesis 32:30, Jacob reported seeing God face to face; in Exodus 24:11, "…sons of Israel: they gazed on God…" In Exodus 33:11, "Yehweh would speak with Moses face to face, as a man speaks with his friend." In Deuteronomy 34:10, "…Moses, the man Yehweh knew face to face." Now, from this, I would assume that there have been people who have seen God face-to-face and have lived, but in Exodus 33:20, Moses is on the mountain with God, and Moses asked God to show him His glory. God told him that he couldn't see God's face, for man cannot see him and live, and that His face is not to be seen. Now, I have quoted biblical references. It appears that the last quotation is a contradiction to the above quotations.

Biblical Scripture was probably written in the common language of man not in the scientific exactness of science.

For example, it's noted in 1 Kings 7:23, the dimensions of a round vessel made for Solomon's temple do not fit the mathematical formula for determining the circumference of a circle, because no decimal points were used.

In Exodus 20:5, when God gave Moses the first commandment, He told Moses he was not to adore other gods, for He is a jealous God. I found this quite puzzling, for is jealously a trait of God? In 1 Corinthians 13:4, a section on the quality of love, it says that love is never jealous. If God is love, how can He be jealous?

In psychiatry, jealousy is not seen as a healthy attribute. Dr. Harry Stack Sullivan, a great leader in psychiatry, believed that jealousy may be a trait of a person who felt inadequate, or unworthy as reported in his book, *The Interpersonal Theory of Psychiatry*. Even with these enigmas, I still believe as in 2 Timothy 3:16 that all Scripture is inspired by God.

I have followed articles about the Holy Shroud that is in the Turin Cathedral. The Holy Shroud has been studied by scientists.

We now have objective evidence of the extremely horrible way Jesus's body was mutilated in the passion and crucifixion. The reason I believe the Holy Shroud is the Shroud of Christ is because all the articles reported that the image of the victim was produced on the shroud by a burst of radiant energy, and they cannot find a cause for producing it. The explanation is quite simple. When Jesus's radiant spirit went from His dead body, it produced a print on the shroud. So it would appear that the Holy Shroud is probably the one that Jesus had had. I shudder to think of the way Jesus died. He was shown absolutely no mercy at the hands of the Romans.

I thought *The Passion of the Christ* by Mel Gibson was one of the greatest movies I have ever seen. I thought I was going to die in that film. I do not believe I could watch it a second time.

At Christmas, I was fortunate to have gotten a week vacation, and I went back to Pittsburgh to spend Christmas with my family. All of my brothers and sisters were in Pittsburgh this year. Years ago, when some of my brothers and sisters had been in St. Paul's Orphanage, they had been cared for by Sister Brigid, a sister of mercy. I had only seen this nun once, but she had left a very great effect on me, because she was a very saintly person. I had forgotten what she had looked like. Sister Mary Paul had given me her address. I sent her a Christmas card to St. Colman's Convent in Turtle Creek, Pennsylvania. When she sent me a card, her new address was St. Paul's Cathedral Convent in Pittsburgh. I decided I would pay her a visit when in Pittsburgh.

When I had first met "Rose," the woman I love, I had felt that I had known her for a very long time. I didn't know why I felt that way, because I had never seen her before.

Well, it's quite extraordinary, but when I went to visit Sister Brigid, she had been the one to answer the door. When she opened the door and I saw her, I was so shocked. I couldn't speak for a moment. She had the exact face of the woman I love, except her eyes are blue, and "Rose's" eyes are brown. During our visit, I told her about it and showed her a picture of "Rose." She was surprised to see the resemblance but believed "Rose" was much more attractive.

Sister Brigid has an Irish brogue and makes one think of a "good fairy." She is the kind of person that one loves instantly, because she reflects the light of God.

From April through June 1979, I did an elective in forensic psychiatry at the Richmond City Jail and the Virginia State Penitentiary. I performed psychiatric evaluations on prisoners. I treated inmates with psychotropic medicines and psychotherapy. I did emergency evaluations. I participated in administrative and medical meetings at the jail and at the prison. I was also on emergency psychiatric call at the main hospital. After this rotation, I decided I would work in prison psychiatry. Because I had served time as a teenager, I believed I had a great insight into the problems that inmates were faced with.

Psychiatric Practice Years

From July '79 through August '79, I had promised one of my psychiatrist supervisors that I would do vacation coverage for him at the Monroe Center for Mental Health. My first day there was my last day there. I had received a very warm welcome when I arrived there. They even had a pizza lunch for me. The caseworker had placed a huge stack of charts on my desk and a stack of prescriptions that had already been filled out.

She told me I would have an "easy afternoon." I informed her that I did not know if I would be able to see all those patients in the afternoon, but I would attempt to see them.

She informed me that I did not need to see the patients, because the staff were already aware of what the patients needed, and all I had to do was "sign the scripts," and sign the treatment team notes.

I informed her that I had never practiced medicine and psychiatry in such an unethical manner, and I was not about to do it now. I told her I would be very happy to see the patients and render appropriate psychiatric treatment. She was quite upset about what I had said, but she did bring in my first patient.

Even though it's been thirty-three years since I have seen that patient, I still remember her. She was an elderly white female with lifelong Schizophrenia. She appeared sedated and confused. I did a mental status exam on her and found that she was disoriented. I did a skin pinch on her forearm, because she appeared dehydrated. I found she certainly was by the positive test. This patient was supposed to be given 3 ccs of a very powerful neuroleptic (antipsychotic medication) Haldol Decanoate IM.

I informed the case worker that the patient was confused, disoriented, and dehydrated, and needed to be taken to Medical College of Virginia ER, to be admitted to internal medicine for treatment of dehydration.

She informed me that the patient needed her injection and would decompensate without it. I refused to order the injection. I then asked to see the clinic administrator. He was upset with me too, because I would not sign the scripts and treatment team notes without seeing the patients. I informed him the only way I would be willing to work in the clinic was to see the patients and do treatments. He informed me that if I was not going to do it their way, I was free to go. I did leave.

I immediately contacted the Virginia State Medical Board in Richmond, Va., and reported them. They informed me that they would do an immediate investigation of the clinic. When my past supervising psychiatrist returned from vacation, I informed him about the situation. He informed me that the clinic had been warned about their practices before, and now they would probably be shut down.

In October, I was fortunate to have another article published: "Intractable Hiccup (Singultus) : Report of Case."

I spent the rest of the summer and fall traveling around the country being interviewed for psychiatrist positions.

In November 1979, I accepted a full-time position as a prison and forensic psychiatrist for the Ohio Department of Mental Health and Mental Retardation, Division of Forensic Psychiatry. I was assigned to the Ohio Pen (CCF) on Spring St. in Columbus, Ohio.

I was extremely blessed to be with two of the most experienced psychiatrists in the system, Dr. Paul Kirch and Dr. Paul Watkins. Both had also been medical directors in state hospitals and were near retirement. Dr. Kirch was also board certified in administrative psychiatry. Working with them was like being in a combination administrative forensic prison psychiatry fellowship. I was extremely grateful for the daily education I received from them regarding the problems we had to face in the system.

The Ohio Pen was a very old prison. We worked in the Saint James Infirmary. Its walls of stone were about a foot thick. In the winter, one would freeze and in the summer roast.

I performed psychiatric evaluations on inmates and did treatment with psychotropic medications. I did emergency commitment evaluations for the court quite often, for inmates to be sent to the inpatient forensic hospital in Lima Ohio.

Court was held almost daily, and I had to give psychiatric expert testimony on the patient's condition. I also participated in the prison staff meetings, especially with the warden, to keep him informed of our work.

I liked the administrators in the division of forensic psychiatry very much. Since prisoner count was at 11:00 a.m. each day, I would go over to the Ohio State Office Tower for lunch and spend time with the administrators. They would keep me up to date with what going on with the department. They were aware I was planning a prison psychiatry career and knew I wanted to learn all I could from them. They would drive me around to the other prisons when they went on problem-solving trips.

Since I love to teach, I obtained a preceptorship with the Department of Psychiatry, at the Ohio State University School of Medicine and Public Health. Medical students in the Phase 1 Curriculum would rotate with me at the prison to learn about psychiatry.

I also started going to the Marion Correctional Institution in Marion, Ohio, once a week to do psychiatric evaluations and treatment of inmates with psychiatric disorders. The warden there was an ex-football player and a "tough guy." He told me he believed psychiatry was BS but he was required to have me see the inmates there.

I would have lunch there with a very good prison psychologist. He enjoyed consulting with me about the patients.

I had a major encounter the first day I was there. I reviewed all the charts of the inmates I was scheduled to see. I noted that one inmate was on Valium, and I am very conservative when it come to giving patients addicting medications. I had a very busy day and was behind schedule. The infirmary was closing, but I told the administrator that I wanted to stay and see the rest of the inmates that day before I left.

"J" was the last patient on my schedule. He was the patient on Valium. He popped his head in the door and said, "Doc I am not going to waste any of your time, just write me a script." I informed him I needed to meet with him before I would prescribe meds. I met with him for about thirty minutes. He was the size of two Rambos! I informed him that I diagnosed depression and would prescribe an antidepressant for him but not Valium, because I did not believe it was indicated, and it was addicting. He had a meltdown.

"You mean to tell me, you kept me here for all this time, knowing you were not going to prescribe Valium for me?" he yelled. I was certain he was going to clean up the office with me. He stuck his finger in my face and continued yelling at me. He told me I was an incompetent quack. He screamed at me, "Did you read my chart?" I informed him I had.

He then said, "Then you have seen that two other psychiatrists did prescribe Valium for me." I informed him that I did.

"Who do you think you are, trying to override the treatment decisions of two psychiatrists?" he retorted. I told him he did have a valid point, but that I still would not prescribe Valium for him. He informed me that he wanted to be transferred to a prison that had a competent psychiatrist. I informed him I would ask the commissioner about it. I also informed him that I was still willing to treat him, but he didn't want that.

I called and left a message for the commissioner. He got back with me and informed me that "J" would be staying at Marion, and if he wanted treatment, he would need to see me. The next time I was there, "J" informed me that the commissioner had sent him a letter that he would need to see me if he wanted treatment. He said he did not want to see me and expected me to get him some help. I told him I would send a referral to the head psychologist, which I did.

Later, the psychologist called me and informed me she was not going to see him, she said, "He's not interested in treatment." "J" came back to my office the following week and informed me he could not get any help. I told him my door was always open if he changed his mind. I had told him I would be willing to do long-term weekly psychotherapy with him. The commissioner had told me I could do that if the patient decided to see me. After a couple of more weeks, "J" came back and said he decided he would see me on a regular basis.

I started doing in-depth psychotherapy. I came to learn about his severe antisocial personality disorder. He had spent most of his life in California with the Maureder Motorcycle Gang. He had murdered quite a few people and had not been caught regarding those crimes. The worst crimes he shared with me were the rapes he had committed. They were sickening! If a young girl accepted a ride on his motorcycle, that meant he was free to have sex with her according to him. He had absolutely no guilt about his crimes, a true sign of antisocial personality disorder.

I stayed true to what I had learned and been taught. If one does psychotherapy as the "masters" have taught, it is character transforming. I am of the treatment group that knows and believes you can effect character change, but it is very hard work and takes a very long time.

After a long time in psychotherapy, "J" informed me he had been feeling bad about what he had done. Bingo! I felt a very great sense of accomplishment! Even though he might still be capable of hurting other people, he could no longer feel good about it. He had developed a sense of guilt! His character had changed! A primitive superego was developing out of a sense of guilt.

What really blew me away about a year later was when the warden stopped me in the hall as I was going to lunch. He informed me he no longer believed psychiatry was BS, I asked him why. He informed me that before I started doing psychotherapy with "J," that "J" would walk down the middle of the hall, and if anyone got in his way, he would clobber them. He informed me "J" had hurt many correctional officers in the past, and he had to be put in isolation for long periods of time. He informed me that since "J" was in psychotherapy with me, he was no longer doing these things. I informed the warden I was very surprised and pleased to hear about all this and was especially happy that he shared this with me. It showed "J" was making progress in the therapy. I wanted to share this extreme case. It points out that therapy does work, even with the most difficult patients, as long as therapists are willing to take the long hard road with the patient.

When I had begun my position at the Ohio Pen, they were under a federal court order to upgrade their treatment practices. After some months, the prison block upgrades were in place. I noted one of the cellblocks had a sign above it, Ward 1.

Dr. Paul Watkins and I took a walk through it. Paul asked me to see how many ways an inmate could hang himself in this so-called Ward 1. I came up with about twenty-five ways. Paul informed me we were now expected to admit our psychiatric emergencies to Ward 1, instead of transferring the patients to Lima State Hospital. I immediately got a copy of the court's orders and read it.

A few day later at lunchtime, the head nurse, one of the best nurses I have ever had the privilege of working with, informed me that we had a psychiatric emergency, and that I was to admit the patient to Ward 1, since it was now open.

By the way, I have had a lifelong sense of humor.

I asked her, "Will you show me where Ward 1 is?"

She informed me, "You already know where it is, and don't be wasting my time!" She was quite busy at this time.

I insisted, "How can I admit a patient to a ward I am not aware of?"

"Do you mean to tell me I have to take you to Ward 1?" she replied.

"Of course," I responded. Off she went in a "huff," and I followed. When we arrived at Ward 1, she pointed to the sign, Ward 1, and said, "There."

I said, "I am totally confused."

"About what?" she replied. I asked her if she would join me in a stroll through Ward 1, and that might end my "confusion." She complied.

Then I said, "You are a nurse, and I am a doctor, and we both have worked on hospital wards, but to me this looks like a cellblock." I informed her I would admit to a ward but not to a cellblock. She then informed me I was under court orders to admit emergencies to Ward 1.

She asked me to go back to the nursing station, and she would show me the document. I complied. I had already read the court mandate. At the nursing station, she took out the court order and said, "Look, here it says you will admit patients to Ward 1!"

I looked at it and said, "Oh my God!" She asked me what was wrong. I informed her she was absolutely correct and that, "Dr. Scarnati is in contempt of a federal court order!"

She replied, "Does that mean you are refusing to admit patients to Ward 1?"

I replied, "Yep."

She informed me she was going to call Central Office about this. I went to lunch.

After lunch, when I was back at my cellblock office seeing patients, I received a call from Central Office. I was requested to walk over and meet with them, which I did. When I got there, the administrator told me, "You will not believe what happened."

I responded, "Tell me all about it."

"Corrections has gone bonkers, they told us you will not admit patients to Ward 1."

I responded, "Sad to say, but true."

"Dr. Scarnati is in contempt of a federal court order." For the next few hours, the "powers to be" met with me. I would not budge.

In addition to the Osteopathic Oath, because I am a member of the Christian Medical and Dental Society, I am also bound by the Christian Hippocratic Oath:

> With gratitude to God, faith in Christ Jesus, and dependence on the Holy Spirit, I publicly profess my intent to practice medicine for the glory of God.
>
> With humility, I will seek to increase my skills. I will respect those who teach me and who broaden my knowledge. In turn, I will freely impart my knowledge and wisdom to others.
>
> With God's help, I will love those who come to me for healing and comfort. I will honor and care for each patient as a

person made in the image of God, putting aside selfish interests, remaining pure and chaste at all times.

With God's guidance, I will endeavor to be a good steward of my skills and of society's resources. I will convey God's love in my relationships with family, friends, and community. I will aspire to reflect God's mercy in caring for the lonely, the poor, the suffering, and the dying.

With God's direction, I will respect the sanctity of human life. I will care for all my patients, rejecting those interventions that either intentionally destroy or actively end human life, including the unborn, the weak and vulnerable, and the terminally ill.

With God's grace, I will live according to this profession.

Since I am also a psychiatrist and a member of the American Psychiatric Association, I am bound by the AMA *Principles of Medical Ethics* with annotations especially applicable to psychiatry:

The medical profession has long subscribed to a body of ethical statements developed primarily for the benefit of the patient. As a member of this profession, a physician must recognize responsibility to patients first and foremost, as well as to society, to other health professionals, and to self. The principles adopted by the American Medical Association are not laws but standards of conduct that define the essentials of honorable behavior for the physician.

Since I am also a member of the World Psychiatric Association, I am bound by:

Declarations on Ethical Standards

As approved by the General Assembly of the World
Psychiatric Association in Vienna, Austria, on 10th July 1983

Having taken sacred medical oaths, I refuse to do anything that would bring harm to my patient, and by the grace of God would forfeit my life if called to do so, rather than dishonor my oaths.

I expected Central Office to terminate me. Around 4:00 p.m., an administrator returned to the office I was in, and informed me that "Everything has been solved!" I would continue to see my inmate patients as I had been doing. I would no longer be required to do emergency admissions, since my fellow psychiatrists had agreed to do such. I was very upset to hear this. I informed the administrator that I was not going to dump my responsibilities onto my colleagues. She informed me they had agreed, and that had solved the problem. When I got back to the prison, both doctors informed me that they would do the emergency admissions. I informed them I was not happy about it, because I did not want them to do my work. They insisted that would be the way it would be done.

I had become a board member of the American Civil Liberties Union (ACLU) when I came to Columbus, Ohio. I had joined the ACLU in Richmond, Virginia, because one of my supervisors, Dr. Ken Solomon, had encouraged me to do so. Ken was a human rights activist and inspired me to join the groups he was in, especially Amnesty International.

When I attended the ACLU board, we discussed civil liberties violation cases. At one of the board meetings, I mentioned the prison situation involving Ward 1. Lou, an attorney and chief board member, asked me if I wanted them to call for a federal investigation. I said I did. Then he asked me, "How do you like your job?"

I responded, " I don't think I want to lose my job."

Then he said, "End of discussion," and went on with other cases.

Toward the end of the board meeting, I told them I did want them to take my case. Lou informed me, "Your job is gone, and you will be fired!" I informed them I really had no other ethical choice. They voted to take my case.

One day, weeks later, Central Office called us and informed us we would not be seeing patients that afternoon but that the Ohio Assistant Attorney Generals would be meeting with us. They informed us that a federal investigation was in progress, and they wanted us to be prepared for the inquest. I knew immediately that it was my plea to the ACLU.

Three state attorneys came over and met with us individually. The young attorney who was with me went over how he wanted me to answer to the feds. It was one of the saddest days of my life. I couldn't believe what I was experiencing. We are the greatest nation on the earth, and yet instead of one standing up for good patient care, as we should be doing, they were doing the opposite.

A few weeks later, I was called to come to Central Office. The feds were in a hearing room. I went in to be questioned about the care of the inmates. The young state attorney, who had proctored me, was sitting across from me. The federal attorney asked me if I was there to give factual information on the inadequate care of the inmates. I answered to the affirmative. I stated giving all facts about the inadequate care. My proctor state attorney, at that point, got up and left the room. I thought to myself, *There goes my job.*

Afterward, I walked back to the prison. Drs Watkins and Kirch informed me that Central Office had a meltdown and was going to fire me. I continued to work, expecting each day that I might be terminated.

On October 21, 1980, I was "commanded" to appear in the United States District Court, For The Southern District of Ohio, Eastern Division, to testify on behalf of the plaintiffs in *Stewart v. Rhodes* (12–5-80) No. C-2–78–220, unreported. I gave factual testimony regarding the inadequate psychiatric and medical care of inmates with psychiatric disorders. Afterwards, I continued to work at the prison.

On my fortieth birthday, I found a very large envelope in my mailbox. It was from U.S. Attorney Stephen A. Whinston, Special Litigation Section, Department of Justice, Washington, DC. It was the *United States' Proposed Findings of Fact, Conclusions of Law, Relief, And Memorandum In Support*. After I read the document, I was crying. It was one of the most wonderful birthday presents I ever received. God had given me a great gift, because I had stood up for proper care of my patients.

The major points were:

> Patients designated as emergency referrals have waited several days before being seen by a psychiatrist.
>
> Emergency referral procedure involving the Central Ohio Psychiatric Hospital have never been utilized, although circumstances indicate it should have been.
>
> Multiple problems were found in scheduling of patients.
>
> Inmates were not receiving medications prescribed for them
>
> The effects of the reduced psychiatric staffing have been felt by all the psychiatrists.
>
> Under current staffing patients are not seen as frequently as they should be.
>
> Other activities by the psychiatrists, such as group therapy, have been eliminated due to the press of caseload.
>
> Current staffing has resulted in the psychiatrists being "stressed" and "overworked."
>
> Psychiatric staffing, in terms of the actual number now working at CCF (OHIO PEN), is inadequate.
>
> Everyone who testified agreed that ward 1 is inadequate as a long term inpatient housing unit.
>
> Solely from a physical architectural standpoint,

ward 1 is not an adequate facility for mentally ill inmates.

The design of the cells in Ward 1 allow the occupants access to bars which could facilitate suicide attempts.

Current staffing provisions for ward 1 are not adequate.

Due to these deficiencies, one of the psychiatrists at CCF (Dr. Scarnati) refuses to order that patients be admitted to ward 1.

This type of confinement adds stress, increases feelings of dissociation, adds to depression, and can produce breakdowns.

Defendants (State of Ohio) have failed to provide adequate mental health staff at CCF (OHIO PEN).

Both Dr. Scarnati and Dr. Leitman testified to the debilitating effects of C-D Block on psychiatric patients.

Dr. Scarnati cited the quality and quantity of staff, the steel bunks, the blind spots, and the bathroom pipes.

Current psychiatric staffing is inadequate.

One of defendants' efforts at trial was to challenge the credibility of Dr. Scarnati. We have found that employees willing to testify about institutional deficiencies have been rare and Dr. Scarnati should be commended for his candor and dedication to meeting the needs of his patients.

Dr. Scarnati offered factual testimony with regard

to referral and scheduling difficulties, medication procedures, and housing conditions. He offered opinion testimony regarding housing conditions in C-D block and Ward 1 staffing, and supervision of Ward 1. In each instance his testimony was corroborated, and in some cases expanded upon, by the other CCF psychiatrists and/or by DFP reports. Dr. Scarnati's testimony should be fully credited by this court.

The violations are clear and undisputed.

Further relief is required to assure full compliance.

It was a blessing that I had not been fired.

In the spring of '81, I decided I was going to go back to Virginia.

I resigned from the Ohio Department of Mental Health. I was pleasantly surprised when the administration attempted to talk me into staying with them. I was grateful for their response, but I wanted a change. Since I like the ocean, I obtained a position near Virginia Beach.

In April 1981, I accepted a position as an inpatient staff psychiatrist at the Hampton Virginia Veterans Administration Medical Center. I was blessed to work with two great psychiatrists and a psychologist, who are my lifelong friends; Dr. Gobi P, from India, and Dr. Tom F from Sira Lanka. Eve, a psychologist, made up the better part of us "Four Musketeers," as we were referred to in a humorous way by the VA. We spent a lot of time together and were great friends. We worked up all the admissions to our ward and did emergency call as needed.

We were also on the faculty for the Department of Psychiatry and Behavioral Science, Eastern Virginia Medical School. We supervised and taught medical students, interns, and residents who did their psychiatry rotation at our VA hospital. I attended the faculty meetings at the medical school.

Since both Tom and Gobi were board certified psychiatrists and I was studying for boards, they helped me immensely for my board patient interview. Thanks to them, I became certified in psychiatry in June 1981 by the American Board of Psychiatry and Neurology.

I spent a lot of time in Virginia Beach during my employment at the VA hospital.

I had a major situation one day when I was on emergency call. I received a call from a swat team in Virginia Beach. They informed me that one of our veteran psychiatric patients was holding people in an apartment complex and was threatening to kill everybody if he wasn't given drugs. They gave me his name, which at first I did not remember that I had seen him in the VA.

They requested that I come and attempt to talk to the patient. I informed them I would do so for them. I then remembered who the patient was. I had seen him in intake. He was demanding to be put on Valium, along with other addicting medications. I informed him I would treat him with appropriate medicine for his condition but refused to prescribe addicting medicines for him, especially since he had a long history of drug dependence. The patient had been very angry at me for not prescribing Valium. He went to another doctor.

Since I thought he might shoot me, I called the VA hospital and informed them I was going to help a swat team and if I got shot, they would need to call in one of the other psychiatrists for call. Well, the VA operator called the chief of staff, Dr. D. As I was getting to leave the apartment, I received a call from him. He told me as a VA doctor, I was absolutely forbidden to get involved with the case, and I was to let the police handle the situation as best they could. He ordered me to stay at home. I was now in a "catch 22." Since I had promised the swat team help, I felt I was obligated to do that. I did not want the patient to shoot anyone, either. I drove down to the swat team trailer and joined them. It was like being back in the military. They had a map set up, and we worked on a plan of what we would be doing.

A short time later, a car pulled up to the trailer; it was Dr. D. He introduced himself to the police and told them he did not want me getting shot. We did develop a plan that was successful. One of the police acted as a "drug dealer," and he was successful in getting the veteran out of the apartment complex.

In the spring of 1982, I looked into the possibility of setting up a Department of Psychiatry and being Chairman of Psychiatry, for Ohio University's College of Osteopathic Medicine in Athens, Ohio. I had had excellent interchanges with the dean and academic department chairs. My goal was to bring my other colleagues with me, to help develop the department. The medical school seemed very interested.

In April 1982, I resigned my position at the VA hospital, because I was certain I would take the offered position at Ohio University.

I took time off for a good vacation.

When I went to OU, I was very disheartened to learn that the dean was going to accept me but not my colleagues. I informed him I was not a department by myself, and minimally would need at least two other psychiatrists to develop a department of psychiatry. His response was that they would hire me, and if things went "well," they might hire others. Since I knew I could not be an adequate department by myself, I did not accept the position. It was quite a disappointment for me, because I did very much want to develop a Department of Psychiatry for OU.

Since I was now out of work, I started to apply for psychiatry positions.

I accepted a full-time position with the Lebanon, Pa., Veterans Administration Medical Center for a full-time assignment at their VA clinic in the Federal Building in Harrisburg, Pa.

I was quite concerned about the inappropriate care the veterans had been receiving. A large number of the veterans were on addicting medications. After they started complaining to me about my titrating them off such inappropriate addicting medications, I called the chief of staff to inform him of the problems. He informed me they had had a GP doing the care before, and now that they had a psychiatrist (me), he expected the veterans to receive the proper care they required.

At the clinic, I performed outpatient psychiatry, did psychiatric compensation examinations, and provided psychiatric consultation to the psychologist, social worker, and other professional staff. I consulted with the FBI on a staff member problem they were having. I participated in staff teaching programs. I prepared quality assurance reports. Since the VA Hospital had a union, I was expected to be a member of the union too and did join.

In the spring of 1983, the main hospital hired a chief of psychiatry.

I was given an unsatisfactory rating from this doctor, because I would not keep the patients on addicting drugs. As one might imagine, I was highly angered by such rating, because I believed I was giving very good care to my patients.

They had a VA so-called, Professional Standards Board meet with me over a period of several months. The board consisted of chiefs of service, which included a radiologist, an internist, and a surgeon. I did not believe they were competent to evaluate the practice of a psychiatrist. I requested that I and my practice of psychiatry be evaluated by the Psychiatric Experts at the Institute Of Medicine in Washington, DC, but the VA would not permit this.

I believed the best way to deal with this untenable position was to educate the three chiefs about proper psychiatric care. Each time I would meet with them, I brought a number of psychiatric publications to the meeting that supported the type of care I was giving my patients.

Around September of 1983, the board had a final meeting with me. They said, "Dr. Scarnati we do not want to hear about the articles you brought in for us today. We are going to put all the cards on the table for you today. We believe you are a good doctor; however, the problem is this: you are not in private practice. You are working for the VA. You have supervisors, and you are expected to follow their directives!" I informed the group that at no time in my medical and psychiatric career, was I going to permit anyone to direct how I was going to treat my patients. I informed them that my standard of care was to substitute my family member in the place of my patient, and if I was not willing to give that care to my family member, I certainly was not going to give it to the patient. I have used this standard all of my medical career. I informed them that I had absolutely no problem in following the directives of supervisors, if it meant better care for my patients, than what I was giving them. I have always taken into account treatment recommendations made by my supervisors. However, at no time, will I ever give patients improper care.

I informed the board that the Nazi doctors at Neuenburg had attempted to slide away from responsibility for their monstrous practices, by informing the court that "They were only following the directives of their supervisors." As we all know, the court did not buy that crap.

The doctors then informed me that I would be fired. At the time, I did not believe that that was going to happen. On October 4, 1984, I received a letter from the VA Medical Center Director that I was to be separated during probationary period on October 13, 1983. The VA probationary period for the VA is two years, and during one's probationary period, one can be terminated without cause. I planned to take legal action against the VA.

I started studying law, because I was going to represent myself. I also applied for unemployment compensation. I did that for two reasons: I could use the money, and I wanted to use the case in the court as a precedent, if I was found eligible to receive benefits. Normally, you cannot receive benefits if you have been terminated.

My union, Local #1966 of the AFL-CIO, had filed a grievance for me regarding my termination.

At first, the State Office of Employment Security rated me ineligible for benefits, because I had been terminated. I appealed their decision. Later at one of the official hearings on November 23, 1983, the VA Chief of Staff did acknowledge that patients had been on narcotics and stimulants. He informed them I was terminated for insubordination.

At the end of November 1983, I received a referee's decision from the Pennsylvania Unemployment Compensation Board Of Review.

Findings Of Fact:

The claimant (Dr. Rick Scarnati) was not insubordinate to his supervisors.

The claimant, during his tenure of employment with this employer, performed his duties to the best of his capabilities and did not willfully or deliberately violate the employer's policies.

Reasoning:

Although an employer may discharge an employee for any reason whatsoever, to deny him unemployment compensation, there must be willful misconduct on the part of the employee. The burden of proving willful misconduct is upon the employer. While willful misconduct has not been statutorily defined, its meaning has been judicially developed to encompass the wanton, and willful disregard of an employer's interest, a deliberate violation of rules, a disregard of expected behavior standards, or negligence manifesting culpability, wrongful intent, evil design or intentional and substantial disregard of the employer's interests or the employee's duties and obligations.

Based on the record, the Referee concludes that the claimant's conduct does not amount to a conscious indifference to the duty owed his employer. There was no detrimental disregard of the employer's interests which was substantially inimical to those interests.

Order:

The determination of the Office of Employment Security is Reversed (in Dr. Scarnati's favor).

Claim credit for waiting week ending October 22, 1983 is Granted. [I did receive unemployment compensation.]

Before I had left the VA, I had contacted the Drug Enforcement Administration (DEA) in Philadelphia and reported the VA Clinic practice of prescribing inappropriate, addicting medications to veterans. DEA Agent Tom C informed me that was a felony. I requested an immediate investigation by the DEA.

On November 29, Agent C got back with me. He informed me he was aware of the "prescription drugs on the street." Sadly for me, he informed me he expected the VA to investigate this. I knew the VA was not going to do that.

On December 1, 1983, I contacted the PA Attorney General's Office of Narcotics Investigation and Drug Control, and complained to J. J. B. about the VA clinic. He informed me that I had raised some "valid issues," and he would call for an investigation. On December 5, I met with Criminal Investigator J E. H for two and a half hours about the drug problems at the VA.

On December 6, J. J. B. sent a letter to Mr. T C, Philadelphia DEA, "Since he (Dr. Scarnati) has now brought this complaint to our Agency and there appears to be some merit to his allegations on the surface, but it is within Federal Jurisdiction, I felt duty bound to officially relay his complaint to you for Federal Investigation."

I had also contacted Mr. Charles E. J, Jr., National Director of Services of the Disabled American Veterans, about the inappropriate care of veterans. On December 8, 1983, he sent a letter to the Chief Medical Director, VA Central Office in Washington, DC, requesting an investigation of my complaint.

Since I had complained to Congressman William J. Coyne about the VA Clinic, he was kind enough to call for an investigation. The Chief Medical Director, VA Central Office sent Congressman Coyne a response on January 13, 1984, informing him that, "A team of clinicians appointed by VA Central Office will conduct a site visit in January 1994, to evaluate the situation presented by Dr. Scarnati."

On January 19, 1984, *The Evening News*, page B3, Harrisburg, PA, published an article about me, "Doctor Challenges VA center dismissal," my filing a lawsuit in federal court against the VA was mentioned, along with my complaint about inappropriate treatment of veterans, and that the VA Professional Standards Board was not presented with documents favorable to my case.

Investigative Reporter Jerry Dubs from *The Patriot* in Harrisburg, Pa., had contacted me about the VA Clinic problems, and I spoke with him for several hours about the problems.

Since I had complained to the Joint Commission on Accreditation of Hospitals (JCAH), the President informed me on February 7, 1984, that they had "communicated with the hospital regarding your(my) concerns," and "will continue to review this matter."

I had met with syndicated columnist Jack Anderson's group in Washington, D.C., regarding problems with the VA. He did a commentary on March 12, 1984, which was published in the nations newspapers. On page A7 of *The Patriot*, Harrisburg, Pa., it was published as follows:

CITIZENS WATCH:

Dr. Richard Scarnati is another whistle blower who found out the hard way what happens when you challenge the bureaucratic routine. He was fired from the outpatient clinic of the Veterans Administration medical facility in Lebanon, Pa., at the end of his one-year trial period last October.

The 43-year old Scarnati, a psychiatrist who joined the Lebanon staff with high recommendations from a previous governmental job, found that patients with psychiatric disorders were being treated with Darvon, a narcotic painkiller; Ritalin, a stimulant; as well as a variety of tranquilizers. In his professional opinion, this was inappropriate medication-and he said so to his superiors.

Scarnati's firing is the subject of an arbitration proceeding. But that's not why he contacted me; he wants to prod the Veterans Administration to do a through investigation of his charges of patient mistreatment.

Last December, state narcotics agents interviewed Scarnati and concluded that "there appears to be some merit to his allegations on the surface." They referred the charges to the Drug Enforcement Administration.

The Veterans Administration assured DEA in December that a medical team would be assigned to look into the charges. But more than six weeks later, Leonard Washington, director of the Lebanon facility, told my reporters that no team had visited yet.

A VA spokesman said a psychiatric expert would visit Lebanon "soon" and report back within three or four weeks.

Reprinted with the permission of The Patriot-News. © 1984. All rights reserved.

The ACLU was so kind to file a suit for me against the VA, under their section: Rights of Government Employees, Scarnati v US in Federal District Court for my refusing to administer certain drugs: United States District Court Middle District of Pennsylvania, Civil Action—Law, No. CV-84–0078, on January 18, 1984.

During the Spring of 1983, my article was published,

The discovery of hell by a prison psychiatrist: a tragic satire on the prison system

The following satire reflects the horrors of the prison system through a conversation between the author and his conscience (Virgil). Some of the moral, ethical, and social issues regarding the prison system are examined. It is evident that the system is in great need of a safer environment for its inhabitants. The author feels that the present system is outmoded and should be disbanded in favor of a more humane one.

One day during lunch break, while I was pondering on the problems in the prison system and feeling quite discouraged, one of the "prison pets," a mouse, darted into the office and jumped on the desk right in front of me. Suddenly, poof! It was as if the mouse had exploded and changed into a most novel creature. Before me was a very large, colorful mouse that appeared to have some of the characteristics of Mickey Mouse and a few features of Pinocchio. He had a long nose, a Peter Pan green hat with a red feather in it, a purple sport shirt, red corduroy mountain-climbing shorts with black suspenders. And he wore black clodhoppers. He did not have a long tail like a mouse, but it appeared to have been frazzled and resembled a bunny's tail.

Suddenly, it occurred to me that I was having a hallucination. I shook my head and rubbed my eyes and blurted out in astonishment, "Oh my God, it can't be! I've only been here a short time with all my plans of doing great things and already I'm burnt out!" To this, he replied: "Get hold of yourself, Doctor. Have no fear, I am the real thing. My name is Virgil and I have been sent here to keep you company so you won't get burnt out." Since then, we have carried on a constant dialogue.

Virgil: Where do you think you are? *Doctor:* In prison, of course!

Virgil: Doctor, if you ponder for a moment you will realize that this is hell.

Doctor: Well, I have thought about it as being hell in the metaphorical sense. I had been in two reform schools and I thought I knew what a prison was like, but I must admit I have never experienced anything as terrible as these dungeons. [These dungeons do bring to mind Dante's *Inferno* and I realized that Virgil was right—this was hell.]

Virgil: "Eternal" hell is really a fun place. It's a series of fantasies like "Fantasy Island" on TV, except that your host is Big Red—the one they call the devil—and you never have to leave. In fact, we love you so much that under our bylaws you are enjoined to stay with us forever. It's so wonderful to live out your fantasy forever.

Doctor: Why do you have a long nose?

Virgil: Like Pinocchio, as one lies, one's nose grows. Except for Big Red—he just becomes more deceiving.

Doctor: What happened to your tail?

Virgil: Big Red frazzled it when I pulled a fast one on him. He's got quite a temper!

Doctor: I always thought hell was a very hot place.

Virgil: Your idea of hell is really whimsical! You aren't going to catch me in the center of the earth in hot beds of coals! The only time you'll see the heat that you associate with hell is when these oddballs start firing missiles at each other. It may seem strange, but the master is really not impressed; he feels it will be an instant fry. He would prefer to see slow, unending burning—like the burning anguish of these scapegoats of social problems.

Doctor: These dungeons certainly are hell. One of the worst things I've ever witnessed was the Prison Industry inside the Atlanta Federal Pen. It is a very large factory with automated cotton looms. The working parts are all metal and what a tremendous noise they make when the parts come together. I could see all the forlorn, apathetic, hopeless faces, mostly black.

I asked how the inmates were able to stand such extremely loud noise and I was told they put cotton in their ears. You know, Virgil, at the end of my 15-minute tour my whole body was tense and I was shaking all over. I must say I don't believe I would have been able to last there for even an hour. I understand the inmate murder rate is quite high at Atlanta.

Virgil: Prison Industry—what a marvelous work of deception! Big Red didn't achieve the title "The Father of Lies" for nothing. It takes years for great achievements. What a grand producer he is! What plays! What grand performances!

We had watched your development with such astonishment at your accomplishments, and I must confess we had almost truly believed that you had followed in the Shepherd's footsteps. The master had been so quiet, but we knew something was brewing because of that smirk of his, his "cat that swallowed the canary" look. On the day you visited our cotton plantation at the Atlanta Pen and saw all our slaves, we knew you were ours. Oh, how the master roared! What fry! Cotton in the ears. Ho! Ho!

Clide the bat was astounded by your response; he knew you had read Mahatma Gandhi's works and had expected that you would begin a death fast to protest the inhumane conditions at the Atlanta Federal Pen. Merving, a toad, knew best, though. He blurted out "Death fast? Fat chance! He's a connoisseur of fine food and wine!"

We were offering you a toast with our finest wine when a faint whisper was heard. "Spiritual dunce!" A profound hush ensued. All eyes turned toward Salome, an extremely charming, delightful she-goat who loves to dance. She blushed so delicately. Giggling followed. I, of course, came to your defense. "Salome, how rude of you! An apology to the congregation is in order!" Then, Salome did such a lovely thing. She proclaimed to all that you would be her paramour forevermore! What "Oh's!" and "Ah's!" Such romance!

You must know you are dearly loved by all. What a bash was held in your honor! The master opened the prize trunk for you. So many treasures! You were awarded a golden key and the most glorious title, "Keeper of Hell." We also announced the creation of a new subspecialty of psychiatry—*hell psychiatry*—and since we know how much you love awards, we made you the Eternal Chairman of Hell Psychiatry. You are our hero. Your praises will be sung forever!

Doctor: Virgil, I am overwhelmed. I don't know what to say!

Virgil: Doctor, your hard work deserves to be noticed. You are in the most challenging of all professions. Prison is worse than a battlefield because, in battles, there are periodic let-ups; not so here.

Doctor: Virgil, it is so incredible to think I am attempting to help people adjust and adapt to hell. Are the patients I help to adapt truly the abnormal ones and the patients who cannot respond to treatment still normal? Should I be snowing everyone with Valium?

It's like a nightmare walking through the visiting area each day, seeing all the apathy and suffering in the faces of the inmates' families. What have they done? Why are they being punished too? It is almost too frightful to ponder these issues. To survive and not become burnt out, one must become blind to all this; one must reach ultimate repression. By doing this, have I become an automaton, a robot that comes and goes and spurts out psychotherapeutic jargon? Am I still a doctor or have I achieved devilhood? Am I one of the "keepers of hell"? Will I turn red and grow horns?

Virgil: Hell has come into existence because of a totally unresponsive, uncaring community. Hell is maintained by decreased taxation, rock-bottom funding, and "out-of-sight, out-of-mind" community responsiveness.

Doctor: When I had just come into the prison system, I was under the delusion that for the most part I did crisis intervention. But in crisis intervention, a patient usually is sent back to a supportive environment. This is not the case in prison.

Does "burn-out" mean that a therapist at that point experiences the release of unconscious, repressed realities of hell, therefore breaking down or returning to humaneness and becoming unfit to continue as one of the "keepers of hell"?

It appears that the "key" of the keeper is total repression of the reality of hell, in order to continue functioning in such a hellish environment.

Virgil: Most of the victims of hell have actually come from hellish environments. They are minorities, drug addicts, alcoholics, the uneducated, and the poor. Therefore, they have had a very early acquaintance to the hellish life of which they are now a part.

Doctor: There are many inmates who demand Valium for their "nerves." As one might expect, hell is quite nerve-racking.

Virgil: It would take a ton of Valium a day to calm their nerves.

Doctor: The inmate is expected to adapt to such impossible situations as rape, providing fingers or toes for the "prison pets," and experiencing an assault while in slumber. Even sleep is a very restless, hellish experience. At times, all this inner heat and turmoil explode into prison riots. Hellish conditions are commonplace. Once, at the Virginia State Pen, maggots were found feeding on one of the inmates.

Virgil: One of our favorite games is "Corrections Versus Mental Health." It keeps the true responsibility off the community. We love sport. The Bible admonishes one to visit the prisons. But you know as well as I do that the only involvement of the community is the "boob tube." They have brains of mush, the vomit the Lord speaks of.

The tube is very highly extolled by the master, for it is a very remarkable spiritual thermometer. One can watch murder; these morons could see the Cambodian refugees and you know what the response has been. No one is emptying out the neighborhood supermarkets to send the food to those poor starving victims. The tube truly is the "idiot box," for with it we have been able to achieve frontal lobotomy without neurosurgery—which, as a physician, you can truly appreciate. The frontal association areas of the brain have turned to mush, and our community has become a moronic group of puppets!

Doctor: Virgil, it appears that a new diagnostic syndrome has evolved out of television—the Mush-Brain Syndrome.

Virgil: In our inner chambers, we have TV World, where one may watch TV all day, every day, forever. It is our most popular and most sought-after treasure. We have a very long waiting list to get in. Since TV hasn't been around for too long, we have to wait for the celebrities to pass through our gates, so we can set up the stage for them. Just think what a joy it is to watch the Muppets all day, every day, forever!

Doctor: I don't like the Muppets.

Virgil: But you do love Charley's Angels, and I know you would love to watch them forever. Don't worry, we make quite sure that everyone is happy!

Doctor: I was sorry to see Shelley Hack get fired; she was my favorite angel.

Virgil: It is most wonderful to find the master in one of his scheming moods. He is as quiet as a dewdrop on a gopher's nose. Those are his only moments of silence.

Doctor: Tell me of one of his great accomplishments.

Virgil: He has so many! As a forensic psychiatrist, I know that you would like to know that Big Red's son is also a forensic psychiatrist. He is the director of one of Satan's most creative enterprises—the infamous Serbsky Institute of Forensic Psychiatry in Moscow. The director, as a true son, has followed in his father's footsteps. He is the ultimate court jester. He is the prostitute of forensic psychiatry. For him, all is fun and games and a masquerade of mockery, for he has the pleasure of dubbing human rights' activists and political prisoners as "insane" and whisking them off for "treatment." As you know, the special psychiatric hospitals such as Serbsky in the USSR have expanded diagnosis to such a degree that all may be labeled "insane." Oh, how grand! Everyone is made ready to partake of the institutes' festivities. And to make matters even more grand, the psychiatrists are high-ranking KGB officers. Such military pomp! The doctors are also directors of professional psychiatry groups in the USSR, adding further mockery to the psychiatric profession.

What makes Big Red scream with fits of delight is that the special psychiatric hospitals are the ultimate torture chambers. Medicines that have helped so many distressed psychiatric patients and have allowed them to regain functional lives are given at such extreme doses to these normal victims that terrible side effects develop—like excruciating muscle spasms. Some patients are "frozen" stiff because their muscles become so tight and rigid. Some develop such restlessness that sleep and rest are impossible to obtain. The effects have been so extreme that some unfortunate victims have killed themselves.

As you know, medicine is probably the most highly respected of all professions and there is nothing that Big Red loves more than to turn it into a grand farce. Doctor, all of your efforts in Amnesty International against the abuses of psychiatry in the Soviet Union are for naught. You can rest assured that Big Red sees to it that no harm comes to his most beloved son.

Doctor: I am afraid that you are right. There is only a small handful of psychiatrists in this country who are willing to take a strong stand toward human rights.

Virgil: As you know, law is also one of the most esteemed professions. We have an extreme love of the law. It is the highest standard of our home; law is inherent in everything we do and we have a law for everything! We have the best legal library in creation—it's a Harvard law student's dream come true. In our home, we have the finest legal minds of all time. Our whole society is law. We want law-abiding citizens.

At the judgments of lawyers and judges, we have the best defense attorneys. The Lord always loses his case. What a dud! All He talks about is love and mercy, which, as you know, have absolutely no place in our legal system. Do you know the best defense we have? It absolutely guarantees our client his rightful place among our legal guild. We play the tapes of the prison visiting room and, when the Destroyer Angel sees the hopeless, pitiful looks of the prisoners' spouses and children, he realizes that the lawyers and judges have always truly been a part of the legal system that gives absolutely no consideration to these wretched victims.

We demand that the legal standard be upheld. We certainly do not want a chaotic society; our law-abiding citizens would never stand for such a thing. Do you know how the Lord feels about the law? He had the audacity to say that He had overridden the law by nailing it to the tree. Since the legal standard is not a standard of heaven, our claim on our clients is rightfully acknowledged as our legal right. And, as you will agree, all our judges and lawyers desire only that the highest legal standard be used in their behalf, and we will defend their legal rights to the utmost!

Big Red has such a fatherly attitude toward his young lawyers. He says they do their utmost in their law practice to mirror his image as "The Father of Lies." For right or wrong, a lawyer will defend a client who he knows is guilty of a crime. This may seem a real travesty of justice, but it is the ultimate proof that he does adhere to the legal standard of our community. Lawyers are also masters of deception. Our legal guild has an eternity of advancement: one studies and creates law forever. We have myriad titles one may achieve in law.

The House of Judges is one of the absolute wonders of our society. When a judge passes through our gates, special ceremonies are held in his honor. Our highest judge, His Most Exalted, Glorified Honor, is dressed in robes of gold. There is a great deal of ceremony in opening court and it takes many days before the main court session actually begins. All honor is given to His Honor.

Doctor: It does appear that the law has reached its highest stage in your land.

Virgil: We love legal jargon and, using legal jargon, the prison proves "beyond a reasonable doubt" that the community has always been ours. We also love Bible verse. As you will recall, Big Red quoted scripture to the Lord during his 40-day fast. Such a marvelous spoof! No one knows scripture better than Big Red. Our Bible class is overwhelmed at his prodigious ability to quote verse. He always quotes verse at the judgments. For example, you have heard the verse, "As you live, so shall you die"? His favorite quote to the lawyers is "You have lived by the law and you will die by the law." We are always adding new verses to our Bible; it is the largest in creation. There is nothing in our society as lovely as that "old-time religion." [Virgil broke out in joyous song, "Gimmie That Old-Time Religion," and I joined in.]

The master is always giving out degrees and honors and the students are overjoyed. We hold claim to the highest number of Bible scholars. Since you've read the Bible from cover to cover four times, we know how much you would love to be part of our Bible class. We are reserving a very special place just for you.

Doctor: You are quite right—I do enjoy reading scripture. Unfortunately, I don't have as much time to read scripture as I used to. There's a lot I'm trying to accomplish before the ACLU has the Ohio Pen closed.

Virgil: Doctor, do you really believe that our community would stand for a pen to be closed? I can promise you that on the day such a thing would happen—which it never will, by the way—the governor would be lynched!

Doctor: I really believe that the future holds great promise.

Virgil: You better believe it! The future is ours! Big Red is so fond of his children. During the Cincinnati Riverfront Coliseum rock concert stampede, he was bursting with fatherly pride. He was so overjoyed that he was speechless. Our youth will do such beautiful things!

Doctor: Virgil, I really enjoyed our conversation, but I'm afraid it's time to go home.

Virgil: Hey, Doctor! Don't forget to bring in a piece of provolone tomorrow. This prison slop will be the death of me yet.

Doctor: See you tomorrow.

Virgil: Be cool.

Two more of my articles were published:

  1 ..."Medication and Psychotherapy",
  2 ..."DMS-III and DMS-III-R: Critical Analysis of Axis IV: Severity of Psychosocial Stressors,"

Law enforcement had been using stun guns for some time, when I received a request from a Consultant to the Coalition of Citizens with Disabilities, Harrisburg, Pennsylvania, to study the issues involved in the use of the stun gun. That consultant was also the President of the Harrisburg, Pennsylvania Chapter of the ACLU. It was believed that Civil Liberties could become an issue in the use of the stun gun. My commentary was published:

"Provocative Concerns Regarding the Use of a Stun Gun" :

The stun gun has been described as a Flash Gordon weapon. One such weapon is the taser, developed by a space-technology engineer with the Federal Aerospace Program The taser is described as a squared-off flashlight-like device costing about $200. The top part of the gun is a flashlight, below which are two pluglike cassettes. Inside each cassette is a dart attached to 15 feet of coiled tine wire for easy release. There are triggers that when pulled turn on the flashlight and set off gunpowder changes that fire the darts and release electric current The taser weighs a little over one pound and is nine inches long. Its power is generated by batteries whose output is usually 8 watts and 7.5 volts Within the taser a powerful transformer generates 50.000 volts when a trigger is pressed. This volt of electricity passes through the wires into the darts which have been shot into the skin or clothing of the victim and "zap" the body. The victim is immobilized and may feel pain. Repeated electrical shocks can be given by pressing the trigger of the stun gun.[1]

For patients with medical and/or psychiatric problems, the stun gun might pose very serious complications and might even result in death.

If the gun was not aimed properly, a dart might strike a victim's eye and cause damage and possible loss of sight

There is great potential for serious harm in patients with cardiac conditions. In a damaged heart from myocardial infarction, the effect of sympathetic nervous stimulation, secondary to the pain of the shock from the stun gun, may not be compensated for by an already damaged heart and prove fatal for the victim by cardiac arrest. Physiologically, it is known that we can effect the heart with electricity. In electrical defibrillation of the heart, usually 440 volts of 60 cycle alternating current or several thousand volts direct current may be required.[2] One does not need to be a physician to realize the great effect a stun gun's 50,000 volt charge could have on the heart.

A number of patients with cardiac conditions have abnormal cardiac rhythms resulting from block in normal impulse conduction within the heart. These patients can be helped with an artificial pacemaker, which is a small battery-operated electrical stimulator planted beneath the skin, the electrodes from which are connected to the heart. The pacemaker then provides continued rhythmic impulses that take over control of the heart.[3] Most likely, the stun gun's powerful charge of 50,000 volts could easily override the pacemaker, resulting in cardiac arrest.

Neurologically, it is known that electricity is a form of energy that is capable of damaging living tissue. The brain, spinal cord, and peripheral nerves may be injured if they happen to lie within the path taken by the current.[4] Because of ethical consideration's, objective research on humans using multiple "zaps" with the stun gun would not be recommended, For patients with seizure (convulsive) disorders or epilepsy, it is known that some individuals may inherit a convulsive tendency. Some seizures may occur following physical stimulation, and in others emotional disturbances may play a significant "trigger" role.[5] It is assumed that the stun gun effects of physical (shock) stimulation and emotional disturbance (fright) could induce seizures in susceptible individuals. The fall itself from the shock of the stun gun could result in head injury that could also result m seizures.

This author is not aware of any studies of the use of the stun gun in children and does not see the desirability of such studies

The use of the stun gun in patients with psychiatric disorders could lead to some morbidity. The patient might feel that he was receiving electroconvulsive therapy against his will. A patient with a paranoid disorder could become terrified at having been immobilized by a "ray gun." A Post-traumatic Stress Disorder could conceivably result from the use of the stun gun.

The literature shows the favorable and unfavorable aspects of the use of the stun gun. A weapon that can be used to protect against crimes can also be used to commit them. In Miami, a woman held up a gas station with a taser, and got away with cash.[6] In New York City, five officers were charged with torturing suspects with stun guns.[7] Stun guns could also be used in muggings and rapes.[8]

Also of concern is the fact that in the hands of criminals it can cause death by indirect means in such a way that it would be extremely difficult for a coroner to determine the actual cause of death.[9]

We are all very much aware of the existence of violence in everyday life. This author, a Prison Psychiatrist who works on a special unit of "so-called" problem prisoners which some have dubbed "the worst of the worst," sees the depth of their hurt. Most of these patients have tragic life histories, rejecting parents, broken homes, and non-supportive social environments. This psychiatrist believes that their potential for violence can only be eliminated by a supportive, empathic, and caring therapeutic environment, this also extends to the world at large.

This psychiatrist does not believe that the control of violence can be accomplished through technology, either by "zapping" a person or by "zapping" a nation by the pull of a trigger or the push or a button The ultimate control of violence on our earth can only come about by the infusion in each one of us of an attribute whose power we have been aware of for thousands of years, that of love.

It has been a number of years since I wrote that article, and yet the problem is still debated. In *Amnesty International*, Fall 2008, Vol. 34, No. 3, page 9 :

Growing Taser Use Confirms AIUSA Warning

A U.S. Department of Justice report released in June underscores some of AIUSA's long held concerns about the dangers of laser stun guns. Most important, the DQJ found that a "significant number" of individuals have died after exposure to the weapon. According to AI research, 320 people have died after being shocked with tasers since 2001. "The Justice Department concerns bolster what Amnesty International has been saying for years: more data is needed," said Dalia Hashad, director of AIUSA's domestic human rights program. "When police use tasers on vulnerable populations, the true impact is simply unknown. This is a cause for alarm."

Manufacturers and law enforcement agencies have touted lasers as an alternative to more lethal weapons. Yet when used on individuals intoxicated by drugs or affected by cardiac conditions—the leading cause of death in the United States— the true impact of tasers is unknown. The DOJ report notes, "Additional research is needed to Improve the understanding of how CEDs (conducted energy devices such as tasers) function I {and} their effect on at-risk individuals.""

The NYPD is one of many police departments across the country that has expanded its use of the stun guns. The number of law enforcement agencies who employ tasers is now estimated at 11,500. AIUSA believes authorities should either suspend taser use pending further research or restrict their use, in jurisdictions that refuse to suspend use to situations in which the only alternative is deadly force.

During the spring of 1984, I had been contacted by Judith, attorney at law, Case Western University, Cleveland, Ohio, and requested to give expert testimony about treatment in a Toledo Ohio Court. I did help out. She informed me on April 17,1984, that the testimony I gave was very important to establish that the patient had been treated improperly.

On May 24, 1984, Dr. M interviewed me for two months of psychiatric coverage at the Harrisburg Institute of Psychiatry, which is affiliated with the Hershey Medical School. I did work there June and July. On August 8, I received a letter from Dr. John F. M stating in part, "From both my personal observation and feedback from our staff, you have been a tremendous help to us and we appreciate your efforts very much."

He was so kind to provide a reference for me:

"Dr. Richard Scarnati has served as an outpatient psychiatrist at the Harrisburg Institute of Psychiatry during June and July 1984 working a total of sixteen hours per week. During this period of time, Dr. Scarnati assisted us with patient evaluations and coordinated and provided much teaching in our intake team process. He has also been involved in the psychiatric care of the dual-diagnosed patients in our SEA Program (MR partial program). His efforts on our behalf have been much appreciated and have been of the utmost quality. He has a tremendous teaching asset and has been well liked by his patients. In relation to our brief contact with Dr. Scarnati, I find him to be a very personable and desirable clinician who would likely make a very worthwhile contribution to any clinical setting in which he may be involved."

The Christian Medical Society, on May 22, 1984 informed me that I had been accepted as a member.

Staff writer Garry Lenton completed a seven-article investigative article series on the Lebanon, Pa., VA Medical Center, and staff writer Jerry Dubs did a three-part series on my charges of improper treatment by the VA. The VA hospital was seen as understaffed. The VA falls short on geriatric care. U.S. Rep. Bob Edgar, D-Lansdowne, did a tour of the VA Medical Center and called it a classic case of benign neglect.

> The July 11, 1984, *The Patriot*, headlined: VA psychiatric care faces new scrutiny.
> *This was the fourth in a six-day series of articles on problems facing Lebanon Veterans Administration Medical Center and its Harrisburg Outpatient Clinic.* By Jerry Dubs/ Staff Writer
> Highlights are:
> Charges that Improper psychiatric, care has been provided at the Harrisburg Outpatient Clinic of the Veterans Administration sent a ripple of concern through the federal government last fall.

...a federal lawsuit, scheduled for trial in September, may bring the charges swirling into the public eye.

At issue is the psychiatric care, particularly drug therapy, given to more than 600 veterans who are treated at the clinic. The quality of care was questioned by a psychiatrist who was fired from the clinic. The psychiatrist has filed a federal lawsuit charging that as improperly dismissed, and that veterans with psychiatric problems were not receiving proper treatment at the clinic.

...VA documents and interviews with medical experts suggest that the quality of care has been less than adequate and perhaps dangerous to some of the patients.

Specifically, the psychiatrist claimed that:

Some patients received a painkilling narcotic for decades, although they did not complain of pain and, in at least one case, a patient was recognized as being addicted to the drug.

At least one patient repeatedly was given five months' supply of Parest , an addicting drug related to Quaalude, that is dangerous if taken in larger than prescribed doses.

Minor tranquilizers were prescribed routinely for extended periods, although they have been shown to cause intellectual impairment when used over a six-month span.

A stimulant, Ritalin, was prescribed improperly to psychotics.

Internal VA documents show that hospital officials were aware of irregularities at the clinic and had instructed the psychiatrist to prescribe medications that he considered improper.

Other documents indicate a practice that psychiatrists describe as being aimed at keeping psychiatric patients "happy and quiet" instead of addressing their problems,

The questions of patient care were raised by Dr. Richard A. Scarnati, a psychiatrist who was employed at the outpatient clinic from September 1982 until he was fired in October 1983.

He said that when he started at the clinic, which treats more than 600 veterans who have psychiatric difficulties, he discovered a "monstrous" situation. "I was very dismayed, A lot of different medications were being given. That was not an acceptable medical practice. Even worse, psychotic patients were being given a stimulant, Ritalin. Some outpatients were given maintenance Darvon, a narcotic, and some patients were on minor tranquilizers for years and years. Minor tranquilizers shouldn't be used for more than a few weeks or months."

In Scarnati's view, the medical practices were at the least unethical, possibly dangerous and perhaps criminal.

A graduate of the Chicago College of Osteopathic Medicine, Scarnati had completed his residency training in psychiatry at the Illinois State Psychiatric Institute in 1977.

He had worked as a consultant on prison psychiatry for the Ohio Department of Mental Health. He had seen problems in psychiatric care while in Ohio and had been part of a legal battle to upgrade the treatment given prisoners there.

He also was familiar with the VA system, having worked in the Hampton, Va., hospital for a year before coming to the Harrisburg clinic. In a proficiency report completed by VA officials in January 1982, Scarnati was noted for "his great concern for, and dedication to, his patients' welfare."

The VA officials in Virginia also described Scarnati as being able "to stand firmly and courageously on convictions he has recognized as right and proper in terms of professional and ethical standards." Those traits were about to land him in trouble.

Dr. Rick Scarnati

As he saw each patient, Scarnati made an independent diagnosis and began taking them off medication he felt was improper or unnecessary. He said he realized that he would not be able to give the patients the therapy he thought they needed.

"The caseload was running away from me. I wasn't seeing the patients often enough. I was constantly requesting [an additional] psychiatrist [for the clinic]; I asked for more help," he said.

...Scarnati continued his work at the clinic, reducing and changing medications to provide what he viewed as proper psychiatric care. Scarnati found that his methods of improving psychiatric care at the clinic were unacceptable to VA Hospital administrators. Reprinted with the permission of The Patriot-News. © 1984. All rights reserved.

The July 12, 1984, *The Patriot*, headlined: Change in psychiatric care resisted.
By Jerry Dubs/Staff Writer

Dr. Richard A. Scarnati's work at the Harrisburg Outpatient Clinic of the Veterans Administration was difficult from the start.

Scarnati's attempts to treat the patients with drugs and psychotherapy that he considered correct met with resistance—from both the patients and VA officials. The psychiatrist was fired from the VA system after a stormy year at the clinic.

He has since filed a federal suit claiming he was improperly fired and the treatment given psychiatric patients at the clinic was improper. His allegations are expected to be aired in September when his case comes to court.

At the heart of Scarnati's claims is the charge that psychiatric care given at the clinic before his arrival and later ordered by his supervisors was improper.

Scarnati said that in the past, medications for VA outpatients were seldom adjusted. He cited one case in which a veteran received drugs over a five-year period without once visiting the clinic for an examination or review.

For the patient's family or guardians, the attempt to lower medication may result in a trying period.

When Scarnati reduced the medication of some of Broughton's (CARE HOME) guests, she said they became "unmanageable."

Early in 1983 she wrote to Leonard Washington Jr., director of the VA's Lebanon Medical Center which operates the outpatient clinic, complaining about Scarnati's care, one of a series of complaints the director began to receive about Scarnati's practice.

In March 1983, Washington wrote to Broughton and defended Scarnati's approach.

"Dr. Scarnati is attempting to treat patients' mental illnesses and their effect on the total person," he wrote. "This is quite different from the treatment approach taken in earlier years in which symptoms were driven underground with powerful medications. Sometimes patients react to changes with anxiety and this is what seems to be happening in your home."

While Scarnati was testing the limits of the major tranquilizers, he was eliminating what he saw as the unnecessary prescription of minor tranquilizers.

Minor tranquilizers, members of a group of drugs called benzodiazepines, were regarded as "miracle" drugs when they were introduced. They are relatively safe and effective, with few side effects.

However, they have disadvantages.

Dr. Nelson Hendler, director of the Mensana Pain Clinic in Stevenson, Md., is a nationally recognized authority on benzodiazepines. He is a psychiatric consultant at Johns Hopkins Hospital, and testified before a congressional committee about the use and misuse of the drugs.

He said that although the Food and Drug Administration has recommended against using benzodiazepines for longer than four months, "I would limit their use to one month."

Extended use of the drugs causes "intellectual impairment and memory loss," Hendler said. A normal dosage of the tranquilizers over a six-month period also can cause depression, he added.

At the outpatient clinic, minor tranquilizers had been widely prescribed.

"I would venture to say that several hundred of the patients were on benzodiazepines for years and years," Scarnati said.

The drugs have limited use in psychiatry.

A warning in the Physicians' Desk Reference in a description of Valium, one of the most frequently prescribed minor tranquilizers, states: "Valium is not of value in the treatment of psychotic patients and should not be employed in lieu of appropriate treatment."

However, there may have been a reason for the use of the minor tranquilizers.

The Harrisburg Institute of Psychiatry treats approximately

1,000 outpatients, Director Yanich said, it employs three full-time and a half-dozen part-time psychiatrists.

Scarnati alone treated 661 patients at the VA clinic, and he was required to complete compensation exams which cut into the time he saw patients.

According to veterans who attended the VA clinic, visits were scheduled three or four times a year, sometimes less frequently.

Staffing at the Lebanon Medical Center, the administrative center for the outpatient clinic in Harrisburg, is below standard, VA officials 'said.

The American Psychiatric Association has a committee that monitors health care provided by the VA. Its chairman is Dr. John Lipkin, who is also an employee of the VA.

While Lipkin was reluctant to criticize the psychiatric care provided by the VA, he noted that, "There is not enough psychiatric care for the people of this country."

He said the VA has a problem competing for the limited number of psychiatrists in the country.

Scarnati saw the widespread use of minor tranquilizers as a means the clinic's previous psychiatrists had used to solve the staffing problem.

"In the grapevine, they said they sort of used the minor tranquilizers to snow the patient, so to speak. It has a zombie effect on the ego. If a patient is taking Valium all the time, his nervous system is depressed. The problem is, that's not looked upon as acceptable treatment," he said.

Scarnati began cutting back on the prescription of the drugs.

He expected problems, so he telephoned Dr. Murray Feldberg, chief of staff, to warn him that some of the patients would "probably be complaining" about the medication changes.

He was right.

One veteran wrote to U.S. Rep. William F. Goodling, R- Jacobus, complaining that he had been taken off Serax, a benzodiazepine.

On March 7, 1983, the same day that Washington wrote to Broughton, he wrote to Gooding about the patient on Serax. He told Goodling that the patient had been treated for psychiatric problems for at least 10 years.

"Over the years he has taken a variety of minor tranquilizers with little change. Dr. Scarnati believes ... that the veteran has become overly dependent on Serax [a minor tranquilizer] and that his use of this agent may need to be interrupted," Washington wrote. "This impression about [the patient] is not new. Dr. Garber, in 1975, commented that Serax appeared to have not been useful in [the patient's] situation. Dr. Pittman, in 1978, felt that [the patient] should be taken off Serax. There are comments in the chart indicating that [the patient] has been taking Serax in larger quantities than the prescribed amount."

While the medical center director was publicly defending Scarnati's psychiatric practice, within the VA system Scarnati was coming under fire.

As early as January 1983, three months after he started at the clinic and two months before Washington would write the letters in his defense, Scarnati was told to change his procedure.

Feldberg and Dr. Andrew Lefko, acting chief of psychiatry service, met with Scarnati on Jan. 28, 1983, to discuss the number of veterans who were requesting transfer from the outpatient clinic to the Lebanon VA clinic.

"Most of them...indicated that you had taken them off their minor tranquilizers," Feldberg wrote in a summary of the meeting.

Feldberg's reconstruction of the meeting included a reference to the practices at the Harrisburg clinic before Scarnati's arrival.

"We acknowledged that the former psychiatrist at the OPC, Harrisburg, had been a very giving individual who found it easier to go along with the demands of his patients than to set limits. We all agreed that the prescribing practices at the clinic needed to be looked into," Feldberg summarized.

The chief of staff concluded his letter with the hope that "the patients will shortly be at a level of sophistication that will permit them to look at and even abandon their longstanding dependency on pharmacological agents."

According to Scarnati, he was instructed at the time to resume giving minor tranquilizers to the patients.

A month before the meeting with Feldberg, Scarnati had written to the American Medical Association to get the professional group's view on the use of minor tranquilizers.

"Anti-anxiety agents, such as benzodiazepines, are rarely indicated for long-term treatment," William T. McGivney, a senior scientist with the AMA, wrote in response. "The benefits of continuous administration [of the drugs] for more than four months have not been fully evaluated, although a few open studies support their effectiveness for up 'to one year.

"Overuse of these drugs may hinder the development of personal coping strategies ... and obscure the source of anxiety."

Bolstered by the AMA opinion and other professional articles on the proper use of minor tranquilizers, Scarnati refused to follow Feldberg's suggestion.

Less than a month later, Dr. Saul Holtzman, chief of psychiatry service, circulated a summary of a Systematic External Review Program Survey conducted in mid-February by VA officials.

According to Holtzman's summary, the VA officials found the wide use of minor tranquilizers improper.

"This is a continuing problem, particularly the use of major together with minor tranquilizers," Holtzman wrote in his summary.

Scarnati felt vindicated.

But the feeling vanished March 25, 1983, when he received a memo from Feldberg.

"Let me give you a few suggestions," the chief of staff wrote. "You need to discontinue any activity designed to curtail the use of minor tranquilizers at the OPC.

"Next, you need to announce your intent to re-examine the use of that agent to all the patients and that you will make a decision about the matter after a reasonable period of exploration. Again I would like to suggest that this period be as long as six months."

Again Scarnati refused.

Three months later, a highly critical proficiency report was completed on Scarnati. Written by Holtzman and countersigned by Feldberg, the report concluded that Scarnati "has not met reasonable expectations in his performance."

In the fall of 1983 he was fired.

In *The Evening News,* July 13, 1984, heading: Fired psychiatrist
asked VA Clinic probe.
By Jerry Dubs Staff Writer:

Highlights of the article are:

Convinced that he was fired by the Veterans Administration because he would not prescribe improper medication, Dr. Richard A. Scarnati tried to have the Harrisburg Outpatient Clinic investigated.

Employed at the VA clinic for a year, the psychiatrist was fired in October after refusing orders to prescribe minor tranquilizers, which he considered unnecessary. He filed a federal lawsuit, arguing that his civil rights had been violated by the process used to dismiss him. He also charged that patients who were treated at the Harrisburg clinic were not receiving proper psychiatric care.

He wrote to a variety of state and federal agencies requesting an investigation of practices in prescribing at the clinic.

He wrote to the Drug Enforcement Administration, the state attorney general, U.S. Rep. William J. Coyne, the Joint Commission on Accreditation of Hospitals, the Disabled American Veterans, the Pennsylvania Psychiatric Society and others.

Nearly all of his complaints took the same turn.

The state attorney general's office sent an investigator to *interview* Scarnati. Joseph J. Bilansky, regional director for the state Bureau of Narcotics Investigation, wrote to the Drug Enforcement Administration on Dec. 6, 1983

"Since [Scarnati] has now brought this complaint to our agency and there appears to be some merit to his allegations on the surface, but it is within federal jurisdiction, I felt duty bound to officially relay his complaint to you for federal investigation."

An agent of the DEA Diversion Group in Philadelphia said the matter was referred to the VA for investigation. "We felt it was a matter for doctors to review .internally," said the agent, who spoke on condition that he not be identified.

Coyne, D-Pittsburgh, wrote to the VA about Scarnati's allegations and received a letter from Donald Custis, chief medical director, who promised a VA inspection of the clinic.

Charles Joecke! Jr., national director of services for the DAV also forwarded the complaint to the VA for internal investigation.

IN THE END, only the Pennsylvania Psychiatric Society promised an independent review of the clinic. That review is expected to be completed late this month, according to Donald N. McCoy, executive secretary for the society.

"Our concerns are based on Scarnati's charges: Who is making the decisions on medical care and the supervision and administration of substances? Are there any established guidelines at the VA that would have permitted this to continue?" McCoy asked.

The VA inspection was conducted Feb. 27–28, more than a year after Dr. Murray Feldberg, chief of staff of the Lebanon VA center which operates the clinic, wrote to Scarnati that "the prescribing practices at the clinic need to be looked into."

According to Robert Putnam, a spokesman for the VA office in Washington, the inspector pulled 200 medical records for review.

THE INSPECTOR'S report is not available. "The materials are, in essence, quality assurance documents and working papers that are not subject to the Freedom of Information Act," Putnam said.

The VA has released only a three-paragraph summary of the report, which defends the prescribing practices at the clinic. The reviewer did note, however: "While a number of patients were treated chronically with benzodiazepines, it seemed well within the community standard."

The number of patients treated chronically with benzodiazepines was not available.

A summary of the VA report, sent to the DAV and DEA, has satisfied those groups that the clinic is operating properly; no further investigations are planned.

BUT THE report contradicts court papers submitted by the federal government, and documents held by Scarnati.

In its answer to Scarnati's lawsuit, the federal government claimed: "It is denied that these drugs [benzodiazepines] are dangerous if taken over a period of time and that many of the patients had been taking these drugs regularly for several years."

While the dangers of the drugs, however well documented, may be a matter of medical dispute, VA records show that patients were given the minor tranquilizers for years.

In a letter to U.S. Rep. William Goodling, R-Jacobus, Leonard Washington Jr., director of the Lebanon VA center, referred to a patient who had received a benzodiazepine for

10 years and, in the VA inspection summary, the investigator referred to patients who were chronically treated with the drugs.

THE VA inspection also failed to address many other questions raised by Scarnati:

A February 1983 quality control survey found the prescription of minor and major tranquilizers to be a problem at the clinic. Yet in March 1983, Scarnati was instructed by VA officials to resume prescribing minor tranquilizers.

Washington's letter to Gooding in March 1983 indicated that doctors had twice before recommended that a patient be taken off a minor tranquilizer that he had received for 10 years. Yet the patient was still receiving the drug when Scarnati started work at the clinic.

A Food and Drug Administration bulletin dated February 1980 noted that "the effectiveness of [minor tranquilizers] in long-term use; that is, more than four months, has not been assessed by clinical studies." Yet in March 1983, Scarnati was instructed to place his patients on minor tranquilizers for "as long as six months."

AT LEAST one of Scarnati's patients, diagnosed as suffering anxiety reaction, twice had received, in 1979 and 1980, refillable prescriptions for Ritalin and Parest. Yet instructions for Ritalin indicate it is not to be given to patients suffering from marked anxiety, and Parest is an addicting methaqualone which psychiatrists say should never be dispensed in large quantities.

At least one patient was diagnosed as having a "prescription drug dependency" on Darvon and Valium. Yet VA doctors continued to supply the patient with the narcotic and the tranquilizer, even though Darvon's approved use is limited to relief of acute physical pain.

The answers to these questions may lie within the VA system. However, they are unavailable.

In response to written questions about the clinic's operation, Washington wrote: "Based on advice of counsel, we cannot respond to the questions ... regarding the outpatient clinic."

Steve Minnichuk, the VA attorney who advised Washington, said VA officials are not allowed to comment on the clinic because of Scarnati's lawsuit against the VA system.

As we have seen, twenty-six years ago, I refused to prescribe the addicting drug Darvon to veterans with psychiatric disorders. Looking at the July 2008 *Health Letter*, by Editor, Sidney M. Wolfe, M.D., *Public Citizen Health Research Group's, Outrage of the Month* title: Why is *Darvon* (Darvocet/propoxyphene) Still Around, Hurting People?

I had refused to prescribe the stimulant Ritalin (methylphenidate) to psychotic VA patients because it would cause decompensation. As one might imagine, I was quite concerned when I discovered research, in which methylphenidate was used as a predictor of relapse, in patients with Schizophrenia (psychosis). I did not consider such research in the best interest of the patient. After I discussed my concerns with editor Howard M. Nashel, he, Dr. Epstein, and I, put our concerns in an editorial page:

"Ethical Considerations in the Use of Methylphenidate (Ritalin) Challenge as a Predictor of Relapse in Schizophrenia" :

Editors' page

It is generally acknowledged that tremendous benefits have resulted from experimentation on human beings. Unfortunately, however, detriments have also abounded. Abuses in experimentation have often resulted from lack of ethical sensitivity on the part of well-meaning researchers, whose primary consideration is to insure scientific progress.

All of us are aware of the terrible scourge of schizophrenia. Numerous psychiatric researchers have been involved in attempting to find a cure for this dreaded condition. New research is constantly dealing with many facets of the problem. An article in the May 1984 issue of the *American Journal of Psychiatry* reports a study concerning the use of methylphenidate (Ritalin). In our opinion, this study raises a serious ethical question.

The authors of the study initially noted the great concern that we all have about the terrible side effects (particularly tardive dyskinesia) on schizophrenia patients of long-term treatment with neuroleptic drugs. The authors were interested in finding a method which could determine whether a schizophrenic patient, who was in remission, and who then was taken off neuroleptic drug treatment, would be at risk of having his psychotic symptoms return. To that end, the authors of the study tested the use of a psycho stimulant drug (methylphenidate) as a predictor of relapse. In particular, the hypothesis that the authors tested was that stable patients, who were given methylphenidate, and who then exhibited transient symptom activation, would thereafter suffer a relapse following the withdrawal of neuroleptic drugs, whereas patients who did not exhibit transient symptom activation would not relapse.

If such a test were successful in predicting which patients would experience a relapse when taken off drug maintenance, the result would, of course, be very worthwhile. Nevertheless, in our opinion, this possible beneficial end result would not justify the means used. We feel that to provoke psychotic symptoms in patients is unconscionable.

The patients in the study had come from the aftercare services of a department of psychiatry. They were stable and well functioning. They had been stable at their current level of remission for at least six months and were receiving neuroleptic maintenance treatment. They had achieved and sustained a level of remission sufficient for them to live in the community as outpatients. They were participating in ongoing vocational activities, such as jobs, rehabilitation programs, or school.

It is well known that methylphenidate and other psycho-stimulant drugs can provoke or exacerbate psychotic symptoms in schizophrenic patients who are acutely ill or are only partially in remission. It has also been reported in the literature that the use of psycho stimulant drugs can cause the recurrence of psychotic symptoms in patients who had been free of such symptoms for quite some time.

Too little is still known about schizophrenia to assume that the only effect on schizophrenic patients from the use of psycho stimulant drugs would be transient symptom activation. Methylphenidate is a very potent drug with many known disabling side effects. It should not be used in any tests with psychotic patients.

Richard Scarnati, B.S. M.A., D.O., Howard M. Nashel, Esq., Gerald N. Epstein, M.D.

I also reported on a very extensive list of Ritalin's hazardous side effects in my publication:

"An Outline of Hazardous Side Effects of Ritalin(Methylphenidate)":

Ritalin (methylphenidate) has been used with much success in attention deficit disorders of children. It has also been shown to be effective in narcolepsy, which is a sleep attack disorder. The literature also reveals a very limited possible effectiveness for Ritalin in very mild depression, senile withdrawn behavior, and apathy.

Even though this clinician believes that Ritalin is effective in attention deficit disorders of children, he has extreme reservations about the use of this stimulant in any other conditions. *The Physicians' Desk Reference* does not list all of the specific side effects of this medication, especially those that have been seen in psychiatric patients. Because Ritalin is a DEA Schedule II Drug with high abuse potential, it may have great legal implications for physicians who prescribe Ritalin in a casual fashion.

Because so many veteran patients had been on the addicting benzo-diazepine, Valium, I completed a very in-depth review of the literature that was published sometime later: in "Critical Issues for Consideration in Prescribing Benzodiazepines."

I was quite dismayed to see on January 3, 1985, the federal court issued a decision in favor of the VA Medical Center (defendants). The essence of the court reasoning was that since I was considered a *probationary employee*, I was not entitled to a full-blown, trail-like hearing, with right to counsel, right to confront adverse witnesses, and cross-examine, before separation from the service.

My ACLU attorney believed an appeal would be futile, and he did not recommend such.

My attorney friends believed I might have a liberty issue in the appeals courts, but it would be very difficult for me to teach myself constitutional law and represent myself. But I did spend thousands of hours doing that. After I failed in the Third Circuit, I went on to file a Petition For a Writ Of Certiorari (Brief) to the U.S. Supreme Court.

Attorney David C. Vladeck of the Public Citizen Litigation Group was so kind to go over my petition; his response was, "While I think you do a satisfactory job of setting out the relevant facts and making your case, I do not think the Supreme Court is going to hear your case."

The Supreme Court Of The United States did docket my Petition For A Writ Of Certiorari on October 7, 1985 as: A-573, No. 85–604. On January 13, 1986, the Supreme Court Of The United States *denied* my petition for a writ of certiorari. All my work in these courts had been in vain. What a baptism of fire I had experienced!

In the winter of 1985, I moved back to Ohio. I accepted a position as a prison and forensic psychiatrist on February 4, 1985, for the Office of Psychiatric Services to Corrections, of the Ohio Department of Mental Health (ODMH). I was assigned to the Residential Treatment Unit (RTU) at the Lebanon Correctional Institution in Lebanon, Ohio, about twenty-five miles north of Cincinnati, Ohio.

My article, Prison Psychiatrist's Role In A Residential Treatment Unit Of Dangerous Psychiatric Inmates describes various treatments.

The state prisons in Ohio are managed by the Ohio Department of Rehabilitation and Corrections, which provides security to the inmate population. At the time, the Ohio Department of Mental Health, Psychiatric Services to Corrections, provided psychiatric treatment for inmates with psychiatric disorders.

Before I began my position at the prison, I attended the State of Ohio, Department of Rehabilitation and Correction (DRC), Corrections Training Academy, in Orient, Ohio. I was not required to do the entire training, but I wanted to, because I believed correctional staff would feel more comfortable with me, knowing I had completed their academy. Both DRC and ODMH were pleased about my desire, because they had not had a psychiatrist who desired such training. I received a certificate on May 31, 1985.

The RTU had been established because of the problems at Southern Ohio Correctional Facility (SOCF) in Lucasville, Ohio (the place of the major prison riot). They had shipped the "trouble-making" inmates to the RTU at Lebanon Correctional Institution (LeCI). The RTU was an "island" unto it's self within LeCI.

The ultimate goal of the RTU was to treat mentally ill inmates who have committed violent crimes, have not adjusted to the prison population, and after successful treatment, return them to the prison population, where they can now cope without being a danger to themselves or others.

My first day on the RTU was my "Baptism in Fire!" When I was let on the RTU, a major emergency operation was taking place. An inmate wanted to fight the sergeant on the block, and believe it or not, the Sgt wanted to fight him. I told him he could not do that. The sergeant asked me who I was and when I said psychiatrist, the sergeant and correctional officers burst out laughing. I, of course, took that in stride. I realized then, I would have a lot of educating to do. I informed them I would be treating the inmate patients on the RTU. I had to immediately order that the inmate who was threatening everyone be placed in restraints and medicated for stabilization.

At the time on the RTU, we had a correctional administrator, a number of correctional officers, and our OPSC staff consisted of nurses, a psychologist administrator, social workers, and an activity therapist beside myself and a part-time psychiatrist. We all did our own work individually as we saw fit and would have a weekly discussion with the psychologist administrator. We were a very experienced group, and I believed with a considerable amount of professional talent.

As time passed, we all got to know each other. At one of our administrative meetings, I brought up the idea of us taking the worse trouble-making inmates with psychiatric disorders in the state prisons and treating them on the RTU. Since we had come from varied backgrounds, I suggested that we brainstorm continuously and come up with the grandest treatment program in mental health. Everyone had smiles; they liked my idea.

We were from that moment on, only functioning as a treatment team. We all developed program ideas.

The RTU operated under a day-treatment model. When the inmate first arrives on the RTU, I would see them for any urgent psychiatric care they might require before a full evaluation. All of their medical needs were addressed by the prison medical physician.

Days after an inmate was admitted, I would do an in depth psychiatric evaluation of him.

I also completed a complete review of his correctional file, so that our team would be aware of the crimes and circumstances surrounding them. Disciplinar reports were read to give an indication of what the patient's weaknesses have been in the correctional setting and is indicative of the areas the patient will need to work on in treatment. These reviews were very important for us to help the patient come to grips with accepting responsibility for his actions and work toward constructive change, in order not to repeat his inappropriate behavior. If the patient had committed the crime while in a psychotic state, we help him learn the importance of remaining in treatment and becoming compliant with taking his psychotropic medications.

As soon as I completed my evaluations, we would meet with the inmate as a team. I was the treatment team leader, and all of us would take part in the interview of the patient. The patient was encouraged to share what he believed was his strengths and weaknesses, and an initial, individualized treatment plan was drawn up for the patient to help him utilize his strengths to deal with his weaknesses. We would get his input regarding treatment, and he would hear our recommendations.

The treatment plan was comprehensive and covered the psychological, biological, medical, social, and spiritual needs of the inmate.

After the initial treatment plan was drawn up, the patient signs it, because it is his contract with the team and his "plan of action" for his individualized treatment program. This also helped to alleviate some of the initial anxiety the patient had to a new situation.

Treatment consisted of psychotropic medications, one-on-one psychotherapy, and group therapies such as arts and crafts, sensory awareness, general education, medication values, developmental psychology, creative problem solving, value clarification, reality awareness, and coping groups. Inmates also attended religious services.

Our overall, most successful, treatment approach was one of an empathic supportive nature.

As a psychiatrist at that time, I did not have the all the varied psychotropic medication we have now, but the treatments could be very effective.

I used antipsychotic medication for patients with major psychosis. If a patient had been medication noncompliant in the past, he was encouraged to take long-acting intramuscular medications. Because a large number of the patients had been medication noncompliant in the community, this was their first experience of having their psychosis under control. As they discovered their ability to function on a higher level, it gave them great satisfaction, and the added insight became a great help in their deciding to stay on their psychotropic medications.

In manic, destructive, socially disruptive, or violently psychotic patients, rapid control of symptoms is very important not only for the patients' and others' safety, but also because the patient has to live with the knowledge of any destructive act he committed while severely disturbed. Rapid control of the symptoms of a patient in catatonic excitement can be lifesaving.

For rapid and maximal antipsychotic action, a highly decompensated inmate may be given a high-potency antipsychotic medication intramuscularly every 30 minutes or every hour, until the acute episode is over. In this psychiatrist's years of clinical experience, I had noted that after the third or fourth injection, the patient is usually somewhat stable. Because many of the violent psychiatric inmates have also had head trauma in the past, and thus may have a seizure disorder; as a result, it may be necessary to increase their seizure medications, because antipsychotic medication lowers seizure threshold. In the acute treatment titrations, benzodiazepines may be give along with the antipsychotic medication, because they increase the seizure threshold, which means it is harder for one to have a seizure.

Many inmates suffer from affective or depressive illness and are suicidal. Because at least 70 percent of depressed patients benefit from antidepressants, it is important that antidepressants be considered for inmates who are depressed.

There is ample clinical evidence that stimulants such as amphetamines and methylphenidate (Ritalin) are effective in the reduction and control of hyperkinetic behavior in children, in attention deficit disorder in adults, and in narcolepsy (sleep attack). Some clinicians have even recommended that stimulants be used in mild depression. Stimulants are not without their problems in the correctional setting. They are a very highly desired item of abuse and would most likely be diverted from clinical use to abuse. Because of extremely severe side effects such as aggression, prescribing stimulants would be quite a challenge in the prison system. If an inmate does have a "pure" attention deficit disorder or narcolepsy and stimulants must be prescribed, then they should be in crushed pill form and given to the patient in liquid to drink. The inmate would need to be closely followed to be certain that he actually did respond favorably, that undesirable side effects did not occur, and that no potential for abuse of such medications exists.

There are a number of critical issues that should be considered when deciding whether or not to prescribe benzodiazepines or minor tranquilizers, such as Valium. Moderate levels of anxiety stimulate adaptive functions that are necessary for coping with problems successfully. Adaptive functions should not be obstructed by medications. We all experience conflicts; the working through of such enhance character building.

Diazepam and chlordiazepoxide may increase aggressiveness in many anxious prisoners. Long-term use of benzodiazepines has been reported to be associated with increased irritability, hostility, and aggressiveness. Rage reactions have also been noted.

Benzodiazepines have a small role in the treatment of the severely and chronically mentally ill, including inmates with psychiatric disorders.

Benzodiazepines may become physically addicting, if used for prolonged periods.

Lithium has been used primarily for mania. It is also be helpful in recurrent depressions, antisocial disorders, and explosive personalities.

Because some of the inmates have initial acute mania, it is also necessary to use a combination treatment such as the major tranquilizer, haloperidol. Lithium carbonate usually takes seven to ten days to take effect and, during the early stage of acute mania, haloperidol is quite beneficial in helping stabilize the inmate. Most of the inmates this prison psychiatrist had treated also have psychotic symptoms. These symptoms are controlled rapidly with the high-potency haloperidol. If the inmate continues to have psychotic symptoms during his illness, it may be necessary to keep him on a combination of both lithium and haloperidol.

This prison psychiatrist has used this drug combination for more than thirty years for patients without adverse reactions. In the beginning of treatment, one may want to start the patient on a high dose of haloperidol and a low dose of lithium. As the patient becomes responsive to lithium, the psychiatrist can start reducing the dose of haloperidol. If the patient's psychotic symptoms remit, it may even be possible to discontinue the haloperidol altogether. This psychiatrist has obtained excellent results using lithium in "moody," aggressive inmates.

Anticonvulsants may offer promising treatment alternatives for inmates without seizure disorders. Anticonvulsants are effective in a significant number of inmates who do not respond to lithium.

Carbamazepine is effective in the acute treatment of mania. It has been used safely in combination with lithium, major tranquilizers, and tricyclic antidepressants. Carbamazepine decreases episodes of paroxysmal outbursts, especially episodes of aggression.

Fortunately, all of the inmates on the RTU on Carbamazepine have seen a decrease of their periodic hostile outbursts.

Psychoanalysis was developed by Sigmund Freud. Because of the intensive, in-depth type of therapy that is involved in psychoanalysis, and the need to see the inmate several times a week, it is usually not possible to do such therapy in prison. This psychiatrist does do elements of psychoanalysis such as free association and dream interpretation.

In psychoanalytic psychotherapy, one modifies behavior by the psychological methods of confrontation, clarification, and interpretation. The inmate must have the ability for introspection for this type of therapy. The fundamental rule of the therapy (i.e., that the patient agrees to reveal all to his therapist) is difficult for inmates. It takes a. long time for inmates to develop trust in their psychiatrist in the prison environment.

This psychiatrist deals with transference reactions of the inmates. The inmate is helped to see that each encounter with a new person is seen as a unique experience that should be taken in that context, and how his inappropriate feelings toward that person affects that interpersonal encounter.

Work begins on discovering with the inmate his major problems or conflicts and ego strengths and weaknesses, and then helping the inmate utilize his ego strengths to deal with weaknesses.

The inmate's current dynamic patterns causing problems are explored as far as possible, and constructive goals are established.

Insight psychotherapy deals with a searching self-scrutiny to discover underlying dynamics to be worked on and resolved, which can lead to personal growth and creative potential for the inmate.

It is desirable to achieve an interpretation of dynamics that will lead to the release of affect in what is sometimes a sudden "ah-ha! experience." This produces an emotional insight blended with cognitive factors.

Usually insight psychotherapy is useful only for the inmate who has fairly adequate ego strength for facing problems. The psychiatrist educates the inmate on how to avoid problems he has been creating or encountering, even without ever knowing the full underlying dynamics of such at times. Transference reactions should be discussed when they are blocking the inmate's progress in therapy.

To get results using insight therapy, the inmate may need to be seen as often as one to three times a week for 30 minutes to an hour. The inmate will need to have some capacity to tolerate frustration and be psychologically minded. The sad fact is that most inmates are not seen this frequently because of staff shortages, therefore this is a rare form of therapy in the prison system.

Supportive therapy was the major form of therapy utilized for inmates treated by this psychiatrist.

Supportive therapy provides the inmate support during a period of illness, turmoil, and temporary decompensation. The goal is to help the inmate's defenses and integrative capacities that have been disrupted. The psychiatrist becomes the role model for the inmate as the psychiatrist helps the inmate to attain independent functioning again. The inmate feels more secure, accepted, protected, encouraged, safe, less anxious, and not alone in his struggles.

This psychiatrist does not encourage too great a regression and too strong a dependency. The frequency of contact may range from daily sessions to as few as once every few months once the inmate is "well." The time of each session may be brief (e.g., a few minutes to an hour or more) depending on the situation.

Focal psychotherapy is a mode of short, insight-oriented treatment. A problem is addressed until a meaningful, acceptable problem interpretation is given to the inmate so that he can work on the problem.

Psychiatrist William Glasser has achieved good results with Reality Therapy with delinquents, and this psychiatrist has found it beneficial for a number of inmates.

In reality therapy the inmate is accepted as he is. For some, this is a totally new experience. The inmate is encouraged to accept responsibility for his actions so that he is able to fulfill some of his needs without harming others.

Responsibility is taught through understanding and discipline. The psychiatrist sets an example, demonstrates appropriate behavior, and instructs the inmate. The inmate is held responsible for his behavior as long as he is not in a decompensated state. The inmates here have developed a sense of self-worth as they have become more responsible for their behavior. The goal of therapy for the inmate is "to do the best you can under the circumstances."

Logotherapy can provide the most meaningful understanding for inmates for coping with the prison environment.

Victor E. Frankl of the University of Vienna Medical School was the leader and originator of the school of Logotherapy or existential analysis, the principles of which were developed by him during his 3 grim years as a prisoner at Auschwitz and other Nazi concentration camps.

Frankl's theory of unconditional meaningfulness of life is phrased in the unconditionally life-affirming words in a verse from a song sung by inmates of the Buchenwald Concentration Camp. "Say 'Yes' to Life in Spite of Everything" (Leslie, 1965). This is a good saying for inmates to think about when they become overly depressed or think about harming themselves.

When an inmate holds firm religious beliefs, there is no objection to making use of the therapeutic effect of his religious convictions, and thereby draw on his spiritual resources (Frankl, 1967).

Quoting or reading from the Bible is often illuminating and helpful for inmates (Hyder, 1973). No ethical system can surpass the altruistic aims expressed in the Beatitudes and the two Great Commandments (Biddle, 1962).

One's life can be fulfilled not only in creating and enjoying but also in suffering (Tweedie,1972). Edith Weisshopf-Joebon states that, by giving unavoidable suffering, the status of a positive value, logotherapy may help counteract unhealthy trends in present day culture where the sufferer is given little opportunity to be proud of his or her suffering and consider it ennobling.

The past should be seen as a storehouse of everything one has brought into existence, whereas the future consists of opportunities yet to be fulfilled. Thus the past is the part of one's life in which he has overcome transiency and achieved eternity (Frankl, 1967). This concept is important for our inmates who believe that their suffering through life sentences has been a waste of their time and lives.

A prison psychiatrist should be a very responsible person, tough, interested, human, and sensitive. He should be able to fulfill his own needs and be willing to discuss some of his own struggles so that the inmate can see that acting responsibly is possible although sometimes difficult. Neither aloof, superior, nor sacrosanct, the psychiatrist must never imply that what he does, what he stands for, or what he values is unimportant. He must have the strength to become involved, to have his values tested by the inmate, and to withstand intense criticism by the inmate. Willing to admit that, like the inmate, he is far from perfect, the psychiatrist must nevertheless show that one can act responsibly even though it may take great effort.

This prison psychiatrist sometimes shared his experience of having served time in two reform schools with selected inmates. He tells them that at age 16, with only a seventh grade education, the court psychologist told him to pursue a trade because his test results showed that he did not have the ability to get a high school education. This psychiatrist also shared his rebirth in the Fire of the Holy Spirit and how his life was transformed to obtain the impossible dream—becoming a physician. The point of this sharing is to convince inmates that their dreams are obtainable.

He also shares with the inmates an inspirational story of a young drug dealer who was caught and spent several years at the Pittsburgh, Pennsylvania's Western Penitentiary, a maximum security prison. He worked as a law clerk at the prison. When he left prison, he attended the University of Pittsburgh, graduating Magna Cum Laude in 1981 with a degree in Biology and Chemistry. He then went on to medical school. He graduated in the top third of his class from Hahnemann Medical College in Philadelphia and is now a surgeon. Because many inmates have been drug addicts or dealers, that story is an inspiration for them to try to better themselves.

The emphasis of logotherapy on realization of meaning and values in human striving as the proper goal of action is an emphasis that is sorely needed in modern psychotherapeutic circles (Tweedie, 1972), especially in prisons. Reading about how others have searched for their own meaning, what they have found and where, can stimulate inmates' thinking (Crumbaugh, 1973).

In treating inmates, this psychiatrist uses inspirational readings that help inmates who are "searching for meaning." The response of patients to the readings is encouraging.

As logotherapy suggests, man is ultimately self-determining; everyone has the freedom to change at an instant. Dr. J. was one

whom Dr. Frankl had at first considered a satanic figure, responsible for mass murders of psychotics during the Nazi euthanasia
program. Dr. J. was later imprisoned in the USSR and gave con-
solation to everyone and lived up to the highest moral standard.
When he learned about this, Dr. Frankl remarked, "How can we
dare to predict the behavior of man!" (Frankl, 1974).

The same can be said of our inmates, even those who have
committed the most heinous crimes; this psychiatrist believes that
they too are capable of change and hence the reason for the RTU.

In summary, logotherapy has a very important place for
inmates—helping them to find meaning in their suffering, and to
accept responsibility for constructive change.

Through group therapy, the inmate displays his behavior
through personal feedback and self-observation; he learns to
appreciate the nature of his behavior and how his behavior impacts
on the feelings of others. He learns that he is responsible for his
behavior and is the author of his interpersonal world.

On the RTU, we had three coping groups per week. They ran
from 1 hour to 1 1/2 hours in length. Six of the higher functioning inmates were chosen for each group. The groups were led by
two professional co therapists, usually a male and a female. The
inmates were chosen for coping groups by evaluation of their
functioning in other lower functioning groups. Yalom's book, *The
Theory and Practice of Group Psychotherapy* (1975), provides the
standard approach that was used in our group therapy.

The co therapists meet with each inmate individually before
he was accepted into the group. The following rules of the group
therapy program were discussed with the inmate:

1.   It is mandatory that strict confidentiality be maintained.
This means that the group members may talk to each other about
what was discussed in group but not to anyone else. All material
heard in the group is to be kept confidential. If anyone breaks this
mandatory rule, he is immediately terminated from the group.

2. The inmates are expected to talk about their problems in the group. This may take some time because it may take a few months before the inmates build up a trusting relationship with the other group members. Some inmates were dropped from the group after 3 months; they never talked about their problems even when encouraged to do so by the therapists and other group members.

3. Absolutely no physical acting out is permitted in the group (e.g., fighting). We do permit the inmates to show appropriate anger and discuss such, but we do not tolerate aggressive confrontations or fighting because it is too disrupting for the group. When an incident occurs, the inmate is taken from the group to his cell. We do not immediately drop the inmate from the group for this because we believe he needs to confront his behavior. The co therapists meet with the inmate before the next group session to see if he desires to continue in the group and if he plans to control his acting out. Fortunately, in most instances so far, the inmate has elected to stay in the group and address his problem.

4. We prefer that inmates deal with problems in the "here and now" because it makes their lives on the unit a little easier to bear.

5. Inmates are expected to have good attendance records. We have a waiting list for inmates to enter the coping groups. If an inmate misses more than three sessions without a valid reason, we meet with him about this, and he is terminated from the group if his attendance does not improve. We find that most of the time the inmates want to be in their group and look forward to it.

6. Inmates on medication are expected to be on medication compliance. There have been a few instances when inmates have refused to take their medications and have decompensated. Because they became so disruptive to the group process they had to be terminated from group therapy at that time.

After the group sessions, the co therapists would discuss the following:

1. Main theme of the group session, what was believed to be the general group content in the session and the evidence for this.

2. The underlying issue of the group session, what was thought to be the implicit aim or intent of the group.

3. A brief discussion of the action of each inmate and the interactions of each inmate with the therapist and other inmates.

4. The reactions of the co-therapists, dynamic analysis of the group therapy session

5. Outstanding events of the session. These may have been comments or nonverbal interactions that seem to express the prevailing mood of the group.

6. Activity of group members outside of the group. Any activity seen either prior to the start of the session or at its termination that is believed to be significant may be discussed.

7. Manifestations of resistance in the group and in individuals are analyzed.

8. If an observer is present in the group session, it is helpful to get their reactions regarding group dynamics.

9. Speculations, probable or improbable, regarding group dynamics may be explored.

In summary, group psychotherapy is one of the most valuable forms of therapy for inmates. Because most of their problems in corrections have to do with their interactions with others, group therapy is the primal place for them to learn how to interact with others appropriately.

Emergencies (Violence Toward Self or Others)

When emergencies occur on the RTU, the inmate is counseled immediately and given appropriate medication if needed. He may or may not be placed in an observation cell depending on the situation. If he does not calm down after counseling and medication, but rather his violence escalates, he is placed in soft leather restraints by the correctional officers. Intramuscular medication such as haloperidol may be ordered every 30 minutes to every hour if needed. Our experience has been that usually after one to several hours the inmate may be safely taken out of restraints and is improved. If he refuses medication and is a danger to himself or others, or unable to care for himself, he is committed to the Oakwood Forensic Hospital for treatment. When he is stabilized, he is returned back to us.

Informed consent for treatment is obtained from each inmate. Discussion with each inmate includes subjects such as: understanding of the treatment; any risks that may be involved from such treatment; expected benefits; possible consequences of not accepting the treatment; available alternative procedures; and the notion that consent is voluntary and that the patient has the right to refuse treatment.

This psychiatrist's role as an educator on the unit has included presentations to correctional officers regarding aspects of mental health in formal and informal discussions.

Because it is also important to upgrade the staff, topics of interest were discussed. When we returned from conferences, we shared the information that we had learned with those staff members who did not attend.

Medical School Faculty Responsibilities:

It is common knowledge that medical care has been a problem in prisons. Many prisons have a difficult time recruiting qualified doctors. It is good experience for medical students to learn to treat prisoners. By working with inmates, the students become less fearful of them and come to realize that they may even enjoy doing so, and be willing to work with inmates when they become doctors.

During that time, I was a volunteer assistant professor of psychiatry in the Department of Psychiatry, College of Medicine, University of Cincinnati, Ohio; and a preceptor for osteopathic medical students from the Ohio University College of Osteopathic Medicine, Athens, Ohio. I developed a senior medical student elective rotation for the special treatment unit.

The senior medical student elective program was statewide in Ohio and was under the Ohio Area Health Education Center Program. The elective program here at the Lebanon Correctional Institution was 1 month long and 40 hours a week for the student. The learning objectives of this elective consisted of the following:

1. Improving professional skills such as gathering clinical data.

2. Improving medical student's positive self-image by helping needy inmates.

3. Increasing understanding of a medically underserved population.

4. Improving creative abilities by improving problem-solving skills.

5. Increasing empathy through personal interaction with inmates.

6. Increasing sense of responsibility for and the recognition of the need for civic responsibility, such as toward child abuse.

7. Learning about inter-action problems with this unique prison system—in other words, security issues versus treatment issues.

8. Developing a greater sense of service to humanity.

9. Learning about human interactions in the prison setting.

10. Learning the holistic approach, which includes the bio-psycho-social-existential-spiritual aspects of prison inmate patients.

11. Increasing ability to function as a professional team member.

12. Increasing understanding of cultural interrelationships, and how they impact on the therapeutic encounter.

13. Increasing understanding of doctor/patient relationships.

14. Increasing understanding of effective versus ineffective communications in the prison setting.

15. Learning about prisoners and their family interactions and problems.

16. Learning about stressors in the prison system.

When student first arrives at the prison, he or she is given a general introduction to the unit, and to the inmates. He or she is also given a tour of the entire prison facility, so that he or she will have some understanding of the operation of the prison.

The student then meets with me, the prison psychiatrist. Together we designed the type of clinical elective that they want to be involved with here, in the prison setting. Some of the activities that the medical student gets involved with on the RTU are: one-to-one doctor/patient interaction, the opportunity of doing patient record reviews, and doing complete psychiatric evaluations of inmates. The student has the opportunity to follow inmates on an ongoing basis for psychotherapy. The student becomes an automatic member of the interdisciplinary treatment team, and offers constructive recommendations to the treatment team and to the inmate. Because we had a number of therapy groups on the RTU, the student may get involved in such if he or she desires. The student also meets with the psychiatrist and discusses his or her patients, and any questions that come up regarding his or her rotation here on the special treatment unit.

All of the medical students who have gone through this program have believed that this has been a very valuable educational experience for them. They have a positive response regarding having served the underserved. They all developed a greater empathy in working with this type of patient, and believed better able to work in this special security environment. They also would be willing to see ex-inmates in their medical practices when they become physicians. The inmates also have enjoyed having the medical students care for them, and help them with their particular problems.

When I first went on Clinical Faculty with the Department of Psychiatry in the School of Medicine with the University of Cincinnati, they wanted me to teach on campus for one morning a week. I did do this for about 1 1/2 years. Most of the freshmen medical students also rotated at the prison with me in their senior year.

This psychiatrist has been in prison work full time for more than 7 1/2 years. Being a prison psychiatrist is very challenging and equally rewarding. It is a very terrible thing to lose one's freedom, but it is hoped that more programs like that of the Lebanon facility can be developed in prisons across the country to help psychiatric inmates rebuild their lives.

I represented Psychiatric Services to Corrections for the Ohio Department of Mental Health's Medical Director's Association from 1987 to 1989. At that time, the department did not have a medical director, and I volunteered to serve in this function for the department. This association comprises the chief physician (medical director) in each of the Ohio State hospitals. I participated in and served in the following projects:

* Review of Medical Staff By-Laws
* Ohio Department of Mental Health Evaluation Instrument for Psychiatrists
* Physical Exam Forms
* Psychiatrist's Time Records
* Release of Information on Patients
* AIDS Problems

In September 1987, I was elected unanimously to the Office of President by the medical directors, for the 1987 to 1988 year. That was quite a compliment to me. All the medical directors informed me that they believed my input was very helpful. As presiding president, I chaired monthly medical director meetings and performed other duties, e.g., obtained speakers for group meeting presentations. One major accomplishment yielded a medical director's position statement recommendation (ten pages), viz., a prescription psychoactive medications, which was ordained for implementation throughout the Ohio Department of Mental Health.

On January 13, 1988, for our scientific presentation program segment, I prepared and presented the following medical research paper:

"Diagnosis and Management of Neuroleptic Malignant Syndrome"

From 1988 to 1989, I remained a member of the Executive Committee, Ohio Department of Mental-Health Medical Directors' Association.

In October 1988, I gave a presentation to the World Psychiatric Association, Regional Symposium, in Washington, DC, entitled, "Prison Psychiatrist's Role with Dangerous Inmates." After that, we received a number of foreign visitors to see our unique psychiatric treatment program.

One of the greatest tragedies I had noted as a prison and forensic psychiatrist was our inability to treat psychiatrically ill inmates who had the right to refuse medications in a non-emergency situation. I addressed this in my publication:

"Questions Regarding the Forcible Administration of Psychotropic Drugs to Treat Mentally ILL Inmates in a Non-emergency Situation"

Two top Forensic Psychiatrists, Dr. Paul Appelbaum, and Dr. Tom Gutheil termed it best, "Rotting with their rights on ..."

It is HELL for inmates to be permitted to remain psychotic in their cells when we have very effective antipsychotic psychotropic medications. Psychotic inmates are a big drain on the limited correctional staff because of the close observation they require. Their psychotic violence that manifests at times because of hallucinations or paranoia, may lead to self harm, harm of other inmates or to the correctional staff. I am fully aware of treatment staff and correctional staff that have been killed by such inmates, and those tragedies could have been prevented if the psychotic inmates would have received beneficial enforced administration of psychotropic medication. The parole board had informed me they would not parole psychotic inmates, and so they "rot" in their cells using up financial resources, when they could otherwise be stable in the community, leading constructive lives. It is also a complete waste of their lives!

Because I believed that treatment in the community mental health centers, even if it be involuntary court ordered treatment, was better than prolonged incarceration for mentally ill offenders, I approached editor Howard M. Nashel about my ideas and we put them together in a Editor's Page:

Comments on involuntary outpa-
tient treatment for offenders:

In colonial America, violent mentally ill individuals were treated as common criminals and put in jails. Although we'd like to think that we are a much more humane society than the one that existed in those times, the fact is that there are today many mentally ill people who languish in prisons without treatment.

Fifteen years ago. Ralph Slovenko stated in his book *Psychiatry and Law* that although a good argument could be made that the state mental hospital systems should take responsibility for mentally ill criminal offenders, it was unlikely that those systems would do so. The fact is that neither the mental health nor the criminal justice system has been able to deal adequately with mentally ill offenders.

A recent survey by the National Institute of Corrections of state and federal correctional systems reveals that six percent of the total inmate population is classified as mentally ill. This seems a conservative figure. Professor Slovenko estimated that 15 to 20 percent of offenders in correctional institutions were disturbed in their thinking, feeling, and behavior. Whichever figure is correct, we're dealing with a large number of individuals.

Are there incarcerated mentally ill criminals who should be released on parole in order to be treated in community mental health centers? There are no doubt many instances when mentally ill prisoners who are eligible for parole are denied it because the parole board considers them to be too dangerous just because of their mental condition. The myth that a mentally ill person is necessarily a dangerous person is strengthened when the person is a convict. Requiring dangerous, mentally ill criminals to undergo compulsory psychiatric or psychological treatment as a condition of parole might make sense if such treatment were efficacious.

Studies have shown that compulsory treatment of mentally ill patients can be as effective as voluntary treatment. In particular, a study by Virginia Aldige Hiday and Judge Rodney R, Goodman that appeared in the Spring 1982 issue of this journal showed that compulsory outpatient treatment of the dangerously mentally ill proved very effective. In the procedure which had been used by the court in the Hiday and Goodman study, the local mental health center would receive three documents:

(1) a court order for outpatient commitment (the term "commitment" is, of course, a misnomer since no confinement of the patient would be involved);

(2) a form letter from the mental health center which would be sent to the county sheriff if the patient had not complied with the treatment plan; and,

(3) an order from the court to the sheriff *to* take the patient into custody and return him to the state hospital in the event of a violation of the terms of treatment.

The specific outpatient treatment plan for each individual would be left to the determination of the community mental health center. By using compulsory outpatient treatment, a patient who had not complied with a treatment plan could be taken back for inpatient care before his condition worsened to the point of becoming extremely dangerous.

Although the Hiday and Goodman study dealt with individuals who were involved in the civil commitment process, we believe that their finding that involuntary treatment can be effective treatment would be applicable to mentally ill criminals. The question of course is: Is society ready to provide treatment in an outpatient setting for criminals who are mentally ill? There are, naturally, certain pros and cons to this proposal. Among the pros is the fact that paroling mentally ill criminals for outpatient treatment would help relieve serious prison overcrowding. Furthermore, if the treatment proved effective, society would benefit. An obvious "con" (no pun intended) would be the additional burden placed on an already overburdened community mental health outpatient system. *In* addition, there are ethical considerations which must be addressed. (See the article by Jeffrey L. Geller entitled "The Quandaries of Enforced Community Treatment and Unenforceable Outpatient Commitment Statutes" in the Spring/Summer 1986 issue of this journal.)

We believe that a pilot program to test the merits of involuntary outpatient treatment for incarcerated criminals is warranted. Howard M. Nashel, Esq. Richard Alfred Scarnati, D.O.

Prison psychiatrist Lebanon Correctional Institution,
Lebanon, Ohio

I had noted early on in treating our most violent psychiatric inmates that they appeared to require much higher doses of antipsychotic medications, and I completed a study:

"Most-Violent Psychiatric Inmates and Neuroleptics":

Highlights are:

In treating violent psychiatric inmates, I had obtained best results using haloperidol and especially fluphenazine decanoate. Fifteen of the 47 patients on the RTU were on fluphenazine decanoate. For the majority of patients with schizophrenia, there are no effective substitutes for neuro-leptics.[5]

Schizophrenic patients exhibit a slowness of information processing. This is not caused by neuroleptics. In normal subjects, neuroleptics increased their speed of information processing. Neuroleptics also reversed the information-processing deficit of schizophrenic patients. The medicated schizophrenic group showed a better overall adjustment in functioning.

To my knowledge, this is the first direct evidence of a significant relationship between slow thought processing and clinical state. Theoretically, slow thought processing creates a vulnerability to information overload and disrupts the normal smooth, sequential flow of information processing.[6]

Most of our RTU psychiatric inmates on neuroleptics have been able to function better since they have been on neuroleptics. They are much better able to participate in the communication in the therapy groups and the educational program.

We have a good medication compliance rate because all the treatment staff, including the correctional officers, encourage the patients to stay on their medications. All of us constantly point out to our patients how much progress they have made since they have been taking their medication and attending their therapy sessions. It takes a lot of hard work and caring about our patients to keep a good compliance rate.

Paradoxically, I have noted interesting effects in several patients. We have a number of very violent patients who have been in the prison for very long periods of time. They have a prison history of constantly being in trouble, fighting, and acting out. They never took their medications. Now, a number of these patients have been medication-compliant because of a therapeutic alliance with their psychiatrist, and have also noted the positive effects of medication on their psychoses. The other positive effect has been that a patient suddenly realizes he has gone for fairly long periods of time without getting into trouble, and feels better about himself and others.

Because my treatment philosophy has been to use the least amount of medication for the shortest period of time, I begin a very gradual lowering of the patient's medication. The interesting finding is that several of the well-functioning patients do not want me to do that, and continue to insist that they be kept on the same dose of medication. Several patients have even asked for higher doses of their fluphenazine decanoate because they feel more is better, but I have been able to show them, by discussing their feelings, that more medication is not needed.

The Los Angeles County Community Treatment Program has also reported excellent results with the use of fluphenazine decanoate in the criminal justice system (diversion program). They reported that their fluphenazine decanoate clinic was the most cost-effective service at their West Central Mental Health Center.[13]

A seven-year follow-up of the Medical Research Council fluphenazine/placebo trial (double-blind study) revealed that, in general, patients continued to be severely disabled by schizophrenia and needed to be continued on their medications.[14]

Brain injury is linked to violent behavior

Medical technology such as computerized axial tomography and nuclear magnetic resonance may reveal brain damage. A person with a history of murder, rape, on aggravated assault, combined with brain damage and sociopathic behavior, has a 90% chance of being violent again.[15]

In pioneer work completed by psychiatrist Dorothy Otnow Lewis, M.D., on characteristics shared by juvenile delinquents who went on to commit murder, all of the murderers had shown symptoms of psychosis. They had been "extraordinarily violent" before they committed murder. Severe central nervous system dysfunction, coupled with a vulnerability to psychotic thinking, created a tendency for the homicidal subjects to act quickly and brutally when they felt threatened.[16] These findings point out the need for early preventive screening for potential violence, diagnosis, and proper treatment. For those with aggression secondary to seizure disorders, the disorders must be properly treated.

Carbamazepine, an antiseizure medication, has been found to be useful in treating aggression. It is said to increase the threshold of the "aggression center," and may be useful in temper outbursts of all kinds.[17]

I have used Carbamazepine in combination with lithium carbonate on one inmate with bipolar disorder who had a history of severe assault. This combination may be additive because lithium carbonate has also been helpful in patients with characterological problems. My patient has not had any aggressive outbursts since he has been on these medications.

Low-dose versus high-dose medication

The role of neuroleptics in reducing relapse rates is well established.

In over 20 years with usage of neuroleptics, some psychiatrists-have not used them to their full potential. Some patients are overmedicated, while others are undermedicated.[19] A usual maintenance dose for fluphenazine deca-noate is 12.5 mg to 75 mg injected intramuscularly every one to four weeks.[20]

Stabilized schizophrenic outpatients have demonstrated relapse rates of 80 to 94% when low doses of maintenance drugs were withdrawn. It has not proven possible to identify with any consistent degree of reliability chronic schizophrenic patients who can be safely withdrawn from maintenance medication.[23]

I always try to use the lowest medication dose possible, although some patients may require high-dose therapy.

I had noted a very favorable result in the overall functioning of some of the most violent psychiatric inmates in the prison system with the use of psychotropic medication in adequate doses. It appears that this unique population requires higher-than-usual doses of neuroleptics. Fluphenazine decanoate has been very effective in helping prevent relapse.

For my patients with insomnia, I preferred to use L-Tryptophan, an amino acid that is a "natural" for inducing sleep: I had "L-Tryptophan A 'Natural' for Inducing Sleep" published.

L-tryptophan is an essential amino acid which is believed to be a "natural" for inducing sleep. It is a precursor of serotonin, a brain amine, believed to be of importance in maintaining sleep. L-tryptophan has many positive effects in the sleep cycle and, in comparison with most medications used by hypnotics, is very safe. It usually does not produce undesirable side effects. As a sleep inducer, reducing sleep latency, it has been found to be effective at a dose of 1 gram.

Sometime after I had been prescribing this in the VA Clinic, the VA informed me they were not going to purchase it for the veterans because it was too expensive. It is interesting to note that in the prison system I was permitted to prescribe it. Sometime later when toxic substance was noted in the Japanese product, I stopped it immediately, because I did not want any of my patients to have bad effects from it.

Because we found a number of inmates on the RTU who desired to learn, I completed a formal study that was published: "Most-Violent Psychiatric Inmates Desire To Study And Learn":

Most of the inmates on this treatment unit have committed very violent crimes and are repeat offenders. The majority of the inmates have a below average intelligence quotient.

The large majority of these patients are considered severely and chronically mentally ill with such diagnosis as chronic schizophrenia and bipolar disorder. Many also are alcoholics and drug abusers and also have personality disorders such as borderline personality disorder along with a major psychiatric diagnosis.

Because a number of these inmates voiced very strong interest in getting an education, a survey was taken to determine the educational interest of the patients. The survey was offered to 23 white and 25 black inmates. All but one inmate completed the survey. The specific questions asked were:

1. Do you like to study and learn?

2. Do you believe you are able to study and learn now to your satisfaction?

3. Have you had any problems getting an education in prison?

4. Have you ever been on a waiting list for school in prison? What prison? How long of a wait?

5. What is your current level of education?

The results of the survey show strongly that most violent psychiatric inmates do have a desire to study and learn. Out of the survey, 40 inmates reported this desire. Twenty-seven (27) patients reported having problems obtaining an education in the prison system. At times, there are waiting lists to get into school, which creates a problem for the inmate with a desire to obtain an education.

The results confirm those obtained in a study of 59 long-term inmates conducted by Timothy J. Flanagan of the Criminal Justice Research Center in Albany, New York. He found that long-term prisoners have a desire to use their time constructively rather than simply serving time, and they want to participate in an education and skills development program (Flanagan, 1981).

The Research Task Force of the National Institutes of Mental Health reported that antisocial children have high rates of reading disability and school failure, although they show no marked intellectual impairment. It is possible that school failure or severe reading problems may precipitate antisocial behavior (Segal, 1975).

In cross-cultural studies of delinquent criminal behavior, it was noted that misbehavior and poor performance in school is a constant characteristic in delinquency (Ferracuti, 1974).

It appears that young people who have poor school performance could end up as delinquents and drop out of school. Because of lack of education and no employable job skills, these young people may turn to criminal pursuits and thus find themselves in the adult prison system. Given this, it is noteworthy that the most-violent psychiatric inmates do have a desire to study and learn, and to better themselves.

One of the major problems our treatment team faced on the RTU, was devil-worship by some of our patients. Over time we had eliminated the desire by such inmates for devil worship by our Bio-psycho-social-spiritual (Holistic) approach to treatment.

I had a desire to do an article that would include input from our treatment staff. I wanted them to have the satisfaction of not only having their name in print but also being involved in a highly worth-while study. I included input from the prison chaplains and Catholic priest. Our article was published:

"Religious Beliefs and Practices among Most Dangerous Psychiatric Inmates,"

By early 1985 the need for a religious component had begun to emerge. Four distinct but recognizable religious ideational groups were apparent on the unit: Group 1, inmates with religious idealizations and auditory and visual hallucinations; Group 2, inmates with marginal religious beliefs; Group 3, inmates who had no beliefs; and Group 4, inmates who claimed to be devil worshippers.

For mentally healthy persons, religious beliefs are part of a rewarding and satisfying life. On the Residential Treatment Unit, pathological religious beliefs of the satanic worshippers were interfering with treatment. Initially, because of security issues, only 8 inmates attended religious services each week on a rotating basis. For awhile that was enough. Any inmate who requested to attend religious services had the opportunity. However, Group 3 and 4 inmates were not requesting to attend services and Group 4 inmates were trying to secretly practice their beliefs. By the fall of 1987, the number of correctional officers who could escort the inmates to religious services had declined, but inmate religious interest had grown.

The new approach was to have religious services on the unit where the inmates lived. In addition, Bible study classes and a fellowship program were held. Satanic worship decreased because those patients were not getting any recognized support for their activities, and other inmates who were involved in constructive religious services did not want to be involved with those practices.

Not long after religious services began to be held on the Residential Treatment Unit, it was noted that pathological religious ideation and hallucinations were decreasing. The staff believed that this decrease was actually due to the religious services because the patients had already been on adequate levels of medication and were involved in mental health treatment.

We believe that the pathological religious ideation and hallucinations were the direct result of devil worship. There was a much higher level of aggression and acting-out before religious services were offered and Bible study became an integral component of the inmates' therapeutic program. There was no specific religious intervention, but the practice of religion and Bible study had a profound therapeutic effect on the inmates' behavior.

When we first started this unit 5 years ago, it was noted before we began religious services on the unit that a number of inmates were involved in devil worship and that we had much acting-out on the unit. Since we started having religious services on the unit, the unit appears to be much more calm and functional. The inmates have been interacting much better than they did in the past. For the majority of the patients, religion played a very important role in their lives. An extremely important point is that 25 of the patients had a history of committing violent acts. It is remarkable that the majority noted a decrease in aggression and violent acts since they became involved in religious services on the unit. Most of the patients believed that they had a stronger, more realistic relationship with God than they did before they started attending religious services on the unit. The majority of the patients $(n = 25)$ believed in God. Most of the patients believed in an afterlife. It is interesting that the majority of the patients believed that they would go to heaven when they died. They seemed to view Jesus Christ as a loving, forgiving God who will have mercy on their souls in the end. It also shows that the patients had a ray of hope and believed that they would be able to change their lives for the better. Most of the patients felt guilty about things that they had done in the past and were trying to do better to make up for their past wrongdoings.

It is also noteworthy that the majority of the patients believed that they had a constructive mission in life. To some people, it may seem remarkable that our inmates believed this way in view of the fact that they had committed extremely serious crimes and have served very long prison sentences. It does show the fundamental core of goodness that is still left in most of them. People in the helping professions can use this basic core of motivation in such patients to help encourage them to do constructive things.

For most of the patients, prayer was very important. They prayed on a daily basis and when they were in stressful situations in the hope that God would help them in their time of need. It is interesting to note that the majority of the patients believed that they were sinners. This certainly falls in the Christian viewpoint that people are all sinners and have a grave responsibility to reform their lives.

The majority of the inmates believed that God is concerned about them. This is very important for this population because several of the inmates never received any visits and the only personal support they received was from the treatment staff. The majority of the inmates believed that religion gave their lives strength and meaning. Another very important aspect of the religious services was that for the majority of the inmates, their religious beliefs prevented them from harming themselves or others. It is interesting that religion influenced the inmates to seek mental health therapy for their psychiatric disorders.

The majority of the patients believed that it was good that the Residential Treatment Unit had a holistic, bio-psycho-social-spiritual approach to their well-being. The majority also believed that it was important for the public to know how they felt about religion. They wanted people to know that religion helped them and that they were working on changing their lives.

The major findings in this study are that the patients did much better when they were also involved in religious services. Their aggression, hostility, and acting-out decreased greatly and they were not harming themselves or others as much as they had done in the past. This demonstrates the importance of religious practices in jails, prisons, and juvenile facilities to ensure that clients are able to practice their religious beliefs and to become involved in constructive religious services during their incarcerations.

The other remarkable thing that can be noted from this study is that even when patients were actively psychotic and were what most people would consider bad, there was always an element of good in them. This points out the importance and responsibility people in the helping professions have to use this good core of the person and to try to draw on that in order to motivate him or her to change his or her life. Those of us on the Residential Treatment Unit (RTU) certainly take this into consideration as we help our inmates to become more adept in their interpersonal relationships and to become responsible members of society.'

I am a life member of the Sierra Club. I love wolves. I first learned of Wolf Park from Robin, who had lived with a wolf family in

Alaska and gave a presentation at the Sierra Club meeting in Cincinnati, Ohio.

I have been to Wolf Park a number of times with Sierra Club members. My first weekend there was noteworthy.

I arrived there late Friday night sometime in the '80s. I had driven there from Cincinnati. Dr. Erich Klinghammer had given me directions. I had driven up Route 65 from Indianapolis. I took the Lafayette exit. I drove about 3–5 miles. I found an old hanging sign, Wolf Park. It was pitch black. You could not see anything. I drove in a short distance and got out of the car. I was in total darkness.

I thought to myself, *If I howl, and there are wolves here, they may howl back. Big mistake!* I howled, and every wolf there howled back. I felt as if I was in the movie *The Werewolf of London*. I expected to be torn apart at any moment. Just then, a light came on from a trailer, and out came Dr. Erich Klinghammer.

He yelled, "Who is stirring up the wolves?"

I responded, "I am." He told me I was just in time for their dinner. I didn't laugh. He took me over to one of the cabins, where I slept all night.

The next morning, my friends arrived. We went into the wolf pen with Dr. Erich Klinghammer. ENO, the alpha wolf, came over to me, stood up, put his front paws on my shoulders, and licked my face. That is how he greets you. Dr. Klinghammer told me to get on the ground and smell him. He smelled like an evergreen. He had two coats of fur. I really liked being with the wolf pack. Be forewarned, they put their noses in your private places. Ha-Ha.

Wolf Park is a very extensive place. I took a hike and came upon the Buffalo habitat. The Buffalo pack was off in the distance. In front of the fence was a buffalo calf. I decided to take his picture. I knew nothing about buffalo. I heard all this racket and looked up from my camera. The mother was charging me! I am unsure if I should have run. I just stood there, and she stopped right in front of me with her head down and gave a loud snort. It was a miracle I was not stomped by her.

Later on I was up on the ridge. I saw ENO in a gully, and I went over to him. I was by myself. He started snarling at me so ferociously his body was shaking. I just walked away. I am sure God protected me.

Later, I was back in the group with Dr. Klinghammer. We went into the coyote pen. Boy, were they funny. There was a large platform they jump up on. They enjoy lining up and having you push them off the platform.

I have been there quite a few times. The last time I was there was in the spring, when they had cubs. I wanted to have a couple of them, but I knew I would not be able to keep them at the apartment complex I was living at.

The staff at the park take you, and your family around to all the pens, and tell you the names and history of the wolves. It's really great.

Me petting Attila The Alpha Wolf

Mother Bufalo With Calf: Mother buffalo had charged Dr. Rick Scarnati

Wolf Park is a nonprofit education and research facility that was established in 1972 by Dr. Erich Klinghammer. Along with research and seminars on wolf behavior, particularly reproductive and inter-pack social behavior, Wolf Park provides interpretive programs to school groups throughout the year by prearrangement. They are also open to the general public from May through November and Saturday evening for Howl Nights. The park is home to several packs of gray wolves, plus foxes and bison. They are incorporated under the North American Wildlife Park Foundation, Inc., which is located in the small town of Battle Ground, Indiana E-Mail Wolf Park: wolfpark@wolfpark.org Wolf Park Battle Ground, IN 47920 (765) 567–2265 Fax 567–4299 www.wolfpark.com/whattodo.html

Another outing I had taken Sierra Club members on was to see the Chinese Golden Monkeys at the Cincinnati Zoo. We were the first to see the exhibit. We had to wait a few hours before the exhibit was completed. We went inside the view area and sat on benches.

A male Chinese Golden monkey was the first to come into the cage area. He looked straight across at me, and he was enraged. I could not understand why he was so upset. I was not doing anything but sitting there. His rage greatly escalated. The next thing I knew, he was running straight at me and jumped in the air, hitting the glass front. He hit it with such force that it is remarkable that he did not break it. We all ran out, and I went to get a zookeeper. I told him what happened; he shut the exhibit down. He informed me there was no way the monkey could see me. It was a one-way glass. What had happened was that the glass was installed at such an angle that it acted as a mirror. And when the monkey came in, he thought that was another male monkey confronting him. The zookeeper corrected the problem, and we all got to see the exhibit. They are very beautiful; they are a deep blue and gold color.

Chinese Golden Monkey that charged
the glass in front of Dr. Scarnati

Over the years, I was involved in human rights. I encouraged Osteopathic Physicians to get involved too by my article,

"Human Rights: A Responsibility of Osteopathic Physicians."

As an Osteopathic Physician and Prison Psychiatrist I had been involved in Amnesty International, a worldwide human rights organization for years. The challenges to Osteopathic Medicine are formidable but I believe with a unified effort of concerned physicians we can meet the challenge.

Amnesty International is a worldwide human rights movement which works impartially for the release of prisoners of conscience: men and women detained anywhere for their beliefs, color, ethnic origin, sex, religion or language, provided they have neither used nor advocated violence. Amnesty International opposes torture and the death penalty in all cases without reservation and advocates fair and prompt trials for all political prisoners.

Amnesty International is independent of all governments, political factions, ideologies, economic interests and religious creeds. It has consultative status with the United Nations, UNESCO, and the Council of Europe, has cooperative relations with the Inter-American Commission on Human Rights of the Organization of American States, and has observer status with the Organization of African Unity.

Amnesty International was the recipient of the 1977 Nobel Prize for Peace. Amnesty International is very much aware of the urgent need for effective international protection of fundamental human rights.

There are constant reports documenting increasing imprisonment of large numbers of political prisoners, escalating use of torture by various governments and executions of political "undesirables." Despite United Nation efforts and international law appeals, the world is without efficient mechanisms to prevent these and other violations of human rights or to protect the victims, One instrument which has proven effective which Amnesty International strives for is to increase the force of an awakened world opinion which can become a very potent force in international intervention *in* human rights crises.

Amnesty International seeks observance throughout the world of the United Nations Universal Declaration of Human Rights, the UN Standard Minimum Rules for the Treatment of Prisoners, and the UN Declaration on the Protection of all persons from torture and other cruel, inhuman or degrading treatment or punishment.

Amnesty International promotes the implementation of universal principles through world wide local groups mobilizing public opinion, letter writing campaigns for the release of prisoners of conscience, protecting their families from hardship and seeking improved international standards in the treatment of prisoners and detainees. In numerous cases, prisoners are released after sustained effort by Amnesty International groups. The international symbol of Amnesty International is a candle surrounded by barbed wire. With the concerted effort of Amnesty International members the candles will never be snuffed out.

In the past a subgroup of Amnesty International has been developed by such dynamic people as Dr. Michael Nelson and an R.N. Phyllis Taylor: the Medical Capacity Committee of AIUSA, The Committee is composed of physicians and health professionals working together for the prevention of torture and the welfare of prisoners of Conscience.

The Medical Capacity Committee has developed protocols for the examination of torture victims. There is ongoing research in developing diagnostic aids for confirmation of alleged torture. This would be an area where osteopathic medicine could offer added expertise in research on lesions complexes that might be found in torture victims. Codes of medical ethics concerning torture have been drafted. Release of imprisoned medical colleagues has been facilitated by physician participation in letter writing campaigns. There have been organized medical and dental services for torture victims in the USA. There is work against medical involvement in the death penalty, and work against the political abuse of psychiatry.

As a Prison Psychiatrist and past Health Coordinator of the Medical Capacity Committee in the Cincinnati, Ohio area my main interest had been in the area of the abuse of psychiatry especially in the USSR. My chosen profession of Prison Psychiatry has been prostituted by the infamous Serbsky Institute of Forensic Psychiatry in Moscow. It was known that the "psychiatric" directors that had been there were officers in the KGB, and the miracle drugs of psychiatry had been used there in such extreme dosages that they become diabolic tools of torture for these "psychiatric "fiends.

A case in point was Major General Grigorenko, a Russian World War II hero. In 1968 when Russia invaded Czechoslovakia, he protested the invasion. He became a super-problem for the Russian leaders because of his esteemed position with his military comrades. It was decided that the best way the General would lose credence was to have him labeled insane. Since the diagnostic criteria was so broad in the Special Psychiatric Hospitals such as Serbsky, and everyone could be labeled Schizophrenic, a diagnostic label was soon put on the General. He was whisked off for "treatment."

A young psychiatrist from Kiev, Dr. Semyon Gluzman looked into the diagnosis of General Grigorenko. He helped demonstrate the fallacies and the distortions of the diagnosis. He also protested the abuses of psychiatry against dissenters. The KGB was most unhappy with Dr, Gluzman and all the Russian Bear's Rage fell upon him. He was given a very heavy sentence for his courageous outspokenness, and to discourage others from joining in his footsteps. Dr. Gluzman has come to know what the Biblical injunction "Gold is tested in the Fire" means. He is not only the "gold" of medicine and psychiatry but he is the "gold" of the Russian people. At an Annual Convention of the American Psychiatric Association, Distinguished Fellowship was awarded to Dr. Semyon Gluzman.

In the January 4, 1980 issue of *Psychiatric News*, Dr, Federico Allodi, Chief of Psychiatry at Toronto Western Hospital, was reported to have interviewed 41 Latin American political prisoners and has documented his findings. He said it affected the medical profession because without the medical and pharmacological technology and the participation of physicians, it would be very difficult to carry out torture. He cites four ways in which a doctor becomes an accomplice: when he (1) participates, looking after the victims so they won't die; (2) remains silent, not denouncing the injuries; (3) does not accurately report cause of death; and (4) helps with knowledge, material, his presence, in any form of torture. He believes torture is a political, medical, and moral issue.

Dr. Nelson and R.N. Phyllis Taylor had reported on a consideration of several states such as Idaho, New Mexico, Oklahoma, and Texas of using a "more humane" way of execution than electrocution, gassing, shooting, or hanging, and that is execution by injection, and a physician is to determine the correct dose of the lethal drug. This possibility is utterly diabolical! It is against every ethical code and oath of medicine. It points out the great need that physicians have to get involved in the quest for human rights and the fight against the violations of medical practice.

As an osteopathic physician, I would like to invite all of you to join the following organization:

Amnesty International, U.S.A
322 Eighth Avenue, New York, NY 10001
(212- 807–8400

The Russian Literary Giant Solzhenitsyn made a comment concerning medical personnel who participate in torture by incarcerating political dissenters in mental hospitals, which I would like to close my article with:

"It is time to think clearly: the incarceration of free thinking healthy people in madhouses is spiritual murder, it is a variation of the gas chamber, even more cruel; the torture of the people being killed is more malicious and more prolonged. Like the gas chambers, these crimes will never be forgotten and those involved in them will be condemned for all time during their life and after their death."

Since I have been in Amnesty International since 1979, I have been involved in a number of projects with them:

- Correspondence written for the Urgent Action Network on Human Rights Abuses.
- Authored "The Psychology of Torture"–regarding the film entitled, "Closet Land." This article appeared in *The Cincinnati Post*, March 13, 1991.
- Served as a Health Coordinator for A.I.s Medical Capacity Committee (Health Professions Network) since 1980.
- Joined Physicians for Human Rights as an active correspondent on August 8, 1988.
- Spoke on Psychiatric Repression (USSR) on January 22, 1980, at the Ohio University Forum.

[Personal concern was voiced against the abuse of psychiatry in the Soviet Union.].

- Gave presentation, "Amnesty International: The Abuse of Psychiatry" at Grand Rounds for the Department of Psychiatry, The Ohio State University Hospitals, Cat.1 CME, February 25, 1981.
- Past Co-Chairman of Work against the Death Penalty, A.I., Cincinnati, Ohio.
- Worked on Death Penalty for A.I. in Norfolk, VA, during 1981–82.
- Served as coordinator for A.I. Is Worldwide Campaign for the Abolition of Torture for a number of years. Completed projects and gave presentations for this campaign.
- Obtained a Proclamation from Mayor Reed, Harrisburg, PA, on August 23, 1984 supporting A.I.'s Worldwide Campaign against torture.
- Performed a workshop on A.I.'s Worldwide Campaign for the Abolition of Torture at the A.I. Area Meeting, Dickinson College, Carlisle, PA, January 28, 1984.
- Wrote an article on A.I.'s Worldwide Campaign for Abolition of Torture which appeared in APA's *Psychiatric News.* July 20, 1984, page 11.
- Gave presentation on A.I.s Worldwide Campaign for Abolition of Torture for A.I. Group, Carlisle, Pa., November 29, 1982.
- Served on project for A.I.'s South African Campaign in Richmond, Va., during 1979.
- Participated in Kidspeace at the St. Francis Center for Peace, June 1989.

- Gave presentation on A.I at University of Dayton, August 28, 1988.
- Assisted the Benefit, "Cry Freedom for Amnesty International", May 26, 1988.
- Gave presentation on human rights issue at the Human Rights Forum at Wright State University, February 23, 1988.
- Assisted presentation of Amnesty International Workshop at the Human Rights Festival, First Unitarian Church, February 14, 1988.
- Gave presentation on Amnesty International's medical group work to the University of Cincinnati's A.I. Student Group, February 1, 1988.
- Presented A.I. programs and presentations at the following Columbus, Ohio sites: Catholic Newman Center (May 8, 1980), Diocesan Commission on International Justice and Peace, Catholic Center (May 21, 1980), Lawyers' Guild (May 27, 1980) and ACLU-Board of Directors (various dates in 80–81). During 1980–81 gave presentation on the Medical Capacity Committee for the A.I. Conference.
- Gave A.I. presentation to students at Mt. St. Joseph College
- Assisted A.I. Midwest Regional Conference, March 9–10, 1990.
- A.I. presentation made at the Cincinnati Friends Meeting, Mt. Auburn Presbyterian Church, February 18,1990.
- Assisted in A.I. Human Rights Day Concert at the Mt. Auburn Presbyterian Church, December 10, 1989.

- Participated in a Student Nationwide "Student Candlelight Vigil for China" at University of Cincinnati, July 20, 1989.
- Assisted at the Human Rights Day Concert, December 6, 1988, at St. John's Unitarian Church.
- Participated in vigil for the International Human Rights Day at the Cincinnati Convention Center, December 10, 1987.
- Assisted with A.I. Riverboat Ride (Boat Ride for Freedom), Cincinnati, Ohio, Sunday, September 13, 1987.
- Assisted the A.I. Booth at Northgate Mall in Cincinnati, Ohio, August 2, 1986.
- Assisted A.I. social, "The Candle Light Ball", Norfolk, VA, August 22, 1982.

During the time my brother Gil was a medical student at the Texas College of Osteopathic Medicine (TCOM), in Fort Worth, Texas, the chairman of the Department of Psychiatry and Human Behavior, requested that I be so kind to develop a forensic psychiatry rotation in Cincinnati for their psychiatric residents. I did so. TCOM appointed me as a Clinical Assistant Professor of Psychiatry from February 19, 1990, on.

I developed a rotation in forensic psychiatry for psychiatric residents that was to include the following training sites: Lebanon Correctional Institution, Lebanon, Ohio, Central Psychiatric Clinic, Court Psychiatric Clinic; Family Counseling; Hamilton, Co.; Court of Common Pleas, Division of Domestic Relations; and possibly, the juvenile court Clinic, Cincinnati, Ohio. When residents were to rotate through the Lebanon Correctional Institution, I was to assist in coordinating their rotations and ensure overall clinical supervision. Unfortunately, even though I spent considerable time and effort in developing the rotation, it never took place, because I did not remain in my employment with the state.

I have been a member of Physicians for Social Responsibility since July 1983. I have:

- Performed legislative alerts.
- Participated in January 1991 PSR Meeting, focused discussion and brainstorming on Persian Gulf War issues.
- Corresponded with an International Physicians Group for the Prevention of Nuclear War (IPPNW) in Chelyabinsk In the Ural Mountains in the former Soviet Union.
- Done research work to address problem of adverse effects on public health due to the Fernald Nuclear Plant.
- Served as congressional point of contact for local Harrisburg, Pa., area PSR.
- Worked on 1990 Southwest Ohio PSR Annual Planning Meeting to help build strong working coalitions with other activist groups.
- Assisted the FRESH/SW Ohio PSR Stress Workshop for victims of the Fernald Nuclear Plant at the Venice Presbyterian Church in Ross, Ohio, October 21, 1989.
- Met with Russian doctors on September 30, 1987, and subsequently corresponded with Dr. Valentine Moiseyev.
- Served on the Steering Committee for Cincinnati PSR in 1985, and Speakers Bureau of Cincinnati, taking part in the Hiroshima Phone-A-Thon on July 31, 1985.

- Represented PSR at a Conference of American Emergency Room Physicians at Kings Island, Ohio in August 1985.

- Gave a presentation to the public, representing PSR, on the Medical and Psychological Consequences of Nuclear War for the Vigil for 38th Anniversary of the bombing of Hiroshima (1983 Ad Hoc Committee for Hiroshima/ Nagasaki Observance in Harrisburg, PA). After the presentation, I was interviewed by Mary McGuire for Channel 27 WHTM TV.

- Gave a presentation for PSR, on the Medical and Psychological Consequences of Nuclear War, on October 1, 1983, for the National Nuclear Weapons Freeze Campaign at the Capitol Area Freeze Walk in Harrisburg, Pa. I marched together with the public after presentation.

- Served on a panel of experts; presented PSR on November 21, 1983, to WSBA 910 On-the-Dial (radio station) in Central, Pa., answering "call-ins" regarding the TV presentation of "The *Day After*." Subsequently I met with the Central, Pa. Nuclear Freeze Group and Congressman George W. Gekas.

- Represented PSR at Rep. Tom Luken's Town Meeting, July 8, 1986.

- Assisted with the PSR Booth for the All-About-Kids Weekend at the Convention Center Booth, August 4, 1989, Fall 1987 and 1986.

Because of my great concern for the potential destruction of humanity, I wrote a paper on

"The Medical and Psychological Aspects of Nuclear War."

The medical and psychological aspects of nuclear war may be described in specific terms in relation to a specific sized nuclear weapon dropped. However, it is believed that most likely as a result of all out thermonuclear war, WWIII, our beautiful planet and everything in it will be completely annihilated. Man will have indeed committed the most heinous crime against humanity and God. We must all work together to see to it that this terrible nightmare does not happen.

The Union of Concerned Scientists is concerned that each day, three to five new nuclear warheads are constructed in our world. And that as each day passes, we are driven closer to the possibility that the gruesome destructive force of nuclear weapons will be unleashed.[1]

The Center for Defense Information believes there are more than enough nuclear weapons as the United States has 30,000 and the Russians 20,000.[2] Nuclear weapons production is a perpetual inflation machine chewing up tens of billions of tax dollars every year.[3]

The United States can explode 12,000 nuclear weapons on the USSR; and the Soviets can explode 8,000 nuclear weapons on the USA. The old concept of "military superiority" is meaningless as there will be no winners in a nuclear war according to Rear Admiral Gene R. La Rocque USN (Ret).[4]

Some professionals have attempted to give us an idea of the destructive force *of* a current nuclear weapon such as a 20-megaton bomb being detonated over a city killing several million people.[5-7]

But a 20-megaton bomb is equal to 1,600 Hiroshima bombs detonated at the same, place at the same time.[8]

It is almost beyond human comprehension to attempt to imagine such a weapon. Does man really think about such a ghastly event? Most likely through the defense mechanisms of denial, suppression and repression, we probably do not think about it for this is the most dreadful thought imaginable.

Physicians for Social Responsibility Inc. have developed a series of national symposia on 'The Medical Consequences of Nuclear Weapons and Nuclear War." Based on medical and scientific analyses, these physicians and scientists have made the following conclusions:

1) That nuclear war, even a "limited" one, would result in death, injury and disease on a scale that has no precedent in the history of human existence.

2) That medical "disaster planning" for nuclear war is meaningless. There is no possible effective medical response. Most hospitals would be destroyed, most medical personnel, dead or injured, most supplies unavailable. Most "survivors" would die.

3) That there is no effective civil defense. The blast, thermal and radiation effects, would kill even those in shelters, and the fallout would reach those who had been evacuated.

4) That recovery from nuclear war would be impossible. The economic, ecologic and social fabric on which human life depends would be destroyed in the US, the USSR and much of the rest of the world.

5) Therefore, in sum, there can be no winners in a nuclear war.

Physicians for Social Responsibility has sent this information to world leaders, including President Reagan and Chairman Brezhnev.[9]

Another group of physicians, Doctors for Disaster Preparedness (DDP) believe that a nuclear shootout is apt to be limited enough for American doctors to make a big difference and, even if not, they should do what they can. They have mentioned being disturbed by the Let's-surrender-to-win-the-war attitude of Physicians for Social Responsibility.[10]

Physicians for Social Responsibility do not have a lets-surrender-to-win-the-war attitude. It was through their efforts that in 1961, as a united medical voice in warning of the hazards of atmospheric nuclear testing, they contributed significantly to the momentum that led to the Partial Test Ban Treaty of 1963.[11]

Dr. Helen Caldicott, pediatrician, mother of three, who almost single-handedly rallied the Australian protest which stopped the French South Seas atomic testing, has commented on plutonium dispersed after nuclear-bomb testing. Plutonium is said to be one of the most carcinogenic substances known. Less than one-millionth of a gram (an invisible particle) is a carcinogenic dose. One pound, if uniformly distributed into each human respiratory tract, could hypothetically induce lung cancer in every person on earth.[12]

"The British Medical Association Report of the Board of Science and Education Inquiry into the Medical Effects of Nuclear War" is a devastating report on the probable effects of nuclear attack on Britain, It was believed that present National Health Service facilities could not cope with the trauma and burn injuries that might be expected from a single 1 mt. weapon dropped on the UK. The warning from the medical profession is clear. Doctors can no more help to save the casualties of a nuclear attack than anyone else. And that survival in a post-nuclear Britain would depend on individual scavenging skills and luck.[13]

The International Physicians for the Prevention of Nuclear War, with 30,000 members in various countries, has reported that civil defense can do nothing to mitigate the spread of disease, the pervasive radiation effect, the potential of widespread famine and the destruction of health care systems. Preparedness, it claims, "deludes the public into thinking nuclear war is survivable."[14]

Dr. Howard H. Hiatt, dean of Harvard School of Public Health and a professor of medicine at Harvard Medical School, believes that no effective medical aid exists for nuclear war survivors. Survivors, if any, would be badly burned, blinded, wounded and have problems of radiation sickness such as intractable nausea, vomiting and diarrhea, bleeding, hair loss severe infection and death.[15]

The response of Hiroshima's medical-care system to the nuclear attack was the following;

"Of 150 doctors in the city, 65 were already dead and most of the rest were wounded. Of 1,780 nurses, 1,654 were dead or too badly hurt to work. In the biggest hospital, that of the Red Cross, only six doctors out of 30 were able to function and only 10 nurses out of more than 200... at least 10,000 of the (city's) wounded made their way to the (Red Cross Hospital), which was altogether unequal to such a trampling...."[16]

In March 1981, the International Physicians for the Prevention of Nuclear War Inc (IPPNW) held their first congress in Airlie, Virginia. There were 73 formal delegates from 11 countries, including 13 from the Soviet Union. Statements were made on the predictable and unpredictable effects of nuclear war, on the inability of surviving doctors to cope with the medical consequences and on the social, economic and psychological costs of the nuclear arms race. Appeals were made to President Reagan, Mr. Brezhnev, the United Nations and fellow physicians throughout the world.[17]

Medical organizations such as the American College of Physicians and the American Medical Association have issued statements about the impossibility of coping with the medical consequences of nuclear war, and some medical schools have included instructions about these consequences in their medical student training programs.[18]

John Birks, a fellow of the Cooperative Institute for Research in Environmental Sciences and associate professor of chemistry at the University of Colorado at Boulder, has reported on the environmental effects of nuclear war. He believes the consequences of nuclear war are almost too ghastly to imagine. That the extinction of thousands of species, if not nearly all life forms, is within the realm of possibility. That even Homosapiens could become extinct. That nuclear war is the ultimate environmental threat. That unless we solve this problem, all other work on environmental problems will be irrelevant.[19]

Dr. H, Jack Geiger, professor of community medicine, City College, City University of New York, and a member of the board of directors of Physicians for Social Responsibility, of which he was a founding member, believes that from a medical standpoint the danger of nuclear war is a public health problem of unprecedented magnitude. That there is no coherent response, no cure. That only one medical and social strategy remains; prevention.[20]

Dr. Robert Jay Lifton, author of "Death in Life: Survivors of Hiroshima," and 'The Broken Connection: On Death and the Continuity of Life," and Kai Erikson, professor of sociology at Yale University and editor of the Yale *Review,* have written on nuclear war's effect on the mind. In looking at the Hiroshima survivors, they not only expected that they would soon die, but they also had a sense that everyone was dying and "the world is ending." Rather than panic, the scene was described as one of slow motion—of people moving gradually away from the center of destruction, but dully and almost without purpose. They were, as one among them described, "so broken and confused that they moved and behaved like automatons...a people who walked in the realm of dreams." Some tried to do something to help others, but most felt themselves to be so much a part of the dead that, as one reported feeling they were "not really alive." A "paralysis of the mind" seemed to haw taken hold of everyone.[21]

It is most probable that World War III, Thermonuclear War, will indeed be the last war fought on earth. With thousands of these nuclear weapons dropped on earth, the war would probably be over in 30 minutes to one hour. Most likely, the earth would be a giant incinerator.

The nightmarish scenario would be that all artists, art, dancers, musicians, music, writers, books, poets, poetry, churches, family members, lovers, pets, plants and everything man holds dear to him would be vaporized. If this author were to be one of the unfortunate survivors of this hellish nightmare, he would know one thing for certain, he would be the victim of a broken heart.

The Roman Catholic bishops' pastoral letter has condemned nuclear war. Roman Catholic Archbishop John R. Quinn of San Francisco passed a resolution praising the bishops' courage in urging a "new theology of peace, which views nuclear war as a most sinful confrontation with our Creator." He believes the bishops' letter was written out of a sense that "we are the first generation since Genesis with the power to virtually destroy God's creation." [22]

A Japanese poet, Sadako Kurihara, is a living "hibakusha," (bomb victim), one of the few survivors of the first atomic bomb. Her volume of poems, Songs of *Hiroshima*, is known throughout Japan. In her poem, "I would be a Witness for Hiroshima," she tells why she turned to writing:

"Because the day was too *much* impressed on *my* retina, *the hellish day of that fatal blaze.*

It was August sixth in 1945, at an early hour of the day;

Men and women were to start their daily work, when unexpectedly

The city and all were blown away;

The seven rivers were filled with naked corpses. [23]

A part of another poem by her is an eloquent warning we must all heed:

"We shall not repeat the mistake."

So we vowed.

But it is you who must vow, America—

You who possess the *bombs*

To burn Hiroshima a million times over,

Do *not perish by your own hand. When a million Hiroshimas* explode *in You, America, Your people will vanish into the far off sky Without even a moment to remember, "Oh, Hiroshima," Then will I send you a message of sympathy In* the names *of the three hundred thousand who perished in Hiroshima and Nagasaki.*

And to your heroes, America, Who tell us they would gladly repeat the act If the President so orders, I send these words:

The hell beneath the mushroom *cloud May be forgiven by God, But never by human beings.* [24]

I also wrote on biblical aspects of nuclear war: "Biblical Prophesy and Nuclear War."

Biblical Prophesy and Nuclear War

The threat of Nuclear War is a major concern of Physicians for Social Responsibility. As a member of PSR, a psychiatrist and a Christian, it is interesting to look at this threat from a Biblical perspective.

Unfortunately, our world has been under the control of Satan for a long time. In Matthew 4:8, he offers all the kingdoms of the world and their splendor to Jesus if Jesus will worship him. In John 12:31, Satan is acknowledged as the prince of this world. 1 John 5:19 states that the whole world lies in the power of the Evil One. In Job 2:2, Satan tells Yahweh he has been round the earth roaming about.

As physicians, our responsibility is to make a proper diagnosis and seek a cure for the problem.

The core problem of potential nuclear war lies with the evil one or Satan. He is the most deadly cancer that we will ever fight. Actually, the three cancers that we must be concerned about are the unholy trinity: the dragon Satan, the Antichrist which is the Beast and his number is 666, and the False Prophet.

There are many who feel that we live during the time of the last world war, the Battle of Armageddon. Revelation 6:4 states that peace will be taken from the earth. From the horrible descriptions revealed in Revelation, one surmises that this is accomplished by means of nuclear war: Revelation 6:14 every mountain and island was moved from its place; Revelation 8:7 all the green grass was burnt; Revelation 16:3 every living thing in the sea died; Revelation 17:19 the cities of the world fell in ruin. 2 Peter 3:7 states the present sky and earth are destined for fire.

Many have wondered where America fits into the Book of Revelation. In Revelation 18: 19, we see that Babylon is destroyed in one hour. In Revelation 18:9, we see that there will be mourning and weeping for her by the kings of the earth who have fornicated with her and lived with her in luxury. If we consider the world at present, there is probably only one country whose destruction would cause so much distress for the rest of the world and this is America. The traits of Babylon are unfortunately much a part of America such as astrology, drunkenness, adultery, free sex, materialism, and adoration of false gods (cults). If America is Babylon and is destroyed in one hour, the destruction would most probably be the result of a nuclear first strike from the Soviet Union. As a psychiatrist, I am very knowledgeable about psychopathology and character disorders. Satan has a very severe character disorder. His main problem is that of pride. It was not enough for him to be "top-dog" angel. He wanted to take the place of God. In Isaiah 14:13–15, we see that he wanted a throne higher than the stars of God and to rival the Most High. And in Matthew 4:8, he wanted Jesus to worship him. And in the end times, Revelation 13:4, the dragon is worshipped. He certainly likes to be in the forefront of events. Many Christians believe that Satan, the Beast and the False Prophet, are here in our midst. Israel was made a nation in 1948. It has been said that that generation would not pass away until God's plan had been fulfilled. Since a generation in Biblical times is 40 years, many feel this world order will end by 1988. The signs of Satan have been with us throughout history. Many believe Hitler was a son of Satan.

If the present world order is to end by 1988, we can be certain of seeing more of the signs of the unholy trinity.

The Pennsylvania Lottery was fixed and on April 24, 1980, the drawing of the Daily Number was 666. The number of the Beast is 666. Since Pennsylvania is the keystone state, was this the "calling card" of the Beast to America?

Because of Satan's character pathology, he likes to attempt to make a farce out of a great accomplishment. In Matthew 4:6, he used a tool of God, scripture to tempt Jesus after his 40 days of fast. He hates the high principles of medicine and has done extensive damage to my profession of psychiatry in the Soviet Union. Since his favorite number is 666, we can expect to see it more and more.

In Section 10, the Section on Travel in The New York Times, Sunday, February 11, 1979, front page, there is an article about: When in Rome, How to attend a Papal Audience. It says that American visitors must obtain their free tickets from the Bishop's office. There is a copy of the ticket on that page, see Figure I, and the number of the ticket is 666. Can this be that the Beast has power in the Church? Or his dislike of the Pope? Or was this just a chance occurrence?

Ticket 666

Professor David D. Acker is the project leader of the Department of Defense team formed to alert managers to current efforts to combat fraud and waste. He had an article entitled: "Putting the Clamps on Government Waste," published in the Defense Management Journal, Vol. 16, No. 1, First Quarter 1980. On pages 42 and 43 there is a combined picture,

Relay Runners

I was most surprised when after I read the article, I did not find any discussion of the runners and what they represented.

I called Professor Acker in Virginia. He told me he did not know where the editor came up with these figures. He said they were not his and he did not know why they were placed in his article. I wrote to the Editor of the Journal, Larry Wilson, asking him why he placed these runners in Professor Acker's article and what they represented. He described the symbology of a relay race where cooperation is of the essence to depict the proper symbiosis of the government-contractor relationship.

He believed there was no significance per se in the numbers on the runners' uniforms. What do you think? Does the Beast have his paws in the Department of Defense? If so, boy are we in trouble!

I then wrote to Editor Larry Wilson requesting that he be so kind to send me the full name and address of the contract artist who did these figures. Editor Larry Wilson called me and told me he had contracted the contract artist, but he said the contract artist told him that he did not remember doing these figures. I sent artist Ralph Butler a certified, restricted delivery letter requesting information on how he came to choosing the numbers for the runners. I never heard from him. I wonder if the Soviet Union's Department of Defense has experienced the Beast's number 666 popping up in unexpected places?

In the Department of the Treasury, Internal Revenue Service's 1980 Instructions for Forms W-2 and W-2P, on page 8, under How to Complete Form W-2P under Box 14, IRA codes are mentioned. It was stated that 666 may be entered. When I contacted IRS about IRA code 666, they would not give me formation about this. Do any of our taxes go to the Beast? Revelation 13–16–18 reveals that the Beast caused everyone to be branded with a mark on his right hand or forehead, and no one was allowed to buy or sell unless he bore this Beast's mark 666.

Brothers and Sisters, I gave my soul to Jesus a long time ago. He is the only one I will serve! I implore all of you with all my heart not to worship the Beast or take his mark. For in Revelation 14:19–12, we see that whoever worships the Beast and its image and receives its mark on his forehead or hand, he shall drink the wine of God's wrath ... their torment will rise forever and ever.

Leviticus19:28 says you shall not tattoo yourselves. The technology to mark us is already here. It will probably be done with a laser or an Infra red marker. We will all probably begin with the use of Debit cards. In USA Today, Section B, front page, Friday, September 7, 1984, mention was made of Visa's new electronic debit cards being in use and will be throughout the USA and Puerto Rico. The "moneyless" society is upon us! Many will "go for it" because without money there will probably be a big drop in crime because without money you can't buy drugs, etc. And then, some "creative" advertising firm will come up with the idea of an "invisible mark" that will be the "in thing." We will probably see something like a young couple in their bathing suits flashing their hand over the "new" mark reception area coke machine on the beach, getting their coke. It will be "so" convenient. It makes me think of the beautiful model Christine Brinkley in that sexy blue dress for the Master Card commercial saying: "MasterCard you are so sheek!" "It's so in!" Yes, brothers and sisters, all the way "in" to hell!

When I have told my friends about these things their response has been, we don't want to hear about "gloom and doom," as a psychiatrist you should be talking about positive things. Reality is very painful to face at times. I too wish "all is right with the world," but it isn't. It is helpful to remind ourselves of the plight of the Jews. As we look back on Hitler's takeover it appears that the Jews did not put up as much resistance as they should have done. They went through the psychological defense mechanisms of denial, suppression and repression believing that things would turn out right.

At times, at some concentration camps, there were really not that many soldiers guarding them. If the Jews would have revolted, they would have made things a lot worse for the Nazis. Remember too that the Nazis used some of the Jews to guard their own people. Also the Roman Catholic Church did not take as strong a stand as they should have taken against the Nazis.

It is true that the things we read about in the Bible concerning the end times are very frightening. But we must not allow ourselves to use the defense mechanisms of denial, suppression and repression. The problem is not going to go away! It is extremely important, that you and your family and friends start thinking about how you are going to deal with the problem when it comes.

I, too, am frightened. It is a very normal reaction to this great calamity that will soon befall us. It is extremely important that we all stand together, for by doing that we will gain emotional support and have the courage to refuse the mark of the Beast.

We must give a lot of resistance to having the moneyless system imposed on us. For in the end we will be giving up control over us.

I am not happy about crime in America but I prefer crime to a "crimeless" society controlled by the unholy trinity.

A friend of mine who has a child said she would take the mark so that her child would be cared for. My response was, "How do you feel your child would feel in heaven knowing that the mom she loves is suffering forever in hell?"

Another said, "I will be the only one in my family who will take the mark so that I can take care of the rest of my family, who will not take the mark of the Beast." No, that will not work either. Absolutely no one must take the mark of the Beast! Also, we have God on our side. In Hebrews 13:5, God himself has said: I will not fail you or desert you.

Yes the unholy trinity will bring very terrible things upon us during their very short reign on earth. As at psychiatrist, I have faced the problem, and have not allowed my defense mechanisms to take over. No matter what the cost to me, I will not accept the mark. I plan with the help of my God to fight this unholy trinity, for as long as I can, in whatever way I can. No, the MX and Bl Bomber are not going to help us in this war.

Brothers and sisters, for this final battle, we must as instructed by Ephesians 6: 10–17 put God's armor on so as to be able to resist the devil's tactics. Stand your ground, with truth buckled round your waist, and integrity for a breastplate, wearing for shoes on your feet the eagerness to spread the gospel of peace, always carrying the shield of faith, salvation from God to be your helmet, and for a sword the word, of God from the Spirit.

At all times, keep in mind the early Christians, standing upright, babes in arms, hands together, singing the praises to God as they walked together into the horrible Roman Arenas.

And most important, during these terrible dark times that are upon us know this, that in our lifetime, the most wonderful joy is to come to pass. Jesus will return on his white horse coming in all splendor and glory to reign with us forever!

Oh Heavenly Father, I ask this through the name of Your most Glorious Son, Jesus Christ, I ask with all my mind, all my heart, and all my soul, that you will send to each of us Your most

Holy Spirit, to help give us the courage, to refuse the Beast and his mark so that all of us may reign with you forever!

In recent years it had been discovered that the number of the Beast is not 666 but 616: Sunday, August 15, 2010 Testing the Faith 666 wrong number of prophetic beast? Newly examined Scripture fragment lends credence to argument it's 616 Posted: May 08, 2005 2:17 pm Eastern WorldNetDaily.com

For centuries, people have been intrigued by the number 666, the "number of the beast," from the Book of Revelation in the New Testament.

Not only is it mentioned in the Bible, it has been associated with the Satanism, universal price codes and the game of roulette, as the numbers on the wheel add up to 666.

Now, the legendary number is getting a fresh look, as researchers are re-examining evidence the number may actually be 616.

In the King James Version of the Bible, the well-known verse of Revelation 13:18 reads:

"Let him that hath understanding count the number of the beast: for it is the number of a man; and his number is Six hundred threescore and six."

While many Bible have footnotes saying the number translated from the original Greek could be 616, experts say new photographic evidence of an ancient fragment of papyrus from Revelation indeed indicates the number is indeed 616, instead of 666.

Scholars in England have been using modern technology to scour some 400,000 bits of papyri which were originally discovered in 1895 at a dump outside the ancient Egyptian city of Oxyrhynchus. Many of the sections have been damaged and discolored, but an imaging process is shedding new light on the sacred text, believed to have originally been penned by John, one of Jesus' 12 apostles.

Fragment from the Book of Revelation shows 616 in the third
line-chi, iota, sigma (courtesy Egypt Exploration Society)

"This is a very nice piece to find," Ellen Aitken, a professor of early
Christian history at McGill University, told Canada's National Post.
"Scholars have argued for a long time over this, and it now seems
that 616 was the original number of the beast."

The papyrus in the spotlight is believed to be from about 300 a.d.

"This is very early confirmation of that number, earlier than any
other text we've found of that passage," Aitken said. "It's probably
about 100 years before any other version."

The main researcher promoting the 616 claim is David Parker,
professor of New Testament Textual Criticism and Paleography at
the University of Birmingham in England.

"This is an example of gematria, where numbers are based on
the numerical values of letters in people's names," Parker told the
UK's Independent. "Early Christians would use numbers to hide
the identity of people who they were attacking: 616 refers to the
Emperor Caligula."

Many commentators have gone with later copies of text which
assign the number 666 to "the beast," believed by some to be the
End-time world power.

Some have also linked 666 with Nero, the ancient Roman emperor known for persecuting Christians.

Parker points out the possibility of 616 was considered by the second century church father Irenaeus, who rejected it.

Regarding this new text, Parker told Britain's Church Times, "This adds weight to those who believe that it is a reference to Caligula's attempt to desecrate the Temple in Jerusalem, by having his statue erected there as part of the cult of emperor worship.

"There may be a reference to it in Mark [13:14], where he refers to the 'the abomination of desolation.' But this was overlaid by the Neronian persecutions. People believed that you could get from '666' to Nero because in Greek he is the emperor Neron Caesar. And 666 is one number less than the perfect 777. The text [showing 616] is quite legible to the naked eye. It was published in 1999, but it has taken people time to catch up."

As I have mentioned, I have studied Revelation all my life. Some time ago, I became aware that Sir Isaac Newton had learned Hebrew in order to research Revelation. He is so brilliant that I believed he would have probably made some unique discoveries regarding Revelation.

Even though his book was out of print, I discovered that the University of Michigan had copies, of *Observations Upon the Prophecies of Daniel and the Apocalypse of St. John.* I purchased a copy from them.

On page 284 we see the mark of the Beast is

but on page 320 we see

We see on page 284 mark 3 crosses, and then page 320 mark one cross. I do not know why the mark of the beast would be different or the significance of the cross or crosses.

On page xviii of Dorland's Illustrated Medical Dictionary, Twenty-sixth Edition, W.B. Saunders Company, Philadelphia.1981, we find: the open A-like letter of his name is lambda and stands for L. The end E-like letter is sigma and stands for S. It is stated that the second version of the beast name is more accurate, and I assume is listed as Lateinoc. Of the three small letters before the 666 are, first: zeta (a Greek letter); second: Greek letter for X; and third: the broken five may be gamma. As we are aware, Sir Isaac Newton was researching on the assumption that the number of the beast was 666. Since we now know the true number of the beast may be 616, then all his research may be for naught.

In my last year of medical school, one of the procedures I was expected to do was circumcision on infant males. I informed my supervisor that I was completely unable to do this procedure, because I believed it to be a barbaric practice and was probably very painful for the infant. I informed him that if he believed I was just trying to get out of work that I would attempt to do double duty on the rotation. He told me they would not force me to do a procedure that I did not believe was right. I did do an article on it:

"Un-anesthetized Circumcision: A Case for Child Abuse?":

Circumcision is an ancient practice being of ritual and religious significance in many cultures.[1] The origin of this practice is unknown, but it dates back to Neolithic time.[2-4]

In the Old Testament, God in his covenant with Abraham mandated: "This is how you shall keep my covenant between myself and you and your descendants alter you: circumcise yourselves, every male among you. You shall circumcise the flesh of *your* foreskin, and it shall be the sign of the covenant between us. Every male among *you* in every generation shall be circumcised on the eighth day...thus shall my covenant be marked in your flesh as an everlasting covenant. Every uncircumcised male, everyone who has not had the flesh of his foreskin circumcised, shall be cut off from the kin of his father. He has broken my covenant.[5] The Jews have kept this covenant for centuries. From the reading it appears that God did not make mention of any use of an anesthetic in the procedure Hopefully, there may have been a physician in the Abraham clan who did use an anesthetic in the procedure, but it is not recorded.

Paradoxically, in the New Testament, Paul states that true circumcision is not the external mark in the flesh, but is of the heart.[6] One would assume from this that physical circumcision is really not that important. For Christians, this is substantiated in Galatians 5:5–7.[7] If we are in union with Christ Jesus, circumcision makes no difference at all, nor does the want of it; the only thing that counts is faith active in love.

Circumcision is still practiced by one-sixth to one-seventh of the world's population, and in the U.S.A., it is the most common operation.[8] In recent times in England, Gardner's 1949 publication, "The Fate of the Foreskin" raised serious questions concerning the practice of circumcision.[9] Even more recently the American Academy of Pediatrics Task Force on circumcision in 1971 and 1975 stated: "...there are no valid medical indications for circumcision in the neonatal period." This position was endorsed by The American College of Obstetricians and Gynecologists in 1978, and reaffirmed by both groups in 1983. [10]

There are serious side effects of un-anesthetized circumcision. It is a fact that circumcision is painful. [11–16] The myth has been dispelled that an infant does not feel pain by showing the newborn definitely has a somatic response to circumcision that consists of increased crying, flushing, vomiting, increased levels of cortisol in the plasma and altered sleep patterns.[17] Other harmful effects noted after circumcision are: less attentiveness and alertness, less optimal motor integration, lower ability to calm following distress, increased irritability or somnolence, being less available for social interaction, emotional withdrawal, going easily from drowsiness to irritability, disruption of the course of behavioral recovery that is expected following birth, and worst of all is the fact that alterations between mother and child interactions have been shown to occur.[18]

Parental actions and feelings of attachment are affected by their perceptions of the infant. If the infant is perceived as unavailable for social interaction, or erratically so during the neonatal period, this would impact on the developing relationship between the parents and child.[19] A rejecting baby affects mother-infant synchrony.[20] There is no doubt that circumcision effects have a harmful effect on mother-child interaction.[21] Quite possibly the harmful effects could be long lasting in the parent-child relationship.

Because of the consistency of these findings, this author joins other physicians who categorically refuse to perform routine circumcision.[22]

Published article titles such as "The Rape of the Phallus," "Penile Plunder," and "A Sexual Rite on Trial"[23] call attention to the controversy and provide physicians with a more thoughtful analysis of this issue.

The AMA has issued a guide on child abuse, diagnosis and care. The points raised are interesting. Signs of physical abuse, emotional maltreatment, and acknowledging the child's distress are mentioned, along with the suggestion that physicians can participate in the primary prevention of child abuse as well by well-baby care and education. The Guide states further, that they should participate in changing hospital childbirth procedures to facilitate parent-infant bonding and support education in child development and care.[24] All of the above points should apply equally to the physician who practices routine un-anesthetized circumcision, which may be seen as an act of torture and would certainly constitute child abuse

All medical associations should take a stand against this ugly practice and insist that it be stopped. For those physicians who do not comply, a loss of their medical licenses and appropriate criminal charges would be in order.

I wish to remind physicians of the first Hippocratic Aphorism "Primum Non Nocere" "First and foremost, do no harm!

On November 20, 1983, I applied to the Astronaut Candidate Program to be trained as a mission specialist for NASA, at the Lyndon B. Johnson Space Center in Houston, Texas. I had high hopes of being one of the first going on the mission to Mars. A lot of the mission specialists are physicians. Unfortunately, I was never chosen.

Each year, I would update my application but in the end I gave up. NASA dropped me on February 24, 1997, because I had not sent in an updated application. At the time, I did not believe I would ever be chosen because of my age. When John Glenn went back into space, I regretted not doing the updates, because he was much older than I.

I had had an interest in the common food additive MSG and decided to do an article on it, which was published:

"Medical and Psychiatric Consequences of the Use of Monosodium Glutamate (MSG)."

Dr. Robert Ho Man Kwok, a senior research investigator at the National Biomedical Research Foundation, noted a strange syndrome whenever he ate in a Chinese restaurant, The syndrome, which he named the Chinese restaurant syndrome (CRS), consists of numbness, weakness, and palpitation 15 to 20 minutes after eating. Dr. Ho Man Kwok cites monosodium glutamate (MSG) as a possible cause of CRS.[1]

Background on MSG

Glutamic acid, a natural component of protein is found in free form in such foods as seaweed,[2] tomatoes, mushrooms, and Parmesan cheese.[3] The largest amount of free glutamate naturally present in foods is about one tenth of the amount used in foods to produce its gustatory effects.[4]

Commercial MSG is manufactured by a yeast fermentation process5, and by fermentation of carbohydrate sources such as sugar or cane molasses.6 Thousands of tons of MSG are manufactured and used in the United States each year. The Food and Drug Administration has placed MSG in the category termed "generally regarded as safe.5

MSG and CRS

A person using MSG as a flavor enhancer consumes as little as 4 g to 6 g MSG per meal. Wonton soup from a Chinese restaurant contains 3 g MSG/200 mL of soup,[2] A typical Western diet contains 0.3 g of free glutamate per day.[3]

The threshold dose of MSG causing CRS symptoms varies appreciably,[2] A controlled dose of 3 g to as low as 0,5 g of MSG is reported to cause symptoms in susceptible individuals.[3,5-9] Prevalence rates for CRS range from 1% to 25% of the general population.[6]

Animal studies using MSG

Research suggests that glutamate is an excitatory neurotransmitter in mammalian cerebral cortex, cerebellum caudate nucleus, thalamus, pontine nuclei, and spinal cord. It also may be a neurotransmitter of cerebral cortical neurons that project to subcortical nuclei and the spinal cord.[10]

The arcuate nucleus of the hypothalamus has an important role in regulation of pituitary gonadal function. MSG administration in male and female mice resulted in an 80% loss of arcuate nucleus neurons followed by reduced reproductive capacities.[11] The lesion of the arcuate nucleus provides substance to the neurotoxicity of MSG.[12] Intrastriatal injection of glutamate results in biochemical changes in rat brains similar to those changes seen in the brains of patients with Huntington's chorea.[13]

Neonatal mice injected with MSG developed severe retinal damage and became blind within several weeks.[2]

These studies caused enough concern about MSG's effects that a recommendation was made to remove it from baby foods.[2,14]

Some late endocrine effects of administering MSG to neonatal rats are as follows: reduced testicular and prostrate weight in male rats; decreased serum growth hormone (GH) in both sexes with a decrease in pituitary GH content; and reduced T_3 and T_4 indices and obesity in both sexes. These endocrine effects are secondary to hypothalamic damage.[15]

MSG-related symptoms in humans

Many symptoms secondary to the use of MSG have been reported in the literature (Table 1).[2,3,16-27]

TABLE 1

Symptoms Reported in Humans as a Result of MSG Use

Vascular (migraine) headaches	Temporal headache
Vice-like pounding in the head	Syncope
Dizziness	Seizures
Pressure Sensation	Confusion
Delirium	Ringing in ears
Numbness	Dry mouth
Hypersalivation	Sore throat
Thirst	Hunger
Lacrimation	Facial anesthesia
Sweating	Flushing and warmth
Tingling	Paraesthesiae
Shivering or Shuddering	Muscle ache
Burning sensation	Weakness
Palpitation	Nausea
Tachycardia (Increased heart beat)	Abdominal pain
Stiffness and tightness	Vomiting
Substernal discomfort	Urgency of urination
Chest pain indistinguishable from true angina	Bladder incontinence
Belief of having a heart attack	Ataxia of gait
Heartburn and gastric discomfort	Severe asthma
Diarrhea and bowel incontinence	Mood change
Irritability and bad temper	Paranoid feelings
Rage	Tiredness
Depression	Weeping
Screaming (in infants)	Hyperactivity
Depersonalization	Trembling
Inappropriate behavior	Anxiety
Panic-like syndrome	

Current theories

Since signs and symptoms observed during intravenous acetylcholine administration are similar to those observed after MSG ingestion; symptoms may be due to a "transient acetylcholinosis."[7]

Accumulating evidence suggests that striatal neurons receive massive input from terminals using glutamate as transmitters. Therefore, it is plausible that glutamate may be involved in the degeneration of striatal neurons in Huntington's chorea. A transport system disturbance for intracellular re-uptake of glutamate may underlie this neuro-degenerative syndrome. This hypothesis could be tested if assaying the high affinity glutamate-uptake capacity of striatal tissue obtained at autopsy from brains of Huntington's chorea patients were possible.[13]

Questions to consider

Usually, elevated levels of glutamate in the bloodstream do not penetrate the normal blood-brain and blood-retinal barriers, but what happens in chronic disease states? Diabetics have "leaky" retinal blood vessels.

Are they at increased risk of developing blindness?[2]

Since neonatal mice injected with MSG have developed severe retinal damage resulting in blindness, a serious question must be considered. What happens in a pregnant diabetic female? Does the MSG in the female's blood cross the placenta to damage her fetus?

And what about drug-MSG interactions?

How many costly, unnecessary medical and psychiatric workups have been done because of reactions to MSG? Several patients have had cardiovascular reactions to MSG. How many of these patients have had to face the stress of believing that they were having a heart attack, when in reality all they were experiencing was a reaction to a food additive? Most of the symptoms listed in this report are commonly seen in psychiatric patients. How many of these patients are really having a MSG reaction?

Conclusions

All these questions need to be answered. I do not believe that MSG is an innocuous substance. Until more definitive studies have been completed, use of this substance may need to be curtailed.

When MSG is used in any type of food substance, such as packaged meats or prepared meals and soups, labeling should be required.

On Saturday June 18, 1988, I traveled to Louisville, Kentucky, with my best friend Marge S, an ex-nun, to hear a presentation by Mother Teresa of Calcutta at the Commonwealth Convention Center. As one might expect, it was one of the grandest religious presentations I have ever heard. It was so wonderful to get to see her, too.

I had been very upset about the student massacre in Tiananmen Square in the People's Republic of China. It was heart breaking! I wrote to President George Bush about it and volunteered to be a part of a liberating army, if he wanted to send one to China. I informed him that even though I was a physician, I was willing to take up arms as an infantry soldier.

When the Gulf War came about, I thought it might lead into the last war at the end of time, the Battle of Armageddon. I believed because I had so much experience, I should go back in the military. I believed I could be a help. The Navy was so kind to offer me a rank as a Commander 05, which is equal to a Lt. Col. in the Army. But before I was called in the war, fortunately the war was over. They wanted me to go to Cuba as a medical officer, but I didn't accept the commission. I informed the Navy I was only interested in going back in if there was a war.

In May of 1991, I attended the American Psychiatric Association Convention in New Orleans, La. During this time, I was interviewed on TV regarding the positive effects of psychiatry and religion on decreasing devil worship and violence on the Residential Treatment Unit for Violent Offenders with Psychiatric Disorders.

Executive Producer/Anchor Mary Lou McCall of Channel 32, WLAE-TV-PBS, interviewed me on May 15, 1991.

Mary Lou McCall had done a documentary film regarding the appearences of Our Blessed Mother Mary in Medjugorje, Yugoslavia.

Our Blessed Mother has been appearing to six children daily in Medjugorje, Yugoslavia, since 1981 with messages of the need for prayer peace, and special messages.

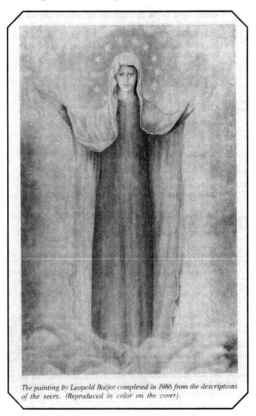

The painting by Leopold Baijot completed in 1986 from the descriptions of the seers. (Reproduced in color on the cover).

The painting of Mary by Leopold Baijot completed in 1986 from the descriptions of the seers (the children that see Mary), Permission given by Rev. Kenneth J. Sommer, SM, Spiritual Director of The Riehle Foundation When I was with Mary Lou, I met a friend of hers, Emily K., a lay missionary in Africa who had been in the Horn Tropics for over twelve years. What a blazing spiritual fire she is! She told me her whole life is Jesus. She told me, "I love Jesus this much," and spread out her arms and said," I want to be cruicified on the cross with him." I told her she was scaring me, and I did not want her to be harmed in her grand missionary service for Christ.

In the spring of 1991, Dr. H, our other prison psychiatrist, met with me and informed me he could no longer handle the prison population patients with psychiatric disorders and requested that I attempt to get us more help. I did request more help. One of the "middleman" administrators met with us and informed us that budget cuts were to take place. We were not only not going to get the more psychiatric help that we needed, but also the psychiatrist's contract was not going to be renewed. We were in total shock! I informed the administrator that there was no way I could see all the patients on the RTU and do the populations of the Lebanon and Warren Correctional Institutions by myself. I was requested to attempt to do such after Dr. H was gone.

After Dr. H was gone, the top administration met with me. They informed me, "We know you cannot do this work by yourself. All we expect of you is come to work every day like you have been doing. Just see the emergencies each day and as many patients as possible." I informed them that that would be impossible, because the RTU patients needed intensive care. I informed them I would attempt to do it for a month and see what happened. I kept a schedule of my RTU patients to be sure that I would see everyone as needed.

As I had expected, at the end of the month, I noted I had not seen all the RTU patients, because my time was taken up with emergency court commitments.

Because I could not give the care I was ethically, morally, and legally bound to give, I decided I would resign. I felt extremely terrible about such, because I had spent years in helping develop the model treatment program. I did not want to resign, but I believed I had no other choice.

I then believed that resignation was abandonment of my patients. I knew I could get another position immediately, but there was no one to stand up and fight for my patients. I knew I had to take drastic measures. I decided to go on strike. I notified the union of my desire to strike.

I met with *The Cincinnati Post* staff reporter Al Salvato and informed him of my plan to strike. I wanted to drum up public support for my strike, in hopes that I would get more help. Al said he was concerned about my safety and planned to be at the strike site with me on the day of the strike.

I made up my strike sign: "On Strike Against The Ohio Dept. of Mental Health For Inadequate Psychiatric Treatment For Inmates With Psychiatric Disorders."

On the morning of Friday June 28, 1991, I took out my strike sign and stood on the prison steps with it. I discovered that day that I had a great bond with the warden. He was the first to show up. He told me I had to get off the prison grounds immediately, because I was not permitted to strike on the official prison grounds. He informed me I could take my sign out on Route 63 in front of the prison. I did do that.

Al Salvato showed up from *The Cincinnati Post*. A state policeman showed up and informed me it was "too dangerous" for me to be out in the highway, and I should stop the strike. He said that in a threatening tone, which I did not appreciate. I told him I had no intention of stopping my strike.

TV camera crews took films of my strike, and the papers across the state did articles on my strike :

Prison psychiatrist picketing Lebanon

By Al Salvato
Post staff reporter

Dr. Richard Scarnati says his courage took months to build.

But once the psychiatrist at Lebanon Correctional Institution vowed to go on strike, he said there was no backing down.

He couldn't, he said, because mentally ill inmates no longer get proper care at Lebanon, leaving them, other inmates and prison staff in peril. Scarnati said he no longer can properly treat inmates, because he is the only psychiatrist left at Lebanon with more than 2,000 inmates and, beginning today, must also treat unstable inmates at Warren Correctional Institution, a 1,000-plus inmate prison next door to Lebanon.

Scarnati contends he is expected to perform "production-line psychiatry" that he predicts will hamper a seven-year-old program that once provided intense therapy to severely mentally ill inmates.

Today, Scarnati pulled a protest sign from his car, and launched a one-man strike against the Ohio Department of Mental Health, for scaling back the psychiatric staff at Lebanon as the prison population soars. The department operates a special Residential Treatment Unit there.

Me on Strike

"On Strike Against The Ohio Department Of Mental Health For Inadequate Psychiatric Treatment For Inmates With Psychiatric Disorders," Scarnati's sign declares.

Scarnati propped up his sign at the prison's entrance and said he'll remain on strike until the psychiatric staff is boosted to ease his case load of 188 patients. He said he had to take a stand today—the first day he is to assume his added duties.

The prison's warden, William Dallman, ordered Scarnati off of prison property but allowed him to continue his picket just off the grounds.

Tom Woodruff, the head of Scarnati's union, calls the psychiatrist's problems "a crisis" that will develop into an emergency at the prison.

But Michael Hogan the state's new Mental Health director, said in a letter to Scarnati last week that he does not consider the psychiatrist's work load excessive. He disagrees with Scarnati that the treatment unit is geared to indepth therapy,

"Since these are essentially outpatient services, the intensity of services is and should be far less in such a clinic than in a hospital," Hogan told Woodruff, president of the Ohio Health Care Employees Union.

Seven years ago, Scarnati was hired at Lebanon and assigned by Mental Health to the unit. Mental Health and the Department of Rehabilitation and Correction teamed to form the unit to aid the growing number of mentally ill inmates heading into prisons.

The unit grew to about 45 patients with Scarnati and another full-time psychiatrist handling most of the therapy; two part-timers also assisted. The part-timers are now gone.

Earlier this year, the department eliminated a full-time psychiatrist. As of today, Scarnati is sole psychiatrist at the Lebanon and Warren prisons.

But the department last month advertised for prison psychiatrists in a newsletter of the Ohio Psychiatric Association. The ad says Ohio is expanding psychiatric services in its adult and youth Institutions. Mental Health spokeswoman Stephanie Hightower-Leftwich declined comment, saying the department cannot publicly discuss personnel matters.

Michael Kirkman, legal director for Legal Rights Services of Ohio, said that agency would investigate Scarnati's claims if inmates complain about being denied mental-health services.

Under the union contract, Scarnati said his job is protected if he pickets in protest of dangerous conditions.

"Some of these inmates may commit suicide before I get to see them," he said. "They may hurt someone. We've had guards seriously hurt here by some of these inmates."

The Prison Psychologist did do an article on my strike:

Inhumane treatment

Regarding the article appearing in the *Post* on June 28, "Prison Psychiatrist Will Picket Lebanon," I am a psychologist working at the prison who agrees that providing only one psychiatrist at the two largest state correctional facilities near Cincinnati (Lebanon and Warren Correctional Institutions) constitutes inhumane treatment of the inmate populations.

The Ohio Department of Mental Health has scaled back the number of psychiatrists to only one who must now treat a prison population at these facilities totaling over 3,000 inmates. In my opinion this is repugnant.

The aim of the prisons is not only to incarcerate these convicted felons and maintain custody of them, but also to provide treatment for their physical and mental health problems.

The Department of Mental Health has abdicated its responsibility for providing sufficient psychiatric care. I believe that one of the major reasons the Department has done this is to cut their expenses.

Their actions art inhumane and must be rectified by increasing the number of psychiatrists at these facilities.

Inaction by the Department of Mental Health may lead to potentially serious psychiatric problems for the inmates.

It may also lead to serious problems for security staff at these institutions in managing these inmates.

HOWARD L. KAMEN, Ph.D. Psychologist
Lebanon

The Union also did a piece on my strike:

The Health Care and Social Service Union

Psychiatrist stands up for ethics

Lebanon Correctional Institute has a prison population of over 2,000. The Warren Correctional Institute, next door, has a population of over 1,000. Prior to June 28, there were two psychiatrists on staff to provide mental health services to those inmates who needed them. One of those psychiatrists resigned.

The Ohio Department of Mental Health ordered Dr. Richard Scarnati, a District 1199 member, to assume the departing doctor's responsibilities. This would have given him a case load of approximately 188 patients, in a prison environment. Dr. Scarnati said, "Enough is enough."

On June 28, Dr. Scarnati began a one-person strike to protest the fact that he would be forced to perform "production-line psychiatry" and hamper the delivery of service to severely mentally ill inmates. The response of the Department was that they did not consider this to be an excessive workload, and that the treatment was not geared to intensive therapy. They refused to listen to his request for assistance.

As a result of the Department's action, or lack of action, Dr. Scarnati, on July 3, 1991, resigned from his position rather than be placed in what he considered an unethical, unprofessional and potentially dangerous situation. The response of the Department to that action was to issue a notice of intent to hold a prediscipinary conference on July 9, 1991. If only they had taken heed to his call for assistance, the situation that now looms at Lebanon and Warren Correctional institutes could have been avoided.

It is the position of the Union that no worker should be forced to work in an unsafe, unprofessional and or unethical environment and will do what is necessary to correct this grave injustice.

I stayed on the strike eight hours a day for three days. I got sunburned the first day. After that I sat under a sun-umbrella. After three days, no one had come to help deal with the problem. There was not the public outcry I had expected. No one cared about the inmates. I decided that since I could not give proper care, I would resign.

When I went back in the prison on the fourth day to resign, as I was walking down the halls to the RTU, all the inmates were banging their cups on the bars out of appreciation for my striking for care for them. The correctional officers were applauding me as I walked by. I was overwhelmed. It felt as if I was going up to receive an Oscar at the Academy Awards.

It was emotionally very painful for me to resign, because I had planned to work there all my life.

The Cincinnati Post did an article on my resignation:

Prison psychiatrist resigns

Plea for staff a 'lost cause' by Al Salvato, Post staff reporter

Prison psychiatrist Dr, Richard Scarnati ended his three-day strike Wednesday at Lebanon Correctional Institution by resigning, saying he alerted the public to inadequate treatment of mentally ill prisoners but his bosses would not listen.

Scarnati resigned alter 7 1/2 years as a prison psychiatrist for the Ohio Department of Mental Health, which operates a special psychiatric unit at Lebanon that provides intensive therapy for the severely mentally ill. Scarnati returned to the unit Wednesday to work two more weeks.

Scarnati said the department, in a budget-cutting move, had eliminated another psychiatrist position. That left Scarnati to handle prisoners at both Lebanon and the adjacent Warren Correctional Institution. Lebanon has about 3,000 Inmates; Warren, about 1,000.

He said new cases at Lebanon had kept him from giving regular treatment to many of the 50 patients in the unit. Scarnati said the department essentially told him to perform "production-line psychiatry" by writing prescriptions without spending enough time with patients.

"I could tell that If I continued to strike, I could not get anywhere with the department," Scarnati said. For three working days beginning last Friday, the psychiatrist stood at the prison's entrance with a sign saying he was "On Strike."

"I think he is courageous for doing what he did and for standing up for his patients," said Tom Woodruff, president of the Ohio Health Care Employees Union. Scarnati is a member of the union.

State mental-health officials have declined to discuss Scarnati's charges, citing personnel policy.

Scarnati said his boss, Mark Madry, wrote to him saying his duties had changed to include seeing new patients at Warren Correctional. It did not address Scarnati's demands to hire more help.

Scarnati decided the department would not budge; he quit.

"I could not go in and attempt to do the impossible. I knew then I was fighting a lost cause."

Mental Health Director Michael Hogan wrote Scarnati recently that he did not consider the doctor's work-load excessive and that the treatment unit is not geared to in-depth therapy.

Scarnati continues to disagree. He said the unit funnels inmates into group therapy hoping to return them to the general population. He said that therapy takes months.

"I gave my life's blood to them (the department). That hurts."

I had warned the department when I resigned that I feared there would probably be riots if the inmates did not receive psychiatric care. My fears, unfortunately, did come to pass as we see from the news:

The Lucasville Siege

Warden warned of psychiatric needs
Mental health problems of prisoners were noted in letter
By Sylvia Brooks, Dispatch Staff Reporter

For months, the warden at the Southern Ohio Correctional Facility near Lucasville has been making pleas for psychiatric help for mentally ill prisoners-but with little success.

At least one of the seven dead prisoners, Darrell Depina, 35, had been on the active psychiatric caseload of the prison in 1989 and 1990, sources say.

The dispatch was shown a March 15 letter that Warden Arthur Tate Jr. sent to his bosses at the Ohio Department of Rehabilitation and Correction. He also sent a copy to the Ohio Department of Mental Health.

Tate protested the "diminished psychiatric coverage that this facility is experiencing, at a time when our psychiatric caseload is increasing."

When asked about the letter, Peter Davis, director of the Correctional Institution Inspection Committee, a branch of the General Assembly, said that two weeks ago, Tate made another "impassioned plea" for help. "We were aware of Warden Tate's concerns, and we shared them, Davis said.

In his letter, Tate said the number of hours a psychiatrist gives to the prison is only about 19 a week.

"A key component in the treatment of psychiatrically impaired inmates is for them to have adequate access to psychiatrists who can assist in their ongoing treatment and care. In my professional opinion, we are not meeting this requirement," Tate wrote.

Tate said there are 301 prisoners with active psychiatric cases, and "these numbers are continuing to increase." He said the prison has "in excess of 75 psychiatrically impaired inmates who are in lockdown status because of their inability to function in an open maximum-security setting."

In the letter that he wrote March 15, Tate also noted, "in the last two weeks," two prisoners had committed suicide by hanging.

Those deaths, he continued, are indicative of "our need for maximum coverage from a psychiatric standpoint, and that hours of coverage be expanded from the traditional 8 a.m. to 4 p.m. schedule."

Tate ended his letter:"This problem as I view it, is acute and requires significant input from both corrections and mental health officials."

Davis said there are two areas in the prison, aside from the general population, where severely mentally ill prisoners are kept. One is in a lockdown block; the other in a section of K Block.

A prisoner was found dead in K Block early Tuesday morning. Authorities are not yet releasing his cause of death. K Block also was the scene of a disturbance Tuesday when the barricaded prisoners of nearby L Block yelled to those in K Block to get involved in the riot. Tear gas was sent into K Block to quell the disturbance.

Davis also said there are some mentally ill prisoners who have never received treatment. He said the Mental Health department likes to handle the most extreme cases—the most psychotic."

He said many prisoners diagnosed with borderline personality disorders, as well as some with manic-depression and depression, do not receive treatment from psychiatrists. The prison provides psychologists but prisoners do not have easy access to psychiatric counseling, Davis said.

It is the Department of Mental Health's responsibility to choose which prisoners receive treatment from a psychiatrist.

The corrections department repeatedly has disagreed with the Mental Health Department about psychiatric cases in prisons across the state, inducing Lucasville, Davis said.

Prisoners who do not fit the Department of Mental Health's criteria for treatment, "are causing a lot of trouble," Davis said.

"There could be a large number of people with mental problems in L Block," for, example, he noted.

He said the corrections department "has been very vocal with mental health on this in recent years. When mental health cut the budget which meant the loss of twenty-two prison mental health positions statewide, the budget of the corrections department was not able to make it up."

Jayn Devney, deputy director of community and hospital relations for the Mental Health Department, said most of the financial cuts made by the department were due to a lack of money.

The sickest people are treated first, because, "given limited resources, we are forced to prioritize," she said.

I was quite upset when I resigned my prison psychiatry position. I had planned on working there all my life. I knew I would sue the Ohio Department of Mental Health.

I applied for unemployment compensation, because I knew they would reject my claim because I had resigned. But I believed if I appealed such denial, the court of appeals would grant me unemployment benefits because I was unwilling to give inadequate care to inmates. I also planned to use that case as a president in the courts when I filed my suit.

Mark Williams Daily Reporter Staff Writer in *The Daily Reporter*, Wednesday, March 3, 1993 on page 5 made mention of me:

FRANKLIN COUNTY COURT OF APPEALS

Psychiatrist eligible for benefits

A state prison psychiatrist, who quit his job because he felt his high caseload kept him from providing adequate help to the inmates in his care, is eligible for unemployment benefits, Franklin County Court of Appeals ruled Tuesday.

The court reversed decisions by Franklin County Common Pleas Court and Ohio Bureau of Employment Services that denied benefits to Dr. Richard A. Scarnati.

Scarnati was a psychiatrist for Ohio Department of Mental Health. For almost all of that time, he was assigned to perform psychiatric services to Ohio's prisons, especially Lebanon Correctional Institution.

When he started working for the state, he was expected to care for approximately 60 inmate-patients. By June 1991, he was serving 104 inmate-patients while trying to provide other services such as psychiatric evaluations prior to parole hearings.

An additional 80 prisoners were added to his caseload from nearby Warren Correctional Institution.

Scarnati already felt he could not provide adequate care to his existing patients.

He attempted to call attention to the situation by declaring a one-man strike that drew letters of support from other mental health professionals. Nothing changed, so Scarnati resigned July 19,1991.

Ordering Scarnati to receive unemployment compensation, the appeals court said the level of psychiatric services steadily deteriorated over the last 10 to 15 years. As the number of inmates increased, the number of psychiatrists available did not keep pace.

"Dr. Scarnati had every right to refuse to continue working under the conditions reflected in the record," the court said.

"The fact that he placed his professional reputation on the line in one last attempt to help the inmates he served (through his strike) is only to be commended. The prison system has suffered a substantial loss in losing a professional who cared enough about the inmates to attempt drastic action to force the improvement of psychiatric care," the court said.

The case number is 92AP-1631.

I deeply appreciate the complimentary comments made above on me, by Judges Tyack, Petree and Close.

I had entered the Court of Claims in hopes of obtaining total justice for my claims, based on the position of the court above.

Even though I spent thousands of hours on this case, I was dumfounded to find that the courts no longer supported my position.

On January 3, 1994, Judge Russell Leach granted the state's Motion For Summary Judgment, because he believed my complaint was not properly before the court, and I was attempting to relitigate issues that had already been determined pursuant to the grievance procedure in my collective bargaining agreement.

I appealed the judgment of the Ohio Court of Claims on January 24, 1994.

The Ohio Court of Appeals, Tenth Appellate District, affirmed the judgment of the Court of Claims, overruling my assignments of error on August 11, 1994. Among other things, they believed that I did not present a claim for relief for constructive discharge; that I and the state's perceptions of the necessary psychiatric coverage clearly differed; that in their opinion, I had not provided evidence that state's position is unreasonable in relationship to patient care; that in their opinion that there is no evidence of specific objective and recognized ethical standards that my position violates, and that in their opinion, that there is no evidence of wrongful conduct by the respondents.

I appealed the judgment of the Ohio Court of Appeals on August 29, 1994, to the Supreme Court of Ohio.

On December 7, 1994, the Supreme Court of Ohio declined jurisdiction to hear the case and dismissed the appeal as not involving any substantial constitutional question. On December 16, 1994, I filed a Motion For Reconsideration In Support of Jurisdiction in the Supreme Court of Ohio; such court denied reconsideration on December 29, 1994.

I appealed to the Supreme Court of the United States on March 16, 1995, with a Petition For A Writ of Certiorari (US Supreme Court Brief). It was for the October Term 1994, No. 94–1553.

The question presented was "Whether A State May Condition Public Employment On A Physician's engaging in unethical conduct in violation of the constitutional rights of his inmate patients, and of his own constitutional rights."

Reasons for Granting the Position

A State Must Not Be Permitted To Condition Public Employment On A Physician's engaging in unethical conduct in violation of the Constitutional Rights of his inmate patients, and of his own constitutional rights.

The Question Presented Is Important

When the public have need of medical care, they expect that physicians will respond in an ethical, empathic manner, and will do them no harm. Would it not then be a violation of public policy for the government to expect the opposite? Did not this government along with other world governments react in absolute horror, when Nazi doctors, responded "Not guilty" at Nuremberg, because they were "just" following government dictates. The position the state placed me in is no different.

Without adequate treatment inmates with psychiatric disorders do decompensate. Life for them becomes unbearable, feeling depressed, hopeless, being psychically tortured by voices, they are prone to harm themselves, and worse, commit suicide.

As a member of the American Osteopathic Association, I am bound by the Osteopathic Oath in which I am to preserve the health and life of My patients, perform faithfully my professional duties, employ recognized methods of treatment, aid the general welfare of the community, sustaining its laws, and not engage in any practices which will shame or discredit myself or my profession.

As a member of the Christian Medical-Dental Society, I am bound by the Christian Hippocratic Oath and am to bring no stain upon the learning of the medical art, will use treatment to help the sick according to my ability and judgment, in purity and in holiness I will guard my art.

As a member of the American Psychiatric Association, I am bound by the principles of Medical Ethics of the American Medical Association with annotations especially applicable to Psychiatry, and I by this code must recognize responsibility not only to my patients but to society, be dedicated to providing competent medical service with compassion and respect for human dignity, and will not be a party to any type of policy that excludes, segregates or demeans the dignity of any patient.

As a member of the World Psychiatric Association, I am bound by the Declaration of Hawaii II ethical values: The aim of psychiatry is to treat mental illness and to promote mental health. To the best of his or her ability, consistent with accepted scientific knowledge and ethical principles, the psychiatrist shall serve the best interests of the patient, and be concerned for the common good. Every Psychiatrist should offer the patient the best available therapy to his knowledge and treat the patient with dignity. If a third party demands actions contrary to scientific knowledge or ethical principles the psychiatrist must refuse to cooperate. The Psychiatrist should stop all therapeutic programs that may evolve contrary to the principles of this Declaration, (I did, I went on strike!)

Petitioner, Dr. Scarnati refused to violate his medical ethics, and the constitutional rights of his patients. The Expert Team commissioned by the state (respondents) found that inmates were not receiving constitutionally minimal mandated care. Can this Honorable Court ignore this? Petitioner thinks not, and prays that this Honorable Court will see to it that the state (respondents) do uphold the Constitution.

As everyone is aware the prisons are growing by leaps and bounds. Adequate medical care is needed. Physicians are fearful of working in prisons because of governmental interference with medical practice; and inmate suits. Since the federal courts have established law regarding adequate medical care, e.g., Estelle v. Gamble, 429 U.S. 97 (1976), it would stand to reason, that this Court would enforce such law by upholding petitioner's ethical stand, refusing the dictates of the state to show "deliberate indifference" to inmates psychiatric disorders, thereby causing cruel and unusual punishment violating their Eighth Amendment rights, therefore, this court's guidelines through legal precedent, are greatly needed for the states regarding physician's right to follow ethical guidelines in administering constitutionally mandated care.

I had received support for potential Amici (Professional Organizations filling briefs on support of my stand on patient care):

On October 12, 1994 NASW (NATIONAL ASSOCIATION OF SOCIAL WORKERS), General Counsel sent me a nice letter:

Dear Dr. Scarnati:

Your letter dated September 30, 1994 to Ann Abbott, Ph.D., President of NASW, has been referred to me for review and response. The issues that are raised in the appeal which you filed with the Supreme Court of Ohio fit within the concerns of NASW. Your actions on behalf of prisoners with mental health concerns were, indeed, admirable.

As you suggested, we will be contacting the other persons or organizations noted in your letter to establish whether an *amicus* brief is being prepared which we could review for possible NASW participation. Unfortunately, we do not have the resources at this time to prepare such a brief.

Again, thank you for providing us your materials and keep me posted on any progress in the preparation of an amicus curiae brief on your behalf. I am also providing copies of your materials to the Executive Director of the Ohio NASW Chapter.

Public Citizen had plans of supporting my position.

I had high expectations that the American Psychiatric Association (APA) would support my position.

Dr. Ted Strickland (Past Governor of Ohio) was a prison psychologist I worked with when I was a prison psychiatrist, and he was willing to testify for me if needed.

After spending years in the courts, I was hopeful the US Supreme Court would decide to hear my case. On Wednesday May 17, 1995, I received the heartbreaking response. My case was not one of the ones chosen to be heard. The court receives about six thousand petitions a year, and only chooses to hear about eighty of them:

I did receive a nice letter from our AOA President Dr. Anderson. He was one of the doctors that had walked across the bridge with Dr. Martin Luther King Jr., in the quest for civil rights.

As a past prison and forensic psychiatrist, I am well aware of government's use of the so-called lie detector, and I had an article published on its use: "A Consideration of the Hazards Involved in the Use of the Polygraph (Lie Detector)."

> Several million "lie detector" examinations are conducted annually in vast areas of medicine, credit, education, government, insurance and employment. Because of the dubious validity and reliability, intrusiveness and infringement on an individual's constitutional and civil liberties, these devices should be banned.

During the time I was in Cincinnati, I received a call from a scientist who was involved in a study with the University of Cincinnati. She was only going to be available for a few weeks and had additional studies to do outside of Ohio.

One of the doctors who had trained with me had recommended me to her. She wanted to learn as much psychiatry as I was able to teach her in a short time. She wanted to incorporate aspects of psychiatry in her work. When I had first met her, I had passed her by. I had looked around and only saw a "teenager" and was about to leave, when the so-called teen came up to me and introduced herself as "Dr." I was quite surprised but did not say anything to her about it. She had advanced education. Even though she was with me for only a few weeks, I fell madly in love with her. On the last day, I informed her I had something personal I wanted to share with her, if she wanted to hear about it.

She responded, "Absolutely."

At this time, I cannot remember everything I said to her, but I remember the deepest parts.

I told her:

"Even though you have only been with me a short time, I have fallen in love with you."

" I am unable to propose to you for a lifetime. The thought of spending such a short time with you would give me agony. "

"When all the stars are gone, a time your mind cannot comprehend, my love for you will remain."

She was crying through most of my proposal.

"God has created so many life forms, that in all eternity, I cannot count them all. And of all his creations, I only want one. And, that is you."

" I want to join my heart and soul to yours in Holy Matrimony for all eternity."

She told me she would think about it, and when she had decided, she would give me her response. Every day she made me wait, I sent her a dozen of roses.

On the third day, she called me, and gave me her response, "Impossible!" That was all she said, just one word. At that moment, all my life dreams shattered. It was the death of joy.

From March 2, 1992, to February 18, 2008, I was a staff psychiatrist for North Central Mental Health Services, 1301 N. High St., Columbus, Ohio 43201. I have done psychiatric treatment for geriatric, adults, and rarely for adolescents and children. I do supportive psychotherapy; consultation; interdisciplinary treatment plan conferences; emergency psychiatry; inservice education; forensic psychiatry evaluations; and acting medical director as needed in the past. I am in charge of the medical student educational program. On February 19, 2008, I became an independent contractor working twenty hours a week.

The academic appointments I have held during my clinic appointment have been:

1) April 15, 1992 to January 8, 2004: Clinical Assistant Professor of Psychiatry. Department of Psychiatry, College of Medicine, Ohio State University, Columbus, Ohio.

2) 1987 to July 16, 1993: Volunteer Faculty, Ohio University, College of Osteopathic Medicine, Department of Specialty Medicine, Athens, Ohio. July 16, 1993, to April 4, 1996: Clinical Assistant Professor of Psychiatry; April 4, 1996, to March 7, 2000: Clinical Associate Professor of Psychiatry; March 7, 2000, to May 6, 2009: Clinical Professor of Psychiatry; May 6, 2009, to present: Clinical Professor of Psychiatry/Forensic Psychiatry.

I have been fortunate to have received a few awards over the years:

1975: Student Medical Writing Contest. Sponsored by the Editorial Department of the American Osteopathic Association. First Prize in Essay Category: "Psychological Considerations of the Physically Handicapped." Honorable mention in Essay Category: "Hospital Safety is Everybody's Business."

1976: Student Medical Writing Contest. Sponsored by the Editorial Department of American Osteopathic Association. Second Prize for Special Category: "The Application of Logotherapy in Osteopathic Medicine."

Special Olympics Certificate of Honorable Mention for Distinguished Services to the Mentally Retarded through Sports, April 1979.

North Central Mental Health Services Staff Award for Outstanding Services, 04/09/93, 02/10/95, 5/1998, 07/09/99, 01/14/2000, 04/14/2000, Special Recognition - 1–12–01.

Certificate of Appreciation: Ten Year Employee, In recognition and appreciation of dedication and service- Oct.11, 02. Dec.5, 02: Special recognition for fiscal year 2002. Employee of the Month (Nov 05). Certificate of Appreciation: Fifteen-Year Employee, In recognition and appreciation of dedication and service, Nov. 16, 2007.

The Psychiatric Society of Central Ohio (A Chapter of the Ohio Psychiatric Physicians Association): The Psychiatric Society of Central Ohio honors Dr. Richard Scarnati, D.O., 2007–2008 President For His Excellent Service To Our Society (September 2008).

The Leading Physicians of the World

The International Association Of HealthCare Professionals Recognizes

Dr. Richard Scarnati As A Leading Physician Of The World

ABI American Biographical Institute, Inc.

2010 Man of the Year in Medicine and Healthcare

Dr. Richard Alfred Scarnati

Who's Who Listings:

Marquis Who's Who Publications:

Who's Who in Medicine and Healthcare, 7th Edition 2009–2010

Who's Who in Science and Engineering 2011–2012 (11th Edition)

The Consumers' Research Council of America has listed me in their "America's Top Psychiatrists" publication, from 2009 on.

I am listed in the American Board of Psychiatry and Neurology of the American Board of Medical Specialties.

I have lifted weights ever since I was fourteen years old. My top lifts were: 315-pound bench press on a standard barbell; 165-pound strict curl on a standard barbell; 212-pound military press on an Olympic barbell.

I have been in a number of weightlifting contests:

1) Thompson Recreation Center, Columbus, Ohio: 1992 Open Bench
   Press, Men's Master Champion Trophy, (215 pounds).

2) Thompson Recreation Center, Columbus, Ohio: 11–11–92, 1992
   Master's Bench Press Open Runner-up Trophy, (220 pounds).

3) Thompson Recreation Center, Columbus, Ohio: 5–22–93,
   Master's Bench Press, (210 pounds).

4) 1993 Champion CRPD Bench Press Meet Trophy, 11–6-1993,
   Columbus, Ohio.

5) 1993 CompuServe Annual Corporate Invitational Bench Press and
   Dead Lift Championship, 11–20–93, 7th Place, (220 pounds).

6) 1994 Central Ohio Bench Press, Dublin High School, Dublin,
   Ohio: 4–16–94, 6th Place Medal, (205 pounds).

7) Thompson Recreation Center, Columbus, Ohio: 11–12–94, 1994
   Master's Champion CRPD Bench Press Meet Trophy, (210 pounds).

8) Performance Fitness Center, Columbus, Ohio: 6–24–1995,

Master's Division Bench Press Contest, 2nd Place
Trophy, (220 pounds).

9) 1996 PAL Bench Press, Columbus, Ohio, 3rd
Place Master's Trophy.

Another of my favorite pastimes is shooting pool. My retired colleague Dr. Walter C, a "Chicago Kid" and musician, is a very good pool player. In the beginning, he always beat me.

He gave me a book on pool playing and has taught me some very difficult shots. Now I am almost as good as he is. We shoot pool once a week after I get out of Mass, and he still probably wins more games than I do.

My brother Bob was a very good pool player in the past. My brother-in-law, Forest, has a "unique way" of shooting pool. At first, I never thought I could ever beat him, but I have beaten him three games straight!

My master's degree thesis was:

A Syllabus for Student Teaching in Physical Therapy (California State College at Los Angeles, 1969).

My American Board Certification is:

American Board of Psychiatry and Neurology, Inc., (1) Certification in Psychiatry, June, 1981 Certificate #22587; (2) Subspecialty Certification in Forensic Psychiatry, April, 1999 Diplomate #1211 Recertification: April 2010 to December 31, 2020.

Fellowship is as follows:

Richard Alfred Scarnati, D.O. was elected to be a Fellow by the American Psychiatric Association on January 1, 2003, in recognition of his significant contributions to Psychiatry; and Life Fellow on January 1, 2007, in recognition of his significant contributions to Psychiatry.
National Appointment (Past): Expert Consultant Pool of the National Institute of Juvenile Justice and Delinquency Prevention.
Joint Commission On Accreditation of Hospitals work:

Field comments relating to the proposed drafts of a single set of standards for hospital based psychiatric services for inclusion in the 1983 edition of the Accreditation Manual for Hospitals (AMH).

Manuscript Referee

In 1983, 1 began doing evaluations of submitted articles to the American Journal of Psychiatry when requested to do so by APA.

I am licensed as a physician in the states of Maryland, Virginia, Ohio, Texas, Florida, Pennsylvania, and Indiana.

I am licensed as a physical therapist in California

I have a Controlled Substances Registration Certificate DEA Registration

My professional memberships are as follows:

American Psychiatric Association: Member—1977 to January 1, 2003. Fellow, January 1, 2003 to January 1,2007, Life Fellow, January 1, 2007 to present.

American Academy of Psychiatry and the Law: Member— November 1979 to Present.

January 30, 1987, to October 1989: Member of the American Academy of Psychiatry and the Law Committee on Psychiatric Services to Correctional Facilities.

Ohio Psychiatric Physicians Association: Member—May 4, 1985, to April 13, 2007. Life Fellow—April 13, 2007 to present. Since 2006 on, I have served as Councilor numerous times.

The Psychiatric Society of Central Ohio (1980–1981) and May 21, 1992 to present: President-elect May 2006 to May 2007, President May 2007 to 2008. Past President 2008–2009.

World Psychiatric Association: Diploma Issued May 1980 to present.

Christian Medical Dental Society: March 25, 1983 to present.

Physicians for Social Responsibility: July 6, 1983 to present.

American Osteopathic Association: 1972 to present.

American College of Neuropsychiatrists (Associate Member): April 1, 1988 to present.

Physicians for Human Rights: August 8, 1988 to present.

Chicago College of Osteopathic Medicine Alumni Association, Life Member.

Amnesty International USA. Volunteer Health Coordinator Medical Capacity Committee of AI 1979 to present.

Common Cause: January 1983 to present.

MENSA (High IQ group): 2-1-1979 to present.

Sierra Club: 10–1981 to present (Life Membership).

Catholic Alumni Club: 2–67 to present.

The American Legion: 8–05 to present.

National Writers Union (NWU) July 26, 2010, to present.

Past Privileges:

Twin Valley Psychiatric System (Central Ohio Psychiatric Hospital) (COPH), Ohio Department of Mental Health, 09/17/92 to July, 05.

Medicare Provider

Medicare, Nationwide Insurance, 09/04/92 to Present.

Medicaid Provider

Ohio Medicaid Program, 09/16/92 to Present.

Credentialed Network Provider

A number of managed care companies contracted with my employer

Over the years in psychiatry we have been fortunate to witness the development of many more advanced psychotropic medications which have benefitted our patients greatly.

The current tragedy is that we are unable to obtain newer psychotropic medications because the patient's insurance companies require pre authorizations in order to obtain such medications. Usually when I call I never reach the person who makes the decision. One notable time I called and had the speakerphone on, while I was writing my patient's psychiatric treatment note, with the medical student also in the room, the speakerphone announced there were 55 calls ahead of mine. Both my patient and medical student were shocked.

This is absolute madness! Who knows more about what the patient needs, than the patient and their psychiatrist?

I have been active in attempting to obtain adequate care for my patients; especially, meeting Senators and Representatives about care problems through meetings set up by the OHIO PSYCHIAT-RIC PHYSICIANS ASSOCIATION.

All my publications are included in the Bibliography.

I have been an avid movie fan all my life. I especially like musicals. My all-time favorite film is Xanadu with Olivia Newton John.

I like a lot of actresses, and my favorites are: Cate Blanchett, Angelina Jole, Meg Ryan, Audrey Hepburn, Julie Christie, Olivia Newton John, Julia Roberts, Cameron Diaz, Kate Beckinsale, Uma Thurman, Jennifer Garner, Lucy Liu, Nicole Kidman, Kristin Scott Thomas, Madonna, Raquel Welch and Charlotte Rampling.

I like a lot of actors and my favorites are: Brad Pitt, Johnny Depp, Nicolas Cage, Mel Gibson, Richard Gere, Tom Cruise, Harrison Ford, Tom Hanks, Clint Eastwood, Gabriel Byrne, Arnold Schwarzenegger, Antonio Banderas, Al Pacino, Robert De Niro, Sylvester Stallone, and Sean Connary.

My current favorite opera singer is a fellow Pittsburgher 10 year old Jackie Evancho who performed on America Got Talent. After I heard her sing AVE MARIA, I came to the conclusion that she is an Angel from Paradise!

I stopped going to films, because the sound is so loud that one gets blasted out of their seat. It's extremely irritating. It's actually dangerous for one's hearing. I have complained so many times at so many places, but no one will do anything about it.

I also like to dance. I enjoy watching the global dancing contests, too.

I like all types of music, especially rock and roll. Some of my all-time favorites are the Beatles, Michael Jackson, Madonna, Sheryl Crow, Lady Gaga, and Abba.

My most favorite song is Amazing Grace.

Amazing Grace lyrics

John Newton (1725–1807)
Stanza 6 anon.
Amazing Grace, how sweet the sound,
That saved a wretch like me.
I once was lost but now am found,
Was blind, but now I see.

T'was Grace that taught my heart to fear.
And Grace, my fears relieved.
How precious did that Grace appear
The hour I first believed.

Through many dangers, toils and snares
I have already come;
'Tis Grace that brought me safe thus far
and Grace will lead me home.

The Lord has promised good to me.
His word my hope secures.
He will my shield and portion be,
As long as life endures.

Yea, when this flesh and heart shall fail,
And mortal life shall cease,
I shall possess within the veil,
A life of joy and peace.
When we've been here ten thousand years

Bright shining as the sun.
We've no less days to sing God's praise
Than when we've first begun.

Amazing Grace, how sweet the sound,
That saved a wretch like me.
I once was lost but now am found,
Was blind, but now I see.

I love art. My sister, Gloria, may be a great artist waiting to be discovered. When she showed me her paintings, I was blown away. I
though I was looking at paintings by the great artists.

I have been fascinated about the Ark of The Covenant, and I sent
the president of Ethiopia a letter about my interest in it:

President Girma Woldegiorgis   P.O. Box 20203
Office of the President   Columbus, OH 43220
Federal Democratic Republic of Ethiopia   9–4-2007

Dear President: I hope you are fine. I am a psychiatric physician in
Columbus, Ohio, USA.

I thank you deeply for having released our three million year old
sister "Lucy" for global exhibit. She belongs to all of us, and your
thoughtfulness is greatly appreciated. As you may be aware, Ethiopia is said to be the origin of mankind.

Dear President, you have another '"treasure" in Ethiopia, the
greatest treasure of all time, The Ark Of The Covenant.

I assume you are aware of the probable history of the Ark.

Over three thousand years ago, God gave Moses the Ten Commandments on Mt Sinai. God gave directions to Moses on the
construction of the Ark, which was then constructed at the foot of
Mt. Sinai. The Ark held the Tablets of Stone (the Ten Commandments). King David brought the Ark of the Covenant to Jerusalem. His son Solomon built a Temple for God to house the Ark of

the Covenant. Only Levite Priests carried and attended to the Ark. The priests who accompanied the Ark gave the Orders of Yahweh (GOD). The Ark was only brought out of the Temple once a year on Yom Kippur, the Day of Atonement for the Hebrew people. The Ark was in the Temple in 701 BC but gone by 626 BC. It had only been in the Temple for about an eighty-year period.

The Queen of Sheba from Africa had heard of the Wisdom of Solomon and visited him. After their relationship, she bore him a son named Menelik. Menelik and his mother returned to Africa. Some years later, Menelik returned to visit his father King Solomon.

Sometime before the destruction of Jerusalem by Nebuchadnezzar, Menelik and a Levite Priest took the Ark from the Holy Of Holies in Solomon's' Temple so that the Babylonians would not destroy it.

They took the Ark down the Nile to the Jewish Temple on the Island of Elephantine in Egypt. All the Jews here seemed to have vanished. Later the Ark was taken down the Nile to the Blue Nile to the Monastery, Tana Kirkos atop a peninsula on the shore of Ethiopia's largest lake, Lake Tana. The Ark was here for 800 years. The Christian monks there are well aware of the history of the Ark.

King Azana then sent for the Ark and it was supposedly taken to Aksum in Ethiopia.

The Queen of Sheba was born in Aksum. Menelik 1, the son of the Queen of Sheba and King Solomon founded the Ethiopian Empire.

The Ark is kept guarded in a small chapel at the Church of St Mary of Zion. Abba Mekonen, a monk, is the keeper of the Ark.

Personally, I believe the Ark is still at the Monastery, Tana Kirkos Peninsula because that is where the Christian Monks are and they would want to be near the Ark. Also it is probably hidden in one of the caves on the peninsula, because it would be safer there than in a church where anyone could get in and steal it.

Your Excellency, I got most of the information on the above from scripture and two films: The History Channel Digging For The Truth: Hunt For The Lost Ark, 2005 AandE Television Networks, and Ancient Mysteries, The Lost Ark by AandE Television Networks, 1994, and also National Geographic.

As you also may be aware, there was a very popular movie made in 1981 about the Lost Ark entitled "Raders of the Lost Ark." Actually, parts were almost documentary in that during the time of the Monster Hitler's reign, the Nazis were in Ethiopia looking for the Ark. Fortunately, your people did not turn the Ark over to these devils.

I am a mystic. I have studied the works of mystics such as Interior Castle by St. Teresa of Avila; The Mystical Doctrine of St. John of the Cross; and Thomas A Kempis' The Imitation of Christ. My holistic care for my patients includes prayer when they desire such. I pray over my patients beseeching the curative Fire Power of the Holy Spirit through my Master, Jesus Christ killing the patient's incurable illnesses such as fatal cancers. Jesus Christ is the center of my heart and soul.

When my father passed away in 1995, I had the most beautiful mystical experiences of my life. At his funeral a blind organist was playing Amazing Grace and Ave Maria. During Amazing Grace I had a mystical vision of Jesus Christ. He was standing with arms open and light was pouring out of Him. The light rays were perfect cylinders. During the Ave Maria, Mary's arms were open to me also. My eyes were closed during these mystical visions and yet they were the clearest and most beautiful visions I have ever seen. One thing about Mary was distressful for me. Her chest cavity was completely open and a very large single vine with very large thorns completely surrounded her heart. I assume she suffers because of all the sin in the world.

I do mystical meditations on the vision of Christ that I saw. One night as I was standing in front of the image of Jesus feeling the Light of Christ pouring into me, a most extraordinary unexpected occurrence took place. Nails went all the way through both my wrists. I felt no pain whatsoever. It was quite a shock! I looked down to see if my wrists were bleeding because I believed I had received the blessing of the stigmata of Jesus. My wrists were not bleeding and so I assumed I may have been blessed with spiritual stigmata. I believe that I have a very close relationship with my master Jesus Christ.

Your Excellency, I implore you in the name of my master Jesus Christ to bring out the Ark of the Covenant. Like "Lucy" the Ark belongs to all of us. Think of the extraordinary spiritual effect on the world's population as they visit the exhibit of the Ark! Your Excellency you would be the most popular guy on the planet for having shared the most beautiful, spiritual, powerful relic with all of us! The Ark does not belong in a dark chapel. It needs to be brought out into the light so its brilliance may touch all of us. Please do this wonderful act. The money that is generated from the global exhibits of the Ark will not only be a great help for the Ethiopians, but I dare say, for all of Africa with your help.

I have heard some strange tales about the Ark. I heard that someone had paid a very large sum of money to see it some time ago. He was taken to a cave where the Ark is actually at and was terrified by seeing angels that were guarding the Ark.

Since I am a psychiatric physician, a Clinical Professor of Psychiatry, and have done over thirty years of psychotherapy and crisis intervention, I volunteer to speak to such angels for the release of the Ark if there are any.

Your Excellency, I also volunteer to carry out the Ark if necessary. I make this statement with great fear and trembling. I am not a Holy Leviticus Priest. I am well aware of the parts of the Old Testament: 1 Samuel 6: 12–20: At Beth-shemish the inhabitants looked into the Ark and were punished. Second Samuel 6:1–11 At Perez Uzzah, Uzzah was struck dead for touching the Ark. I will be on my knees praying and begging God not to strike me down for wanting to bring out His Holy Ark.

Your Excellency it is my prayer that you will decide to bring out the Ark for all of us to see all its wonders.

May God bless you and your people.

Best wishes,

Dr. Richard Alfred Scarnati, BS, MA, RPT (CA), DO, LFAPA
Diplomate of the American Board of Psychiatry and Neurology and Forensic Psychiatry Subspecialty
Clinical Professor of Psychiatry, OU College of Osteopathic Medicine
Life Fellow, American Psychiatric Association
President, the Psychiatric Society of Central Ohio
US Army Veteran
Member:
American Psychiatric Association
American Academy of Psychiatry and the Law
Ohio Psychiatric Association
The Psychiatric Society of Central Ohio
World Psychiatric Association
Christian Medical Dental Society
Physicians for Social Responsibility
American Osteopathic Association
American College of Neuropsychiatrists
Physicians for Human Rights
Chicago College of Osteopathic Medicine Alumni Association, Life
Member
Amnesty International USA
Common Cause
MENSA.
Sierra Club (Life Membership)
Catholic Alumni Club
Public Citizen
ACLU
American Legion
NAMI (PROFESSIONAL DIVISION)

Years ago I saw a special presentation on our bicentennial by TV anchor Ted Koppel. He said he wanted to present the best example of America that we had.

He presented Dr. Susan Nagele, a physician and Mary Knoll, lay missionary in Africa. There was this large hut. A number of poles were holding up a straw roof. There was a line of patients that you could not count. Dr. Nagele was at one end treating a patient, while big black flies were biting her. She had "only" been there eight years! I was blown away by her grand medical care to humanity. She is the Mother Teresa of medicine!

Dr. Susan Nagele is the grandest doctor I have ever known. I suspect that some day when she arrives at the gate, Jesus will say something like this, "Come here Susan, I have been waiting a long time to give you a big hug. See that Castle of Light over there by the lake. That is your new home. And, by the way, we don't have any flies here!"

Another physician I greatly admire is my younger brother, Gil. In his teens, he was studying to be a priest but ended up in the highest of all priesthoods, that of medicine. He spent his medical career in compassionate treatment of HIV/AIDS patients. I visited his office in Dallas. It was a cottage with a white picket fence. The patient lobby was most pleasant; the sunlight comes pouring in. Gil informed me he likes a nice environment for his patients. His patient brochure tells it all:

Dr. Gil Scarnati attended Georgetown University, where he earned a Bachelor of Science degree with a double major in linguistics and German. Upon, graduation he was awarded one of Georgetown's highest distinctions, the University Regents Citation.

He went on to obtain a Master of Science degree in Counseling Psychology from Virginia Commonwealth University and subsequently worked as a therapist and psychology instructor at the junior college level.

He received his Doctor of Osteopathy Degree from Texas College of Osteopathic Medicine and thereafter completed an internship in General Practice at Dallas Memorial Hospital.

Stemming from his European heritage, Dr. Scarnati has acquired fluency in four languages. He has also danced professionally, initially with the Washington D.C Ballet and subsequently as a soloist with the Northwest Florida Ballet.

The goal of this general medical practice is to offer discreet, confidential care to the community, with special attention to HIV and AIDS.

In the past decade, advances in the biomedical sciences have transformed AIDS from a mysterious, rapidly fatal disease to a treatable illness. Now more than ever, there is a need for competent, compassionate physicians who can implement these advances and apply this progress to treatment programs that offer hope and an improved quality of life.

Much of the routine care and medical management of HIV/AIDS can he appropriately handled by the general family practitioner familiar with the clinical manifestations of this disease continuum. Nonetheless, there exist certain and specific circumstances where the intervention of specialists is warranted. Referral to and reliance upon the expertise of these specialists form an integral part of this practices' approach to HIV/AIDS diagnostics and therapeutics.

"Here at whatever hour you come, you will find a light and help and human kindness." Albert Schweitzer, 1875–1965. Inscribed on the lamp outside his jungle hospital at Lambarene. (My brother used this quote as the standard for his care of his patients).

It is heartbreaking for me to report that my brother had a rare, progressive, degenerative disease, nemaline rod myopathy. In spite of it, Gil was pursuing a Doctorate Degree in Neuroscience from the Graduate School of Biomedical Sciences at the University of North Texas. There he had two desires, one was to find a cure for AIDS, the other was to make me a white rabbit. I had lost BUMO, my white rabbit when I was ten. Tragically, Gil died on February 11, 2011 at age 57.

My brother

One of the most complimentary things written about me was from my CEO Dr. Don Wood:

Employee of the Month

Rick Scarnati

You always find him walking slowly in the halls, with a chart in hand and a patient behind him - even after five o'clock. Dr. Scarnati has been working on behalf of North Central clients for the millennium. He has so much experience that he always has an anecdotal story to suit every situation. His productivity is impressive. His contributions to the med clinic, our agency and the community are immeasurable.

CEO

November 11, 2005

North Central

About Me

On September 2008, I received an honors plaque from The Psychiatric Society of Central Ohio:

The Psychiatric Society of Central Ohio, Honors, Dr. Richard Scarnati, D.O., 2007–2008, President, For His Excellent Service To Our Society.

The high point of my week, for most of my life, has been attending Mass and receiving Holy Communion. John 6:52–54, "I (Jesus) tell you most solemnly, if you do not eat the flesh of the Son of Man and drink his blood, you will not have life in you. Anyone who does eat my flesh and drink my blood has eternal life, and I shall raise him up on the last day."

I attend Mass at St. Andrew's Catholic Church, in Upper Arlington, Ohio. From time to time, I have a religious dinner discussion with my good pal, Rev. Mike Watson the Pastor.

God has blessed me with wonderful doctors, along with being highly blessed with a wonderful brother and sister-in-law, Bob and Babs, who take compassionate care of me after I have medical procedures.

Many people along the way have told me that I should write a book about my experiences and finally, I have done so. I hope that my story will be an inspiration to young people who have been in trouble and don't believe there is any hope for them.

Hebrews 12:6; the essence is that the Lord trains the ones that He loves and He punishes all those that He acknowledges as His sons, and suffering is a part of one's training.

I have had to work so very, very hard with a very great deal of sacrifice and the narrow path with Jesus is not an easy one to tread. I require a lot of help from Him just to carry the minute cross I have been given.

If you desire something worthwhile, you must work very hard to get it. Nothing comes easy. You have to be willing to stick it out, no matter what; and with the help of God, you will make it.

Jesus, long, long ago in my desolation, isolation, and despair, I cried out to You, and You heard me. You came to fill the void in my heart and soul, comforted me, guided me, and gave me rebirth by the Holy Spirit.

Jesus, I had no idea what You meant when You told me in my heart that You would lead me to all my dreams. Jesus, my dreams were such impossibilities. Being a physician was so very far away from me; it was like reaching for a star.

Jesus, as you know, Luke 12:48 essence is, When a man has had a great deal given him, a great deal will be demanded of him; when a man has had a great deal given him on trust, even more will be expected of him.

Master, I am of the latter.

Jesus, the debt I owe, I cannot pay. I cannot enter the Gate into Life without your mercy and love.

Jesus, know this; that of all the gifts You have given me, even that of the highest of all priesthoods, the grandest of all professions, that of medicine, the gift I cherish the most, and in place of all, is You.

> Jesus you are:
> My Beginning
> My Mind
> My Heart
> My Soul
> My Bright Star of Dawn
> My Living Water
> My Bread of Life
> My Wine
> My Blood
> My Word
> My Light of the World

My Way

My Servant

My Lamb

My Dayspring

My Carpenter

My Teacher

My Author of My Faith

My Holy One

My Witness

My Lord

My Master

My Door

My Rock

My Cornerstone

My Shepherd

My Light of the World

My Wonderful Counselor

My Almighty

My Everlasting Father

My High Priest

My Anchor

My Prophet

My Way

My Truth

My Lion

My Prince of Peace

My King of Kings

My Immanuel

My King of the Jews

My Judge
My Messiah
My Advocate
My Mediator
My Savior
My I Am
My Alpha
My Omega
My Amen
My End
My Resurrection
My Redeemer
My Love
My Joy
My Everlasting Life
My Eternal Song

Bibliography

I   Scarnati, Richard A., "Recreation Therapy for Persons with Cystic Fibrosis: A Review," *American Corrective Therapy Journal*, 23:7-13, January February, 1969.

II   Scarnati, Richard A., "The Role of the Physical Therapist in Special Education", (Article of the Month), *Rehabilitation Literature*, 32:130-37, May, 1971.

III   Scarnati, Richard A., "Special Olympics", *Journal of Health, Physical Education and Recreation*, 43:49-50, February 1972.

IV   Scarnati, Richard A., "A Critical Evaluation of the Techniques of Manual Muscle Testing", *The D.O.*, 15:175-90, November 1974.

V   Scarnati, Richard A., "The Use of Lithium Carbonate in Heroin Withdrawal: A Case Report", *The Journal of the Pennsylvania Osteopathic Medical Association*, Vol. 28, No. 2, pp. 26-29, 49, March/April, 1984.

Lithium use with heroin addicts described, Psychiatric News 17 (5): 46, 54, 1977.

Lithium carbonate seen as help in heroin withdrawal. Psychiatric News 12 (17): 1, 1972.

Scher J: Lithium carbonate in opiate detoxification: a preliminary report. Paper presented at the Second International Symposium on Drug Abuse, May 29,1972, Jerusalem, Israel.

Altamura A: Therapeutic attempts with lithium in young drug addicts. Acta Psychiatr Scand 52: 312–319, 1975.

Flemenbaum A: Affective disorders and "chemical dependence": lithium for alcohol and drug addiction. Diseases of the Nervous System 35: 281–285, 1974.

Green A, Mayer R, Shader R: Heroin and methadone abuse: acute and chronic management, in Manual of Psychiatric Therapeutics. Boston, Little, Brown and Co., 1975, pp. 203–210.

Singer I, Rotenberg D: Mechanisms of lithium action. N. Engl J Med 289: 254–260, 1973.

Bozarth M, Wise R: Heroin reward is dependent on a dopaminergic substrate. Life Sciences 29: 1881–1886, 1981.

Brambilla F, Casaneuva F, Lovati C, Penalva A, Madeddu A, Martinez-Campos A, Muller E: Lack of tolerance in heroin addicts to the neuroendocrine effects of an enkephalin analogue. Life Sciences 29: 493–501, 1981.

Way E, Shen F: Catecholamines and 5-hydroxytryptamine, in Clout D (ed): Narcotic Drugs Biochemical Pharmacology. New York, Plenum Press, 1971, pp. 229–253.

Gershon S: Lithium, in Arieti S (ed): American Handbook of Psychiatry. New York, Basic Books, Inc., 1975, pp. 490–513.

Yokel R, Wise R: Increased level pressing for amphetamine after pimozide in rats: Implications for a dopamine theory of reward. Science 187: 547–549.

Cole J, Davis J: Antianxiety drugs, in Arieti S (ed): American Handbook of Psychiatry. New York, Basic Books, Inc., 1975, pp 427–440.

Hollister L: Summary: benzodiazepines 1980: current update. Psychosomatics supplement to 21: 32, 1980.

Brophy J: Psychiatric disorders, in Krupp M, Chalton M (ed): Current Medical Diagnosis and Treatment. Los Altos, Lange Medical Publications, 1981, pp. 603–656.

Hollister L: A look at the issues: benzodiazepines 1980: current update. Psychosomatics supplement to 21: 4–8,1980.

Rickels K: Clinical comparisons: benzodiazepines 1980: current update. Psychosomatics supplement to 21: 15–20, 1980.

Hartman E, Cravens J, List S: Hypnotic effects of L-tryptophan. Arch General Psychiatry 31: 394–397, 1974.

VI   Scarnati, Richard A., "Psychological Problems of the Physically Handicapped", *The D.O.*, Vol. 17, No. 3, p. 142, November 1976.

VII   Scarnati, Richard A., "Transcendental Meditation: A Case Report of a Physician's Response, to Transcendental Meditation" *The Christian News*, August 20, 1979, Vol. 17, No. 34, p. 13, Cols. 1-3.

VIII   Scarnati, Richard A., "Intractable Hiccup (Singultus): Report of Case", *The Journal of the American Osteopathic Association*, 79 (2): 127-29, October 1979.

IX   Scarnati, Richard A., "The Discovery of Hell by a Prison Psychiatrist: A Tragic Satire of the Prison System", *The Journal of Psychiatry and Law*, Vol. II, No. 1, pp. 75-85, Spring, 1983.

X   Scarnati, Richard A., "Medication and Psychotherapy" (Letter), *The Psychiatric Times*, Vol. 3, No. 7, pp. 29 and 24, July 1986.

XI   Scarnati, Rick, "DSM-III and DSM-III-R: Critical Analysis of Axis IV: Severity of Psychosocial Stressors", *Osteopathic Annals*, Vol. 14, No. 5, pp. 37-39, SeptemberOctober, 1987.

XII   Scarnati, Richard Alfred, "Provocative Concerns Regarding the Use of a Stun Gun", *Journal of the American College of Neuropsychiatrists*, Vol. 2, No 9, p. 7, Spring, 1988.

Ferretti F: Zap! The New York Times Magazine 13–16, Jan 4, 1976

Guyton AC; Textbook of Medical Physiology, Philadelphia, W B Saunders Company, 1976.

Guyton, ibid.

Gilroy J, Meyer JS: Medical Neurology, Toronto Ontario, The Macmillan Company, 1969.

Chusid JG Nervous System. Current Medical Diagnosis & Treatment, Edited by Krupp MA, and Chatton MJ, Los Altos. California, Lange Medical Publications. 1981.

Ferretti, loc cit

Berry CM. Benedetto R, Stun guns: Safer than nightsticks, police say, USA Today 3A, May 7. 1985.

Berry, ibid,

Sahw W. Electronic Stun Gun, Law and Order 24: 22, 24–26, 28, August 1976.

It has been a number of years since I wrote that article and yet the problem is still debated. In Amnesty International, Fall 2008, Vo1.34, No. 3, page 9.

XIII   Scarnati, Richard A., Howard M. Nashel, and Gerald N. Epstein, "Ethical Considerations in the Use of Methylphenidate (Ritalin) Challenge as a Predictor of Relapse in Schizophrenia", "Editors' Page", *The Journal of Psychiatry and Law*, Vol. 12, pp. 313-314, fall, 1984.

XIV   Scarnati, Richard A., "An Outline of Hazardous Side Effects of Ritalin (Methylphenidate)", *The International Journal of the Addictions*, Vo1.21 (7), pp. 837-841, 1986.

XV   Scarnati, Richard A., "Critical Issues for Consideration in Prescribing Benzodiazepines", *Osteopathic Annals*, Vol. 13, pp. 19-23, November 1985.

XVI   Scarnati, Richard A., "Prison Psychiatrist's Role In a Residential Treatment Unit of Dangerous Psychiatric Inmates", *Forensic Reports*, Vol. 5, No. 4, pp. 367-384, Oct. Dec. 1992.

For specific references please see the journal article

XVII Scarnati, Richard A., "Questions Regarding the Forcible Administration of Psychotropic Drugs to Treat Mentally Ill Inmates in a Nonemergency Situation", *Osteopathic Medical News*, Vol. 6, No. 4, pp. 41 and 46, April 1989.

XVIII Nashel, Howard, and Richard Alfred Scarnati, "Editor's Page, (Comments on involuntary outpatient treatment for offenders)", *The Journal of Psychiatry and Law*, Vol. 15, No. 2, pp. 173-175, Summer, 1987.

XIX Scarnati, Richard Alfred, "MostViolent Psychiatric inmates and Neuroleptics", *The Journal of Psychiatry and Law*, Vol. 14, Nos. 3 and 4, pp. 447-68, 1986.

For specific references please see the journal article

XX Scarnati, Richard A., "L-Tryptophan A "Natural" for Inducing Sleep", The Journal of the Pennsylvania Osteopathic Medical Association, Vol. 27, No. 3, pp. 13-17, Summer, 1983.

XXI Scarnati, Richard A., "Most-Violent Psychiatric Inmates Desire to Study and Learn", Forensic Reports, Vol. 5, No. 3, pp. 283-5, July September 1992.

Ferracuti, F., & Dinitz, S. (1974). Cross-cultural aspects of delinquent and criminal behavior. In Aggression, Vol. 52, Ch. 15 (pp. 287–303). The Association for Research in Nervous and Mental Disease.

Flanagan, T. J. (1981). Dealing with long-term confinement: Adaptive strategies and perspectives among long-term prisoners. Criminal Justice and Behavior, 8, 201–222.

Segal, J., & Boomer, D. S. (Eds.). (1975). Research in the service of mental health: Summary report of the research task force of the National Institute of Mental Health (pp. 37–38). Task force staff and coordinating committee with Herbert Yahraes. Rockville, MD: U.S. Dept. of Health, Education, and Welfare.

XXII Scarnati, Rick, Mark A. Madry, Alfreda Wise, Henry D. Moore, Jr., Mark C. Schmieder, and Matthew L. Stephens,

"Religious Beliefs and Practices Among Most Dangerous Psychiatric Inmates", Forensic Reports, Vol. 4, No. 1, pp. 1-16, January March, 1991.

XXIII Scarnati, Rick, "Human Rights: A Responsibility of Osteopathic Physicians", Journal of the American College of Neuropsychiatrists, Vol. 1, No. 8, pp. 7-8, Winter, 1987.

XXIV Scarnati, Richard A., "The Prostitution of Forensic Psychiatry in the Soviet Union", The Bulletin of the American Academy of Psychiatry and the Law, 1980, Vol. VIII, No. 1, pp. 111-113.

XXV Scarnati, Richard A., "Gluzman", Psychiatric News, April 18, 1980, Vol. XV, No. 8, p. 2, Col. 1.

XXVI Scarnati, Richard A., "The Medical and Psychological Aspects of Nuclear War", Buckeye Osteopathic Physician, Vol. 54, No. 12, pp. 15-17, May 1985.

For specific references please see the journal article

XXVII Scarnati, Richard A., "Biblical Prophesy and Nuclear War", Christian News, Vol. 24, No. 36, p. 8, October 6, 1986.

XXVIII Scarnati, Rick, "Unanesthetized Circumcision: A Case for Child Abuse?" Journal of the American College of Neuropsychiatrists, Vol. 4, No. 2, pp. 11-12, June July, 1990.

Holve R.L. and others: Regional Anesthesia During Newborn Circumcision: Effect on Infant Pain Response. Clinical Pediatrics 22:813, 1983.

Wallerstein E: Circumcision: The Uniquely American Medical Enigma. Urologic Clinics of North America 12:123, 185.

Wallerstein, ibid.

Warner E. Strashin, E.: Scientific Section: Review Article: Benefits and Risks of Circumcision, CMA Journal 125:968, 1981.

Genesis 17:1–15.

Romans, 2:28–30.

Galatians 5:5–7.

Warner, loc. cit.

Wallerstein, op. cit., p. 124.

Wallerstein, ibid.

Wallerstein, op. cit. p. 125.

Warner, op. cit., p. 972.

Armstrong, H: Circumcision (letter). CMA Journal 127:459, 1982.

Holve, loc, cit.

Dixon S, and others: Behavioral Effects of Circumcision without Anesthesia. J. Dev Behave Pediatr 5:246, 1984.

Poma, PA: Painless Neonatal Circumcision. Int J Gynaecol Qbstet 18:308–9, 1980.

Warner, loc. cit.

Dixon, op. cit. pp. 248–49.

Dixon, op, cit, p. 249.

Thoman, EB: A Rejecting Baby Affects Mother-infant Synchrony in Porter R, O'Connor M (eds): Parent-Infant Interaction. Ciba Foundation Symposium 33, Amsterdam, Elsevier, 1975, pp. 177–200.

Marshall, RE and others: Circumcision effects upon mother-infant interaction. Early Hum Dev 7:367–374, 1982.

Wallerstein, op, cit, p. 124.

Wallerstein, op. cit., p. 131.

AMA issues guide on child abuse diagnosis, care: Expanded role for MDs advised, American Medical News, P. 46, August, 16, 1985.

XXIX Scarnati, Richard A., "Medical and Psychiatric Consequences of the Use wof Monosodium Glutamate (MSG)", *Osteopathic Medical News*, Vol. 4 (3), pp. 40, 43, 52, March 1987.

Kwok RHM: Chinese restaurant syndrome. *N Engl J Med* 1968; 27, 8: 796.

Reif-Lehrer L: Possible significance of adverse reactions to glutamate in humans. *Fed Proc* 1976; 35: 2205–2211.

Allen DH, Baker GJ: Chinese restaurant asthma. *N Engl J Med* 1981; 305: 1154-1155.

Colman AD: Reply to: Possible psychiatric reactions to monosodium glutamate, *N Engl J Med* 1979; 300: 503–504.

Schaumburg HH, Byck R, Gerstl R, et al: Monosodium L-glutamate: Its pharmacology and role in the Chinese restaurant syndrome. *Science* 1969; 163:826–828.

Ebert AG: Adverse effects of monosodium glutamate. Letter, *J Asthma* 1983;20:159–164.

Gann D: Ventricular tachycardia in a patient with the "Chinese restaurant syndrome." *South Med J* 1977;70:879–881.

Colman AD: Possible psychiatric reactions to monosodium glutamate. *N Engl J Med* 1978;299:902.

Asnes RS: Chinese restaurant syndrome in an infant. Clin *Pediatr* 1980; 19:705–706.

Young AB, Penny JB, Dauth GW, et al: Glutamate or aspartate as a possible neuro-transmitter of cerebral corticofugal fibers in the monkey. *Neurology* 1983:33:1513–1516.

Holzwarth-McBride MA, Hurst EM, Knigge KM: Monosodium glutamate induced lesions of the arcuate nucleus. *Anat Rec* 1976;186:185–196.

Holzwarth-McBride MA, Sladek JR, Knigge KM: Monosodium glutamate induced lesions of the arcuate nucleus. *Anat Rec* 1976;186:197–206.

Olney JW, De Gubareff T: Glutamate neurotoxicity and Huntington's chorea. *Nature* 1978; 271:557–559.

Neumann HH: Soup? It may be hazardous to your health! *Am Heart J* 1976;92: 266.

Bakke JL, Lawrence N, Bennett J, et al: Late endocrine effects of administering mono-sodium glutamate to neonatal rats, *Neuroendocrinology* 1978:26:220–228.

Kaplan HI, Sadock BJ(eds): *Comprehensive Textbook of Psychiatry*, ed 4. Baltimore, Williams & Wilkins, 1985, vol 2.

Kenney RA, Tidball CS: Human susceptibility to oral monosodium L-glutamate. *Am J Clin Nutr* 1972:25:140–146.

Cochran JW, Cochran AH: Monosodium glutamania: The Chinese restaurant syndrome re-visited, *JAMA* 1984:252:899.

Reif-Lehrer L: A search for children with possible MSG intolerance. *Pediatrics* 1976;58:771–772.

Gore ME, Salmon PR: Chinese restaurant syndrome: Fact or fiction? *Lancet* 1980; 1:251–252.

Andermann F, Vanasse M,Wolfe LS: Shuddering attacks in children: Essential tremor and monosodium glutamate, *N Engl J Med* 1976;295:174.

Reif-Lehrer L: Monosodium glutamate in tolerance in children. *N Engl J Med* 1975; 293:1204–1205.

Freed DLJ, Carter R: Neuropathy due to monosodium glutamate intolerance. *Ann Allergy* 1982:48:96–97.

Schaumburg HH, Byck R: Sin cib-syn: Accent on glutamate. *N Engl J Med* 1968; 279: 105–106.

Morselli PL, Garattini S: Monosodium glutamate and the Chinese restaurant syndrome. *Nature* 1970;227: 611–612.

Leung A: Wonton, straight up, *JAMA* 1985:253:1880.

Goldberg LH: Supraventricular tachyarrhythmia in association with the Chinese restaurant syndrome. *Ann Emerg Med* 1982;11: 333.

XXX Scarnati, Rick, "A Consideration of the Hazards Involved in the Use of the Polygraph (Lie Detector)", *Journal of the American College of Neuropsychiatrists*, Vol. 1, No. 4, 5, pp. 21-24, Spring, 1987.

XXXI Scarnati, Richard , "Columbus chapter honors Justice Evelyn Stratton," *OPPA-INSIGHT MATTERS*, Vol. 32, No.3, p.6, Fall 2007.

XXXII UMI, Books on Demand, From: ProQuest Company, 300 North Zeeb Road, Ann Arbor, Michigan 48106–1346, USA, 800–521–0600, www.umi.com *Observations Upon the Prophecies of Daniel and the Apocalypse of St. John, In Two Parts.* By Sir Isaac Newton, Printed by J. Darby and T. Browne in Bartbolomew-Clofe. MDCCXXXIII. Pp. 284, 320.

XXXIII *The Cincinnati Post,* Friday June 28, 1991, p.13A, Prison psychiatrist picketing Lebanon.

XXXIV *The Cincinnati Post* Monday, July 8, 1991, P. 6A, Inhumane treatment.

XXXV SEIU, AFL-CIO VOL.2 No.4 1199 SEIU SOLIDARITY (NEWS BULLETIN) p.4, Psychiatrist stands up for ethics.

XXXVI The Cincinnati Post Thursday, July 4, 1991, p.8A , Prison psychiatrist resigns.

XXXVII The Columbus Dispatch Thursday, April 15, 1993 Page 6C, The Lucasville Siege.

Permissions

FORENSIC REPORTS (Articles), reprinted by permission of the publisher

(Taylor & Francis Ltd, http://www.informaworld.com).

BUCKEYE OSTEOPATHIC PHYSICIAN (Articles),reprinted by permission of the publisher Ohio Osteopathic Association.

OSTEOPATHIC MEDICAL NEWS (Articles), reprinted by permission of the publisher American College of Osteopathic Internists.

CHRISTIAN NEWS (Articles),reprinted by permission of the publisher Christian News.

JOURNAL OF THE AMERICAN COLLEGE OF NEUROPSYCHIATRISTS (Articles),reprinted by permission of the publisher The American College of Osteopathic Neurologists and Psychiatrists.

JOURNAL OF PSYCHIATRY & LAW (Articles),reprinted by permission of the publisher Federal Legal Publications, Inc.

THE JOURNAL OF THE PENNSYLVANIA OSTEOPATHIC MEDICAL ASSOCIATION (Articles), reprinted by permission of the publisher Pennsylvania Osteopathic Medical Association.

SOLIDARITY (Volume 2 Number 4) (Article), reprinted by permission of the publisher SEIU District 1199 WV/KY/OH.

AMAZING GRACE,IN THE PUBLIC DOMAIN, Constitution Society.

WORLD NET DAILY (Article), reprinted by permission of the publisher World Net Daily.

E.W. SCRIPPS COMPANY("Scripps") publisher of the Cincinnati Post(Articles), reprinted by permission of the publisher E.W. Scripps Company.

COLUMBUS DISPATCH (Article), reprinted by permission of the publisher The Columbus Dispatch.

AMERICAN ACADEMY OF PSYCHIATRY AND THE LAW (Articles), © American Academy of Psychiatry and the Law. REPRINTED WITH PERMISSION.

JOPERD (Article), reprinted by permission of the publisher JOPERD.

THE PATRIOT-NEWS (Articles), Reprinted with the permission of the Patriot-News. © 1984. All rights reserved.

listen|imagine|view|experience

AUDIO BOOK DOWNLOAD INCLUDED WITH THIS BOOK!

In your hands you hold a complete digital entertainment package. In addition to the paper version, you receive a free download of the audio version of this book. Simply use the code listed below when visiting our website. Once downloaded to your computer, you can listen to the book through your computer's speakers, burn it to an audio CD or save the file to your portable music device (such as Apple's popular iPod) and listen on the go!

How to get your free audio book digital download:

1. Visit www.tatepublishing.com and click on the e|LIVE logo on the home page.
2. Enter the following coupon code:
   5d09-0723-6e0c-9243-140d-4cb9-be8b-5bcc
3. Download the audio book from your e|LIVE digital locker and begin enjoying your new digital entertainment package today!